Intuition
and
Ideality

SUNY Series in Systematic Philosophy
Robert Cummings Neville, Editor

Whether systematic philosophies are intended as true pictures of the world, as hypotheses, as the dialectic of history, or as heuristic devices for relating rationally to a multitude of things, they each constitute articulated ways by which experience can be ordered, and as such they are contributions to culture. One does not have to choose between Plato and Aristotle to appreciate that Western civilization is enriched by the Platonic as well as Aristotelian ways of seeing things.

The term "systematic philosophy" can be applied to any philosophical enterprise that functions with a perspective from which everything can be addressed. Sometimes this takes the form of an attempt to spell out the basic features of things in a system. Other times it means the examination of a limited subject from the many angles of a context formed by a systematic perspective. In either case systematic philosophy takes explicit or implicit responsibility for the assessment of its unifying perspective and for what is seen from it. The styles of philosophy according to which systematic philosophy can be practiced are as diverse as the achievements of the great philosophers in history, and doubtless new styles are needed for our time.

Yet systematic philosophy has not been a popular approach during this century of philosophical professionalism. It is the purpose of this series to stimulate and publish new systematic works employing the techniques and advances in philosophical reflection made during this century. The series is committed to no philosophical school or doctrine, nor to any limited style of systematic thinking. Whether the systematic achievements of previous centuries can be equalled in the 20th depends on the emergence of forms of systematic philosophy appropriate to our times. The current resurgence of interest in the project deserves the cultivation it may receive from the SUNY Series in Systematic Philosophy.

Intuition and Ideality

David Weissman

State University of New York Press

Published by
State University of New York Press, Albany

© 1987   State University of New York

For information, address State University of New York
Press, State University Plaza, Albany, N.Y., 12246

Library of Congress Cataloging-in-Publication Data

Weissman, David, 1936–
    Intuition and ideality.

    SUNY Series in Systematic Philosophy
    Includes index.
    1. Intuition.   2. Thought and thinking.
3. Ontology. 4. Idealism. I. Title. II. Series.
BD181.W36 1987   121'.3   86-14476
ISBN 0-88706-427-2
ISBN 0-88706-428-0 (pbk.)

10 9 8 7 6 5 4 3 2 1

To my children

Contents

Acknowledgements

I am grateful to the President and Fellows of Wolfson College, University of Cambridge, for their hospitality during the two years, from 1979 to 1981, when I was a visiting member and fellow; to the Center for Dewey Studies at Southern Illinois University for the senior fellowship which they granted me during 1981 and 1982; and to the Research Foundation of the City University of New York for their support, in 1979 and 1986, at the beginning and end of this project.

My family and friends have endured this obsession with me. I am also grateful to them.

Introduction

T his book is motivated by three assumptions and a question. My first assumption is that thinking is not usually making. The world has an existence and character which is independent of the things we think and say of it. Some thinking and talking is a kind of making, as we invent the laws or encourage the expectations which distinguish our culture. All the rest is only a way of talking or thinking about matters which are discovered, not made. Perception too is not a way of making the world. It does alter the world, as seeing an apple creates in us the color it is seen as having. But the apple was already determinate in every respect. It may also be true, as quantum physics implies, that some other properties discovered in the world result from the ways that we affect it, as when measuring for velocity or position. But here too, the world is determinate in every regard. It is either qualified or not, at every moment and place, with each of the infinity of possible properties.

My second assumption is that mind is located in the middle of the things known, as one of them. Mind is, more likely than not, the activities of a physical system. Its connections to the other things known are physical and causal, as we alter the things about us, or accommodate to them.

My third assumption is that nothing known to mind, its own states included, is known directly. Knowledge of every sort is mediated by signs. These signs may be natural (as perception is natural) or conventional (as the signs of ordinary and improved languages are conventional). We use our signs to formulate hypotheses. Hypotheses are meaningful because they signify possible states of affairs; they are true when the possibilities are realized as actualities having some

1

physical relation to us. The signs composing these hypotheses are usually the conventional ones of thought or language; but percepts are also used as signs, as when smoke is construed as the sign of fire.

The mediating effect of signs and hypotheses is all the more apparent when the factors signified are the variables of a deep science. Physics is an example, when it speculates that atoms or force fields are the basis for observable effects. Here the mediation is doubled: Signs and hypotheses mediate our knowledge of the world; things specified by our hypotheses are known by the way of the observable differences they make. The mediation is not simpler when we know our own minds. For mind is not a theatre where a single auditor regards the events occurring before him or her on a stage or screen. I assume, to the contrary, that experience is made when mind or brain applies a set of schemas for differentiating and organizing its sensory data, all the while generating a skein of well-informed thoughts or words. Mind also turns to monitor itself, hypothesizing about some part of all that is present within it.

These are my three hypotheses. Together, they say that mind is located within the world, with access in thought and action to the world and itself. Every channel of information is, I assume, mediated by signs and hypotheses. These proposals might require several books to justify them. That is the advantage of declaring them immediately as assumptions. I shall not argue for these claims, though I recommend them for the following four reasons.

(1) The arguments of my previous book, *Eternal Possibilities,*[1] convince me that the world is determinate in every respect, for reasons which are independent of what we say and think of it. We do not require that thought or language should assume the responsibility for making it determinate. That is so because determination originates within the complexes of properties, existing as possibles, which prefigure our world and its states of affairs. Every complex of possibles is determinate, because each one of the infinity of possible properties is, or is not, a constituent within the complex. Our actual world is the instantiation of one such possible world, so that every determination of the one is inherited from the other. Thinking about the world as though it were determinate is not, therefore, a condition for making it determinate. These determinate thinkings are only our hypotheses. They are true or false of a world that is indifferent to them, and determinate already.

(2) The combination of understanding and control achieved by science, technology and ordinary practice are inexplicable if we do not suppose that nature's protean character is radically constrained by a relatively small set of variables and relations having distinct ranges of determinable values. These variables and relations are not directly inspectable, however capable the thinker. Ordinary perception and our reflections upon it do intimate the presence within nature of many or all these factors; but special genius and many generations may be required before we can formulate the hypotheses which identify them. There is no basis for the claim that we might know the world's generating and sustaining variables by direct inspection. Practice is a first clue to their identity. Science is our most reliable source of information about them.

(3) Science, like our plans for action, is expressed in the conventional signs of natural language, as supplemented or replaced by mathematics. The hypotheses comprised of these signs are the instruments used for representing these variables and relations. This is additional reason for saying that our understanding of the world is mediated, never direct.

(4) Computer science and cognitive psychology begin to identify the sign generators within our brains. Brains are parts of bodies, so that mind is the set of activities occurring within a network of physical processes.

These four points together have this implication: We live and act in the middle of things, representing many of them correctly, while having only mediated access to anything that is known.

My one motivating question is relevant here. Why is it that so few thinkers share the belief that we are located in the middle of things as one of them? Every amoeba tests its world. We do that too, and all the more effectively; but then, inexplicably, we let the project lapse. We do not carry on, past practice and science, to a specification of nature's most general features. The philosophic inquiry which does that might be an organizing matrix for all of our questions about nature, with practice and science to provide the basis for our claims about it even as philosophy integrates their discoveries within the framework which it provides. So, we might hope to locate their more particular claims within the context of nature's categorial form and conditions, as matter and space-time are some aspects of categorial form, while eternal possibilities, some of them instantiated here, are one sort of condition. All of this, or variations upon it, might be commonplace as we elaborate upon the character of this environment, our world. Yet, the metaphysics of nature hardly exists. Why is that so? One imagines several answers.

One reply will be that my three assumptions are, individually or collectively, false. I am not deterred by this response, because all the rest of this book will show that the principal reason for saying it is more absurd than any part of my three assumptions. A different answer will be that the question makes a false assumption. It supposes that there is no plausible set of naturalistic categories, and no tradition of inquiry within the metaphysics of nature. But what of the pre-Socratics and Aristotle? The very names confirm the point: We are asked to espouse ancient themes, though little or nothing has been done to revise them in ways making them applicable to nature as it is known to our science and practice. Philosophers who reject the method discussed in this book do always go back to Aristotle. He supplies them with categories having a basis in nature. But then we never do sustain an inquiry that would prove the cogency of these ideas, or some others invented to replace them. Aristotle and Aristotelians are the resource for a study that is lapsed, not the center of a thriving inquiry.

What of Hegel and Whitehead? They speak unequivocally for the philosophy of nature. Notice, however, the reason for Hegel's fascination with nature: He regards it as the opaque and recalcitrant obstacle to the dictum that nothing can exist if it is not disclosed to a thinking mind. Nature is a challenge to subjectivity. Can we turn it inside out, proving that nature is not an alien thing-in-itself by establishing that everything within it is or can be manifest to inspecting mind? Hegel's philosophy of nature, like his phenomenology, is impelled by this objective. Thought is to move beyond immediacy, particularity, and contingency, to mediated but concrete universals. Everything that was hidden is to be exposed, as mind affirms that nothing is real if it cannot be perceived.

This last assertion must be false, if my third assumption is true. For thought never sees nature laid bare, with all its structure disclosed. This could not happen if all our knowledge of the world is mediated by signs and hypotheses. Hegel's reasons for believing that all nature must be inspectable are topics for later chapters. More relevant here is this other fact: We do not have a metaphysics of nature founded on Hegel's requirement for full disclosure, though we do have a science which thrives because of rejecting that principle—e.g., as atoms are not disclosed, though we do have hypotheses to represent them.

Whitehead too is not so much a solution to my problem, as he is one symptom of it. Whitehead populates the world with "drops of experience." That is his response to these two questions: how do we know the world, and what is its character. Both questions are settled if we start from ourselves, characterizing our own experience, then stripping it down before generalizing to everything else. Whitehead's actual occasions are merely the reduced versions of human experience.

Whitehead's use of the hypothetical method is sometimes regarded as paradigmatic for metaphysics. It is worth repeating therefore, that his hypotheses about actual occasions are only generalizations from the experiences we know to the claim that every other thing is like us. We are no farther into the world than Descartes left us when he described the thinking subject. Whitehead was a man of deep scientific learning. But that is different from being a metaphysician of nature. Whitehead has emphasized his "reformulated subjectivist principle." We should take him seriously. One aspect of his disabling subjectivist bias is considered in Chapter Five.[2]

My question is still unanswered: what is there to explain the fact that we have no metaphysics of nature? There must be something very potent suppressing our interest in having one. For what other explanation might there be for the fact that philosophy is mostly oblivious to nature when materialism seems adequate to all or most of what is actual? Life and mind may have exclusively physical conditions. So do cultures express our diverse accommodations to the requirements of our bodies and circumstances. Still, philosophers avoid the issue or ignore it, with the result that we have little or nothing to say of matter for hundreds of years. There are exceptions, as Descartes' claims about matter are more powerful and systematic than most everything that follows him within the philosophic literature. Hobbes and Marx are materialists, though not in the systematic terms that are required of a comprehensive metaphysics. They may have supposed that science would provide this more systematic account, though we expect since Aristotle that science will use fundamental notions without supplying complete explications for them. So, it accounts for change by formulating the laws of motion, meaning the constraints that operate within motion. This is not, however, a complete specification of all the considerations that are relevant to it, as we also want to know whether motion is continuous or discrete. It is scientists and philosophers together, sometimes with mathematicians, who answer questions like this one. There was no likelihood, therefore, that science would resolve all the questions about matter and nature by itself. Philosophers who want a metaphysics which provides for nature while locating human beings within it should expect to supply some part of the theory. We don't do that. Something operates within us to extinguish philosophic interest in all those things whose existence and character are independent of the ways we think about them.

What is this impediment? I call it the *intuitionist method*. A philosophic method is a procedure for generating and testing claims about some aspect of reality. The intuitionist method requires that everything real should be present or presentable, in its entirety, to the mind. Anything that is not presentable is not real. Those things which are presented are "grasped," "seen," or "inspected."

Intuitionist method has two consequences. First is the certainty that mind achieves when it thinks or perceives the given. There is no distance between mind and its objects when they are set directly before it. Error is eliminated with the gap that would have existed if mind were trying to confirm its assertions about matters of fact standing apart from it. Second is a corollary to the demand that nothing should be acknowledged as real if it cannot be inspected. Imagine that all our contingent claims are false, because none of the things they signify do exist. There would still be the world comprised of mind, its sensory affects, and the ideas or theories used to create a thinkable experience. Here is a case where intuitionism has justified a comprehensive idealism.

We are reminded that intuitionism is a two-edged sword. On the one side, it is a radical scepticism, where nothing exists if it is not thought or perceived. On the other side, it is an uncompromising idealism, where everything which does exist has satisfied the requirement that mind should think or perceive it. This combination of scepticism and idealism has the implication that mind itself cannot exist if it is not seen to exist. Intuitionism is founded in this self-confirming perception. It develops as mind discovers within itself, or creates, the data or structures with which it thinks the world. Idealism is, therefore, the culmination of intuitionist method. Not every intuitionist, but all the systematic ones will want to show that the world's differentiations and unities, even existence itself, is incorporated within our minds or God's, so that mind may have direct and confirming access to them.

This program is achieved as intuitionism devotes itself to either one of two autonomous realities; to the sensory given as it is thought or perceived, or to mind itself. David Hume is an intuitionist of the first sort. Reality, he says, is constituted of nothing but impressions and ideas. Kant objects that experience is pervaded by the relations which mind imposes as it thinks the sensory given; but the outcome is almost the same: The thinkable world is identifiable with the phenomena that are given to, and synthesized by perceiving, thinking mind. The other basis for intuitionist reality is the intuitionist's self-perception. Leibniz and Whitehead generalize from Descartes' characterization of the thinking subject, saying that all of reality is only the array of finite minds totalized by God's mind.

One reason for the difficulty of metaphysical thinking is the anomaly of having to think about the world by superimposing the theories of intuitionist metaphysicians on the world known to science and practice. For how should we construe Leibnizian monads or Whiteheadian occasions in a way that makes them applicable to pots and pans, let alone to the subtler variables of physics and biology? We may persist in using the intuitionist ideas as though we might someday establish their applicability to nature; but no one ever does that. The incompatibility is so deep that intuitionist metaphysicians hardly bother to pretend that the world they describe is identical with the one known to science and practice.

Consider, for example, time and cause. Intuitionists of every sort describe these two in ways that are limited by our powers for inspecting a perceptual or conceptual given. But how shall we inspect the past and future; or causal dispositions, efficacy, and necessity? None of them is inspectable, with the result that intuitionist notions of time reduce it to a span of inspectable time—e.g., James' "specious present" and the "becoming" of Whitehead's actual occasions. Causality reduces to constant conjunction. Many philosophers, including distinguished philosophers of science, agree that these truncated ideas are the appropriate ones for thinking about nature. Anything more, they say, violates the (intuitionist) requirement that we must not speculate about matters that cannot be observed.

What is the authority with which these philosophers speak? Are they scientists or craftsmen infused with a respect for nature's autonomy; or is it true instead that they appropriate scientific theories for the purposes of intuitionist understanding? The answer is apparent when philosophers of science tell us that we may dispense with causality in the world so long as we can think about the world as though causality were a factor within it. How are we to do this? By using well-confirmed and formalized scientific theories for generating test sentences having conditional form. No matter then if intuitionism has disqualified itself from telling what causality might be as it operates within nature. It is good enough that we are able to think of nature as though it were a coherent, causal process.

This is the place where intuitionism expresses itself as "instrumentalism." Instrumentalism is not, as it may first seem to be, a doctrine focused upon the gadgets or machines used for operating within the world. It is, instead, the view that thoughts or sentences are mind's principal instruments as we create a thinkable experience. So, it is enough that we be able to think of nature as though it were organized causally; and enough that we have a physics appropriate for thinking of nature as though it were constrained by certain immanent laws. We do not require, in addition, that cause should be a factor within nature, or that physical laws should be immanent constraints within a real space-time.

We see the beginnings of instrumentalism in Descartes, where the idea of two equally primitive substances, mind and body, is quickly superseded by the deeper claim that mind is primary as it turns upon both itself and nature. For neither one can exist if there are not clear and distinct ideas of it. Mind quickly establishes that it has direct and assured access to itself; but mind never does achieve a comparable access to nature. Extended substances are known only as we have clear and distinct ideas of them, where it is only the honesty of a perfect God which guarantees that there are objects corresponding to these ideas. Descartes' successors can dispense with God and his work, meaning the extended world. It is enough for them that we have a theory adequate for making our experience coherent. Does that theory direct our behaviours, making us effective as we organize experience in ways that satisfy our interests and needs? This is, if so, all the theory we need.

Notice that intuitionism, especially as expressed in this instrumentalist way, has important moral consequences. Instrumentalism is a kind of world-making. We create a thinkable world, but more than that, a world that satisfies our interests and values. No wonder then if intuitionism makes us contemptuous of the things created, but also vain. They exist, after all, only because we have thought them, and only then because our objectives have made it useful that we think them. Our authority and importance are by comparison boundless and unconditioned. We advance confidently into a world where nothing can surprise or defeat us, because we have made the world in ways that make it transparent and congenial. Intuitionism, idealism, and instrumentalism converge, here, in our self-adoration as world-makers. We almost forget that we live and die as we accommodate to a world we have not made.

My objective in writing this book may be plainer now. I hope to describe the intuitionist method and its idealist consequences so that both may be discounted in favor of a different method, one that enables us to describe reality as we live within it. That other method is the one of formulating and testing hypotheses. We are familiar with this method as it is used in science and practice. I suppose that we might use it to formulate a metaphysical theory that is applicable and adequate to nature's categorial form and conditions. Scientific hypotheses are true or false within the domains to which they apply. I suppose that metaphysical theories should also be true or false, and testable.

There are many metaphysical hypotheses formulated already within the sciences, as we look there for specifications of matter, space-time, energy and the hierarchical organization of natural phenomena, from the inanimate to the organic, mental and social. The evidence for and against these metaphysical hypotheses is empirical evidence of the sort that is familiar within the experiments used for testing less general hypotheses. Categorial form includes all of these most general specifications of nature's form. It also includes those factors which are exhibited within natural processes, but not explicitly characterized by the law sentences of our scientific theories. The laws themselves are a useful example. How are they immanent within nature? Suppose that we formulate hypotheses about their place there. What empirical data, what experiment, will count for or against the hypotheses? The answer I suggest is that our hypotheses are testable if they tell what factual difference would obtain if the solutions they propose are correct. We say, for example, that there are no laws immanent within nature, meaning that natural laws are only the law sentences of our theories. One difference this entails is that nature should be chaotic, because of having no internal constraints. It is not chaotic, so that we have evidence against the claim that the hypothesis is true.

My assumptions about the uses of hypotheses derive from Peirce. Metaphysical uses of the hypothetical method, Peirce called it *abduction,* are elaborated in the sequel to this book, entitled *Hypothesis and the Spiral of Reflection.*[3] The current book anticipates some of those claims; but its principal task is the one of identifying intuitionist method, its presuppositions and consequences.

There are some misunderstandings likely to result from my characterization of intuitionist method. Here are three of them.

First is the exasperated, "Did anyone get it right? Is all the history of philosophy tainted by this intuitionist bias?" My answer is that we do have an independent but largely suppressed and outdated naturalistic tradition. It originates in the pre-Socratics and Aristotle. It survives in Thomas, through the Middle Ages, to Hobbes. Peirce almost liberates this tradition from intuitionism. Dewey alternately repudiates and affirms it. Some others, including Paul Weiss and Justus Buchler, speak for the tradition. Several philosophers of physics, biology and scientific method elaborate and defend it. But otherwise, the tradition hardly exists. Certainly, the philosophers who are best-read in this century do little or nothing to elaborate upon our understanding of nature as it is known to science and practice.

This is sometimes plainest where we expect that philosophy will finally declare its impatience for intuitionism because of its respect for science. There are, for example, the many books describing one or another of the topics which are vital to nature, e.g., space and time. Why is it that their writers emphasize the formal character of scientific theories while saying rather less about their nominal topics? We might understand this emphasis as the caution of philosophers who believe that scientific theories are the only legitimate characterizations of nature. They may believe that our merely philosophic accounts of it risk being described as theory distorting popularization, or as fatuous speculation. Still, this caution does not explain the disproportionate emphasis upon the mechanics of the theories used for thinking the sensory data, coupled to a reluctance for saying anything substantive about nature. Could it be true that most of our modern philosophy of nature is, more exactly, a specification of the alternative rules that might be used for creating a thinkable experience? That would speak for the abiding influence of intuitionism among us.

Does it follow that the history of philosophy is useless to a metaphysics of nature, because of being either antique in its characterizations of nature, or oblivious to it? This is a second misunderstanding, for that is not implied. Some intuitionists, e.g., Plato as he distinguished Being and Becoming, Forms and the flux—use the intuitionist method for making distinctions which may be critical for any valid metaphysical theory. There are also intuitionists who describe some aspect of nature with marvelous facility, though their own metaphysical theories are not applicable to the matters described. Whitehead does that in *Process and Reality,* in the chapter entitled "The Order of Nature." This is the place where Whitehead describes nested and overlapping stable systems of the sort known to thermodynamics, though his theory of actual occasions leaves him with nothing to say about the relations which pervade these systems. He resorts to God, saying that God thinks each system and all systems together as a differentiated totality. This is one of several cases where intuitionist philosophers make discoveries which confound their own theories.

A third misunderstanding may result from one assumption which I make about philosophic inquiry. I suppose that people who use a philosophic method may do so while giving little or no thought to either the method or its implications. While some philosophers are scrupulous in telling what they do and why, these others are less self-conscious. They are more likely to be eclectic, using bits and pieces from various methods and theories without regard for the coherence of their practice or beliefs. This eclecticism is apparent in some of the philosophers whom I describe as intuitionists.

It may seem outlandish, however, that philosophers should be charged with idealism and intuitionism, when these thinkers would say that they have never heard of the method and detest its commitments. These may be philosophers who think of themselves as realists. Yet, everyone is a realist to the degree of believing that hands, feet and Naples do surely exist. This is the natural and naive realism of unreflective belief. Difficulties arise about the status of these things only as philosophers try to formulate the conditions for their existence. It is here that intuitionism is a critical factor. For there is a tension between the alleged reality of the things about us, and the requirements of every philosopher's theory about them. How does he provide for the reality of things-at-hand or Italian cities in the terms approprate to his theory of being or language? It may be true that each of us is always a realist in the ordinary business of life; but it is too late to be a philosophic realist if one's theory entails that Naples or any other thing has no reality apart from the conditions for our thinking it.

It is not convincing, therefore, when idealist philosophers renounce their idealism while continuing to use the intuitionist method. Idealism is not only a theory that one professes. It results just as surely from using the intuitionist method. Why is that so? Because intuitionism reduces reality to the inspectable given. We may reasonably ask if a philosopher's idealism is the expression of a more or less tacit intuitionism; and we may look for the evidence which would confirm that this is so. Eclectic thinkers may not exploit or endorse every aspect of the method or its implications. Still, intuitionist method is not easily divided, so that we might pick and choose among its parts. The method has a decided integrity, one that affects its presuppositions and its implications. Philosophers who use the method for purposes they like, should not be surprised if it commits them to some things they do not like.

Several of the philosophers whom I describe as intuitionists appear to be defended from this charge by their own disclaimers. Heidegger, for example, writes as follows:

> By showing how all sight is grounded primarily in understanding, we have deprived pure intuition of its priority, which corresponds noetically to the priority of the present-at-hand in traditional ontology. 'Intuition' and 'thinking' are both derivatives of understanding, and already rather remote ones.[4]

What Heidegger calls "pure intuition" is the unmediated apprehending of sensory data, or anything else that might be set before the mind. There is no pure intuition, he ways, because mind has already taken up the matters perceived for some purpose of its own. These things are perceived as read-to-hand, not merely as present-at-hand.

This is an objection to the claims of unmediated perception. It is not, in any way, a repudiation of intuition. This is plain when Heidegger writes of the condition for being:

Being is presence as the showing itself of outward appearance. Being is the lasting of the actual being in such outward appearance. This double presence in-sists upon presence, and thus becomes present as constancy: enduring, lasting.[5]

Certainty thus first and alone determines the reality of what is real.[6]

When truth has become certainty, then everything which is truly real must present itself as real to the real being that it is.[7]

What really is shows itself in the light of the truth which has become certainty, as the *cogitare* of the *ego cogito*.[8]

Intuitionism is just the claim that everything real is and must be present or presentable to a mind. The passages just quoted affirm that this is Heidegger's view. It is incidental to this claim that the matters set before our minds are schematized, or not, by prior acts of thought, though intuitionists typically hope to confirm that these acts too are inspectable. Heidegger's disclaimer is, therefore, no evidence against the charge that he is an intuitionist. These same considerations apply to everyone whose rejection of unschematized perceivings is coupled to the view that nothing is real, whether schematized or not, if it is not inspected or inspectable. This question will arise again when Carnap's views are the ones at issue.

The source for the four quotations above is Heidegger's essay, "Metaphysics as History of Being." This essay is the deepest apology for intuitionism known to me. It is hard to imagine a more effective argument for defining reality in terms hospitable to inspecting mind. Most everything that I have wanted to say of intuitionism is said there, though with this difference. Heidegger believes that intuitionism is and must be the authentic expression of Being. I suppose, to the contrary, that the existence and character of things are independent of the fact that we think about them. Our hypotheses are representations, meaning that they are signs for possible states of affairs. They are not re-presentations of the things they signify, as though we might still capture the things thought and known for inspecting mind. I shall assume that Heidegger's intuitionist emphasis on the *presence* of things to mind is consistent with his antipathy for the claim that experienced time is limited to the *present*.

I have wanted to describe intuitionist method in a way that is more dialectical than historical. The result is a morphology, not a chronicle. There are examples to illustrate particular claims about this method's focus and development; but I have ignored great swathes of history where intuitionism is dominant. My examples are usually the philosophers of our time. The principal exception is Descartes. He is necessarily the starting point for any consideration of intuitionist method. All of modern intuitionism starts in the *cogito's* self-discovery. Even Platonic intuitionism comes to be grounded there, as mind confirms the clarity and distinctness of its ideas before applying them. All of the philosophers I cite move within this Cartesian tradition whether or not they acknowledge him as their point of reference.

My examples from twentieth century philosophy may seem dated, since none of them derives from recent books and articles. It might be said that intuitionism is all but extinguished among us. That is not so.

Bas van Fraassen has argued in a recent book that, "Empiricism requires theories only to give a true account of what is observable, counting further postulated structures as a means to that end."[9] He would have us understand that "postulated structures" are merely the conceptual devices used to focus and organize our thinking about the observables. van Fraassen's "empiricism" is, like the one of Hume, a kind of intuitionism. I mean that his "observables" are only the data set before our inspecting minds. So, this goat is a set of appearances. The goat's thinghood is only one of the postulated structures for thinking in an organized way about goats. Hume and Kant argued in similar ways as they described the relations and empirical schemas used for organizing phenomena. van Fraassen is like them when he identifies reality with the observables, reducing all the rest of it to the concepts used for telling a coherent story about the world.

I shall be distinguishing intuitionists from one another in the following way. Some emphasize the contents set before inspecting mind. Others emphasize the forms used for thinking content. van Fraassen belongs with Hume among the intuitionists of content, or with Kant somewhere in the middle among those who believe that experience is made equally of sensory content and organizing forms. Jacques Derrida is, unequivocally, an intuitionist of form. He agrees that we do use theories and interpretations as though we might represent real differences within the world. But that is a deception, one that we discover as we remark the succession of conflicting interpretations. Rather than devote ourselves to any one of them, expecting that it might be true in some literal way, we are to turn ironically upon our conceivings. What do we find? Only style or the barely disguised motives of those who encourage us to use their interpretations for thinking about the world and ourselves. All the differentiations and unities ascribed to the world are only the ones that thought projects as it creates a thinkable world. The world, itself, is an "abyss." Interpretation is like the bicycle of the high-wire aerialist: pedalling fast is the only way to save ourselves from falling into it.

How shall we carry on deceiving ourselves when reflection discovers that every interpretation has only style to recommend it, and power to enforce it? The perpetually renewing source for our many interpretations is left mysterious. There is only "differance."[10] a principle or activity which generates the succession of interpretations, as though we might be fooled for a while, every next time. Could we break this cycle where interpretations are used, exposed, rejected and replaced? No, the cycle repeats itself forever, because we need a set of forms for making the world thinkable, hence presentable.

Derrida and van Fraassen may disagree with one another as much as I disagree with both of them. But their affinity is genuine. Both of them suppose that reality reduces to whatever matters are set before an inspecting mind: to sensory content for van Fraassen, to thinkable form for Derrida. The two of them are my evidence for saying that intuitionism flourishes among us.

The six chapters of this book are an extended reason for believing that we should reject their method. Chapter One is an exposition of Descartes' intuitionism. I argue that his method, like every one, presupposes a psychology and an ontology. A method's ontology is the domain to which it applies. Its psychology is the set of faculties required for using the method. Descartes' intuitionism has the effect of conflating these two, so that method's domain reduces to the qualifications of thinking substance. Mind, as self-encircling, self-sustaining consciousness, is made to be the crucible for all the rest of Being.

Chapter Two is a survey of some dialectical cycles within intuitionist thinking. These include the cycles of content and form, mind and experience, and the justifications for intuitionist method.[11] Chapter Three is a list, with commentaries, of those factors which are constitutive of intuitionist method. Chapter Four is a more detailed account of the intuitionist ontology and psychology. I have wanted to establish the basis for all of those metaphysical theories which suppose that mind is first in knowledge, and first in Being.

This concern for metaphysics is my principal motivation. Why is metaphysics oblivious to nature? Intuitionist method and its psycho-centric ontology are the cornerstones of my explanation. Chapter Five considers their influence upon Hume and Whitehead as they formulate notions of cause and effect. I propose an alternative theory of substance and cause in order to confirm that many important things are neglected when reality is identified with the things presented for inspection. Chapter Six expresses these concerns in a different way. There is, I argue, an enduring intuitionist project. Philosophers enact it by trying to establish that the differences, the unities and even the existence of the world might be provided for within a thinking mind. We are not surprised, perhaps, that philosophers might have argued for this claim in the distant past. I argue that the idea follows directly from the psycho-centric ontology of intuitionist method, and that it survives in contemporary linguistic philosophy.

My arguments within these chapters are meant to have a practical effect. We should renounce intuitionism and its ontology. Hypothesis is a better method. There is no other one available to us as we think and act within a world whose existence and character are independent of the ways we think about it.

The analytic Table of Contents is a survey of the argument. Its headings are dispersed within the text.

Chapter One

Method, Mind,
and Ontology

1. The alleged neutrality of philosophic method

P hilosophic method often feigns a neutrality which is meant to qualify it for application to every subject matter. We are to imagine that no biases are hidden or imposed as we think philosophically about any thing whatever, whether actual or possible, real or imaginary. But no method is neutral, and every method's authority is parochial, because each one makes assumptions of two kinds which limit its application. On the one side are claims about the domain, or ontology, to which the method applies. On the other side are assumptions about the character that mind need have in order to use the method. Method, mind, and ontology are reciprocally related, so that the shift in either one may require an alteration in the other two. These three together form a kind of circle. It confines the assertions which can be made by using the method. We may hope that one method, with its presuppositions about mind and ontology, may describe a circle so wide as to comprehend all the questions and truths which are or could be significant for philosophers. There is a method of that sort, that is, the one of using signs to represent any possible state of affairs. That method is described in the sequel to this book, *Hypothesis and the Spiral of Reflection*. The current book is devoted to an alternative candidate for universality: Intuition, not hypothesis, is the method usually preferred as philosophy supports its claims to knowledge. This first chapter starts with Descartes, using him to illustrate both the reciprocity of method, mind, and ontology, and the intuitionist method he espouses. Method's constraining effect helps to explain certain anomalies in Descartes' views. There are the claims he would like to make—e.g., about God, and the scruples of his method. These two are sometimes opposed, as method precludes various ontological claims which theory affirms. Should we cripple theory so that it will not violate the strictures of our method; or should we have a method adequate to the formulation of any theory? This is the question animating all the discussion in both books.

2. Descartes' method

For what purpose, and with what presuppositions do we apply a philosophic method? Consider these answers:

A method is necessary for investigating the truth of things[1]

This is Rule IV of Descartes' *Rules for the Direction of the Native Talents.* It is an abstracted but concise restatement of Rules I and II:

The goal of studies should be to direct the inborn talents toward producing solid and true judgements concerning everything that presents itself.[2]

It is proper to deal only with those objects concerning which our inborn talents seem sufficient to achieve a certain and indubitable cognition.[3]

Rule IV is modern, whereas Rules I and II are baroque. It tells succinctly what method's purpose is, while they are too much preoccupied with the psychology and ontology of method's application. Those issues are irrelevant to truth, so that we do better for purposes of method to emphasize Rule IV, caring only about the procedures and criteria for making and asserting judgements.

This last sentence is a précis of the bias which is common to modern readers: Method is to be disassociated from questions of psychology and ontology; first, because psychologism is a threat to the integrity of every normative property, truth especially; second, because functionalism establishes that method is distinguishable from its realization in agents of any particular design. Rule IV encourages this modern emphasis. But then Rules I and II, together with the other Rules and his commentary, show that Descartes never supposed that method should be set apart from assumptions about mind and the objects of inquiry. To the contrary, Descartes cannot describe his method without telling what mental activities it requires and what sorts of entities are appropriate to its applications. The bearing of psychology and ontology on Descartes' method is my first topic. Later, I shall consider functionalism and psychologism, asking how they affect the reciprocity which I claim for method, mind, and ontology.

Here is Descartes' account of method, with psychological and ontological commitments ignored. He advises, in Rule V, that we should

> reduce by steps complicated and obscure propositions to simpler ones and thereafter try to ascend through those same steps from an (understanding) of the simplest of all things to a cognition of all others.[4]

Descartes supposes that method is applied as we turn reflectively to reconstruct our beliefs. We are to find clarity and certainty, hence justification, for beliefs which are otherwise complicated and obscure. Reconstruction begins as we identify the simple ideas from which more complicated ones are derived. The clarity and distinctiveness of simple ideas is our first objective. Later, we are to derive successively complex ideas from the simple ones. These are the demonstrated truths. They, with the simple truths, are the whole content of knowledge. It may happen that reconstruction fails to clarify every one of those obscure ideas which philosophy inherits from the less reflective strata of thought and experience. For we are thinkers emerging from the remoter parts of Plato's cave. Our first beliefs are shadows and imitations, with only a glimmering in them of the truths they prefigure. There may be nothing to redeem in some of them. Reconstruction will give perspicuous expression to whatever content they do have.

Every reference to psychology and ontology is suppressed, first in the last quotation above, then in my gloss of it. I have quoted only a part of the Rule, also deleting a word for which the more neutral "understanding" is substituted. These editorial liberties suggest the extent to which Descartes' views are mutilated when method is isolated from mind and ontology. For Descartes never hesitates to tell, when saying what he requires of method, how mind behaves in achieving knowledge. Nor is he vague in specifying the kinds of objects to which method is applied. Here, for example, is the complete statement of Rule V:

> All method consists in the order and disposition of those things toward which the keen vision of the mind must be turned in order to discover any truth. Undoubtedly, we shall exactly employ this rule if we reduce by steps complicated and obscure propositions to simpler ones and thereafter try to ascend through those same steps from an intuition of the simplest of all things to a cognition of all the others.[5]

This says that truth is achieved when the "keen vision" or "intuition" of mind is turned upon "simpler" things and their relations. These simples are described in the exposition to Rule VI as "absolute natures."

> I shall call absolute whatever contains in itself the pure and simple nature, relevant to the question asked: so that everything that is considered as independent, cause, simple, universal, one, equal, similar, right, or others of this kind, is absolute: moreover, this same first nature I call the simplest and easiest because we use it in resolving questions. . . .[6]

Method is the discipline of mind as it discovers, apprehends, and organizes "absolute natures." These natures stand before the mind as ideas. Mind is their appropriate medium, because natures originate as ideas in the mind of God.

Descartes supposes that method, mind, and ontology are distinguishable but inseparable, method being mind's preferred but still natural way of treating the matters set before it. But then Rule IV, so spartan and modern, is misleading for its apparent implication that method is independent of psychology and ontology. Why do we misread Descartes' views about method, wanting him to say, as we believe, that method is separate from those other two factors? There are two motives for this persuasion. One is functionalism, the view that logical operations are distinguishable from the media in which they are, or may be realized. The other is psychologism, the objection that truth must not be confused with any state of mind as mind believes correctly that some thought or sentence is true. Let me tell what functionalism and psychologism imply, while saying that neither one is an obstacle to the essential reciprocity of method, mind, and ontology.

3. Functionalism

Functionalism is the doctrine that form has a specificable, "logical" integrity, as we may state a method's procedures and even its truth conditions, without indicating the kind of system or agent whose method it is, or the kinds of entities to which the method applies. Deduction is an example. Its rules are representable in ways that are neutral for psychology and ontology, though deductive procedures are realizable in systems as different as computing machines and human minds. The difference between silicon chips and neurons is not ontologically problematic, as both are physical systems. Functionalists will likely prefer, therefore, that we make their point by using a more dramatic example, one that emphasizes the irrelevance of ontology to method by comparing two applications which differ categorially. Suppose that some god creates a world by deriving more remote historical events from preceding ones. His method is the one that we apply when thinking deductively, but the ontology of the result is different, as this god's mind is different from our own. The abstract specification of method, together with the truths proved by it, will have been blind to these differences. Minds and machines, sentences and history: Each of these systems or domains will be appropriate to its application. We are reminded of Wittgenstein's remark that a phonograph record, sheet music, and live performances have the "same form"; meaning, a form differentiated from all its expressions as it exists in "logical space."[7]

Would it have mattered to Descartes that a method may be considered in this abstract way, without reference to the character of the agent applying it or the entities to which the method applies? Should we agree that the method is distinguishable and separable from its psychology and ontology? Notice as we answer that it is not method but only its logical crux that is alleged to be separable. We must be careful, therefore, that a method's applications are not conflated with its formulable essence. Functionalists rely upon this conflation when they say that a method is separable from its applications, and consequently from the psychology and ontology which are required whenever the method is applied. But then it is apparent that abstracted form has displaced those various applications which it summarizes and represents. This cannot be the last word. For what is method? Is it merely an abstracted form, or is it rather that procedure which is applied or is so embedded within an agent and domain that it may be applied?

Descartes would have emphasized this point. He would have understood that there might be a generic though perhaps analogical similarity in the way that God and humans think. He would have appreciated the functionalist description of a system whose "logical states" allow for diverse realizations. But Descartes would have been dissatisfied by an abstracted, schematic account of method, because method as he understood it is the discipline of human thought. It is the procedure that we apply when resolving our intellectual confusions. Perhaps God too is constrained to think in the way prescribed by a method. But then it will be true of God as of us that applications of a method cannot be understood in a comprehensive way by appealing to an abstracted representation of it. Not method abstracted, but only method applied: that is and must be our point of reference in considering the separability of method from psychology and ontology. Does God make history by deriving later events from earlier ones? Then his method is the same generically but different specifically from the one used by minds and machines as they prove sentences by deriving them from other sentences. We cannot specify the differences between these applications without citing the mind applying the method—e.g., God's or our own—and the domain to which the method applies. Method's applications presuppose considerations of both kinds, for method is distinguishable and separable from psychology and ontology only as we ignore its applications, restricting ourselves to the abstracted form.

Remember by way of confirming this point that the aim of Descartes' method is true judgement. Method abstracted, method as the functionalists describe it, is spinning its wheels, producing no judgements. Functionalists do expose a method's form, sometimes including a generic account of its procedures and a specification of the least condition to be satisfied if its judgements are to be true. But their account is not a complete specification of all the factors which are required if the method is to be applied. Nor are these additional factors the mere contingencies of its application. For method applied, method as it produces true judgements, is the act of a mind that is structured in ways that are appropriate to its domain. A functionalist might remark the similarities between *nous* inspecting Forms and the mind described by Hume as it regards its impressions. But it is not inspection in the abstract, only the *inspectio* of a mind qualified to reflect upon one or the other of these things which produces true judgements. The reciprocity of method, mind, and ontology is fundamental as we consider method applied, not merely form abstracted.

4. Psychologism

Is the reciprocity of method, mind, and ontology more vulnerable to the charge of psychologism? By *psychologism,* I mean the identification of extramental entities, relations, or norms with mental states. Concepts are psychologized when meaning is reduced to use or the interdefinability of terms, with no reference beyond a concept to that extramental referent which it signifies. So, "red" is meaningful because it signifies a certain property, whether instantiated or not. The word does have a use, but its meaning does not reduce to that use. Truth, hence knowledge, is psychologized when we describe it as the interanimation of sentences, without regard for the relation of a thought or sentence and that other usually extramental entity or event which satisfies it. Norms are psychologized when they are identified with stipulations or attitudes, as when justice is reduced to the idea of what might or should be, thereby losing its power as a demand having force upon us, whether or not we acknowledge it. Psychologism defeats our hope of knowing a world which is independent of mind for its existence and character, for it supposes that thought never can reach beyond the mind to things which are represented within it but are independent of it. Meaning, truth and norms, with the objects of our knowledge, are reduced to one or another of mind's contents, attitudes, or behaviors. Even the knowledge of our own mind is compromised when the status or activities to be known are displaced by whatever things are interposed in the act of knowing them. Thought then takes these representations, not their referents, as its objects. The result is psychologism: the systematic confusion of signs with their objects.

Psychologism is a term of abuse. Realists use it as they deny that mind might create the things known, or the standards which need be satisfied if knowing is to be adequate to its objects. Realism affirms this contrary view: that knowing mind exceeds its own activity, touching ground in a reality which is independent of mind for its existence and character. Thought reaches beyond itself by construing its contents as signs having objects distinct from them, where representations designate real possibilities. Yellow dog and golden mountain are possibilities of this sort, the one actualized, the other not. The thoughts or words designating these things have intentional meaning because of referring beyond themselves to the possibilities they signify. These possibilities are the senses—i.e., the meanings—of our thoughts and words. Thoughts or sentences are true when the possibilities signified are instantiated. The correspondence of a representation and state of affairs is, therefore, the satisfaction of the sign by its object.[8] Norms too may have a realist interpretation, as we say that the idea of justice has both representational and deontological force: it represents a possibility which should be realized. Psychologism would reduce all of these things to mental states, depriving them of external reference. Mind would have the responsibility for making and containing all the discriminations which realists locate within the world.

Descartes rejects psychologism because it aborts knowledge: ". . . for certainly were I to consider these very ideas only as particular modes of my thinking and not refer them to any other thing, they could scarcely provide any matter for error."[9] Or for truth. Is there some difficulty in averting this result when our method has essential commitments to psychology and ontology? The saving answer is that reciprocity in method, mind, and ontology is indifferent to the opposition of realism and psychologism. Some methods are psychologistic and some are not. The difference is a result of the method itself. It is independent of the fact that every method has psychological and ontological assumptions. Descartes' own views are a useful example, because his remarks about truth are unstable, despite his antipathy to psychologism. Ideas are true, he says, if they are "clear and distinct." This is an ambiguous phrase, one having a strong interpretation which opposes psychologism and a weaker interpretation which implies it.

The strong reading holds that altering or negating a clear and distinct idea is impossible because of generating a contradiction. Contradictions are impossible in two respects: They cannot exist or be conceived. We are to apply the test of clarity and distinctness to our ideas, inferring from the conceivability or inconceivability of some idea to the necessity or impossibility that the thing conceived should exist. We safely make this transition from ideas to the world because, as Descartes believed, every consistent idea signifies, however obscurely, something external to us which is "like an archetype."[10] There is, he says, no less reality in this "cause" than is present in the idea of it.[11] The contradiction within an idea is paired to, and represents, the contradiction that would result from altering or mixing archetypes—i.e., essences—in ways that violate their integrity. The necessities discovered within our clear and distinct ideas are to be regarded in a parallel way, as necessities representing necessities in things. These may be necessities of essence or of existence—e.g., as it is necessary that two and two are four, and necessary that God exists, if it is a contradiction that the sum of these numbers be other than four, and a contradiction that God not exist.

The strong interpretation saves truth from psychologism, because of establishing that the negations of necessary truths are contradictory. These necessary truths obtain in all possible worlds. Mind has not made them, and it cannot undo the contradictions which result when these truths are negated. We merely discover that some ideas and judgements are the one or the other, contradictions or necessary truths. Descartes assumes that we will distinguish truth, itself, from our ways of representing particular truths, and also from clarity and distinctness, the criterion used in testing for truth. That test together with our ideas and judgements is located within our minds. Truth is something more, namely, the correspondence of some idea or judgement to that archetype it represents. Psychologism is no threat to this strong reading of Descartes' view, because truth exceeds our thinking as mind entertains true ideas and makes true judgements.

Descartes turns from this logical test of necessary truths to an arguably psychologistic one as he evaluates our ideas of contingencies. Most ideas or judgements are not necessary truths, as nothing impossible results if we alter or negate the ideas of Sun and wax. Altered ideas do violate the identity of the originals, because of being different from them, but these variants do not contradict the originals, being only their contraries as red and blue are contraries. Nor is a contradiction entailed if we imagine that the Sun is larger or smaller, hotter or colder. Compare this to necessary truth, where no change can be imagined in an archetype without producing contradiction—e.g., as it is contradictory that a Euclidean triangle should have internal angles equal to more or less that 180°.

How shall we decide the truth of contingent claims when variations of their objects are not contradictory? This is the place where

Descartes is vulnerable to psychologism, for his notion of clarity and distinctness is weakened to suit the contingencies at issue. So, an idea is clear and distinct, hence true, it if is set unambiguously before the mind's eye. We remark its content, noting what distinguishes it and also the respects in which it differs from other ideas. We make a true judgement if these conditions are satisfied. Ideally, as in the wax experiment, we discern a founding geometrical structure, understanding the wax's more apparent and qualitative features as the protean expression of this deeper form. This is the level at which we might hope to apply the strong, logical test of clarity and distinctness, proving that some of the properties of the geometrical structure are necessary in the respect that negating our idea of it would produce a contradiction. But this is Descartes' aspiration, not his achievement. His ideas of the many contingencies never reach to that deeper, geometrical level. There never is an occasion for applying the strong criterion to them. Only the weaker reading is appropriate, as ideas are clear and distinct if they are set plainly before our inspecting minds, each one exhibiting its distinctive content and organization. These are the ideas or judgements to be regarded as true when we have also supposed that God intervenes to save us from deception by creating the particulars which satisfy our clear and distinct ideas.

Descartes' vulnerability to psychologism is here. Clarity and distinctness would be insufficient as a test of truth "if it could ever occur that anything I were to perceive just as clearly and distinctly would be false. . . ."[12] There are two defenses against this possibility: The logical reading of clarity and distinctness saves us from error in the case of necessary truth (their negations are contradictions); God defends us from deception when the truths are contingent. Suppose, however, that we are Cartesians who have denied God's existence, or merely that God stands surety for our clear and distinct ideas. Mind will be as before: it will have nothing before it but its ideas and sensory data, with no access to the world of things signified by those ideas. There will, however, be this difference: Mind will have no way to confirm the applicability of its ideas to the matters whose existence and character are independent of it. Where truth was to be the correspondence or satisfaction relation between ideas or judgements and their referents, our atheism will deprive us of the only device known to Descartes for establishing that any idea is true of these mind-independent matters of fact. The result will be that truth shrinks. No longer a relation between ideas or judgements and the things they signify, it will reduce to being a property or relation of ideas. Clarity and distinctness will no longer be the evidence for a relation which reaches beyond mind into the world, but only the evidence of something distinguishing within the ideas or judgements themselves. What could that something be? This issue is left to post-Cartesian intuitionists. It is resolved when, for example, the truth of contingent claims is made to devolve upon their coherence with other claims, so that truth reduces to the relations among sentences. We have an example of this reduction in one interpretation of scientific theories, where the truth of higher-order sentences within a well-confirmed theory is described as a function of the support they receive from test sentences. On this interpretation, the support of test sentences is not regarded as evidence that the higher-order sentences are true of something beyond themselves—i.e., the world. Psychologism demands that all the conditions for truth be retained within the mind; and this interpretation complies. Truth, it says, is only a relation of sentences. This counts as psychologism, because it reduces truth to the coordination of those thoughts or sentences with which mind thinks the world, hence to a state of mind. This is the outcome we should want to resist, because it leaves us with the bearers of truth when their relations to the things truly signified are ignored or denied.

It is critical that we avert psychologism if we hope to preserve the idea of truth as it applies to our knowledge of those things which are independent of mind for their existence and character. Is there any reason apparent now for supposing that psychologism is implied if a method has psychological commitments? There is nothing in this account of Descartes to suggest that these two considerations are related in any way beyond the fact of being designated by a similar word. Indeed, such evidence as we have from Descartes proves their independence. This is plain when Descartes is turned the one way or the other, away from psychologism or towards it, as we affirm or deny God's existence. With his method and its psychological assumptions constant, this independent claim is enough to make that difference. The fact that method does presuppose certain claims about the competence of the mind applying it is, therefore, no invitation whatever to the psychologizing of reality, truth, or moral standards.

There is only this one complicating factor: Descartes would himself be driven to psychologism *by his method* if this additional assumption—i.e., that God defends us from deception—were mistaken. This is so because Descartes' intuitionism reduces thought to the inspection of ideas and sensory data, with no access to the world beyond this given. We may determine in an *a priori* way that necessary truths reach beyond our minds, applying to all possible worlds. There is, however, nothing but their perspicuous and coherent presentation to count towards the truth of contingent ideas. God's guarantee is the only thing saving them from psychologism.

We may argue for the reality of God by saying that a finite effect (i.e., our minds), must have an infinite cause. We may justify our belief in God's guarantee by saying that a perfect being would not deceive us. But then it is all-important that we be right about God's reality and intentions, for being, truth and every value are reduced, in the absence of his guarantee, to the horizons of this conceptual, sensory and personal given. Even the necessary truths are likely to be reinterpreted. Rather than describe them as truths obtaining in all possible worlds, we shall likely say that they are merely tautologies, meaning that these logical truths are created as mind applies certain of its own conventions. Truths of every sort will be psychologized, because of being deprived of an extra-mental referent. It is most consequential, therefore, that Descartes' intuitionism does risk the psychologizing of reality, truth, and values.

Does it follow that Descartes' method is subverted in this way just because of presupposing a psychology? No, it does not. There are these three things to consider. First is the fact that a method may have an inherent psychologistic bias. Intuitionism is a method of this sort whenever this method identifies the objects of knowledge with those things which may be set before and within our minds. It then identifies truth with some attitude of mind, with relations among thoughts or sentences, or with the relation of thoughts or sentences to the matters inspected. If all of these factors are present within an inspecting mind as its qualifications, then truth too will be a mental state. There will be no way, short of God's guarantee, to avert psychologism. Second is the point made some paragraphs above: a method presupposes a psychology just because mind must have certain faculties appropriate to using the method. This by itself is no less innocent than saying that a singer needs a throat and lungs. Psychological presuppositions do not by themselves entail psychologism. Third is the fact that the psychologistic tendency of Descartes' intuitionist method is enforced by the psychology which it presupposes. He assumes that intuiting mind is equipped with a sensorium for receiving content, and the power for inspecting it. Evidently now, it is not the fact of presupposing a psychology which makes a method susceptible to psychologism. That is a bias already inherent within some methods. The psychology they presuppose can only reinforce the tendency already current within them. Even Descartes' method can be saved from psychologism by making the *ad hoc* assumption that God guarantees the truth of clear and distinct but contingent ideas.

Other methods avert psychologism altogether, as Peirce's abductive method requires that we formulate and test hypotheses about matters whose character and existence are independent of the ways we think and talk about them. Hypotheses are meaningful because of representing possible states of affairs. They are true when the possibilities are instantiated. There is nothing in this of psychologism, though an appropriate psychology is presupposed: mind makes and uses signs, then designs and conducts the experiments which test the hypotheses. Accordingly, it is not the reciprocity of method, mind and ontology, but only Descartes' own method, which risks psychologism.

5. Descartes' intuitionism

We often say that Descartes' method is deductive: *more geometrico,* he calls it. This characterization is misleading, because of being incomplete. It emphasizes the construction of complex ideas from simple ones, as theorems are complex ideas deduced from simpler axioms. It ignores the fact that our knowledge of simple natures, e.g., that I am a thinking thing, is not any kind of deduction. What is that disciplined activity, that method, which is responsible for exhibiting these simples, and for constructing the deductions which may themselves be apprehended as certain and self-evident? The words which signify this activity are the ones introduced in the paragraphs above, namely *intuition* and *inspection*. These are Descartes' own words, so that *intuitionism* is an appropriate characterization of the doctrine which affirms that all our knowledge derives from intuition. The *more geometrico* is just the mind's procedure for organizing the things inspected. Intuition is the more fundamental, defining activity: we intuit the simple natures, and then assemble the more complex ideas directly before our inspecting minds.

Descartes' *Rules* are a handbook of this formal procedure. The *Meditations* is the more conspicuous example of intuitionist practice. The difference between them is especially important because of obliging us to correct our exaggerated emphasis upon the formal, deductivist character of Descartes' method. Little or nothing is deduced from the simple apprehension of the *I am,* or the immediately subsequent perception that I think. Here, in the *Meditations,* the one emphatic claim about method is its reliance upon intuition. Mind turns upon, discovers and inspects itself.

Some of Descartes' remarks help to make this point. They tell what he claims for intuition, and how intuitionism affects his commitments to psychology and ontology.

"All knowledge", Descartes says, "is certain and evident cognition."[13] These secure cognitions are the basis on which to reconstruct beliefs which may be true, though we are unable to determine from our confused beliefs whether they are categorically or merely probably true. First among the secure and absolute truths is the one acquired in self-knowledge:

> For that I am the one who doubts, understand, and wills is so manifest that nothing could happen by which it may be explained more evidently.[14]

This self-knowledge is to be the starting point for reconstructing all of our other beliefs.

There is, however, this ambiguity: what role shall our self-knowledge play within these reconstructions? Is the *I think* to be one of the simple natures from which more complex ideas are constructed? Or is there some other role assigned to mind? The deductivist emphasis among Descartes' interpretors encourages us to expect that complex truths about us will be derived from the *I am* or the *I think.* But that never happens. Mind never reflects upon itself in this way, so as to deduce one or another claim about its own nature. Descartes never requires that it should, for three reasons. There is first the motive left over from the First Meditation: the discovery that I am is already the sufficient barrier to a universal scepticism. Second, mind is not so much an idea to be known as it is the activity which is foundational for our knowledge of every other thing. Ideas of those other things, and the sensory data which are their effects upon us come before the mind to be appraised. Mind is their measure. Are they clear and distinct, hence a basis for the reconstruction of our beliefs? Mind ponders and decides. A third reason for not applying deduction to the idea of mind's simple nature is the wastefulness of doing that. Nothing could be more evident than mind's own nature. That is the point of the last quotation above, and also of this next one:

> Neither can this method be extended to teaching how these operations of intuition and deduction are to be performed, because they are the simplest and primary; they are so much so that unless our intellect were already able to use them beforehand, it would not even comprehend any of the percepts of this very method, however easy they are.[15]

We are to know what intuition is without instruction. Anyone failing to observe it in himself need only be reminded of his powers for direct inspection. We might help to direct him by citing examples where something is known by inspection, or by using allusive language, saying that mind "sees" or "grasps" whatever matters stand before it. But there is no argument by which to prove that we do have a power for the direct inspecting of ideas and ourselves. There is no argument required, because no one reflecting upon his thinking, whatever its object, would require that the existence or character of this intuiting power be proven or explained to him.

Notice, however, that intuition is complex, having three constituent factors that are mentioned or implied in the quotation just above. First is the claim that knowledge is acquaintance: we know as the mind's eye sees. Second is the assumption that something is given for seeing: it is set before the mind as the content or object of our intuition. Third is the claim that our power for inspecting a content is reflexive, so that we know ourselves to have intuition in the moment of using it. Descartes supposes that these three factors are distinguishable but inseparable. Acquaintance must have its object, as light is not luminous if there is no object reflecting it. That object or content is equally reliant on mind's apprehending of it, as it may exist only by virtue of being perceived. Nor is my self-acquaintance incidental to my inspection of the matters set before me. That is one of the principal claims of the *Meditations,* where knowledge of oneself is the foundation upon which every other knowledge claim is based. This most elemental fact is, indeed, more immediate to me than any other content or object on which I might reflect. My self-perception is unmediated, occurring at the moment and in the act where those other objects are perceived. Yet, it is not possible that I might reflect upon myself while having an otherwise empty mind. It is because I am conscious of something else, because that other thing has excited my awareness, that I discover myself. Accordingly, Descartes' intuitionism requires that knowing mind should have two objects before it: some content more or less clearly perceived, and itself.

6. Plato and Descartes

Descartes' emphasis upon acquaintance is reminiscent of Plato in the *Seventh Epistle* where every discursive account of matters known is transcended as mind sees the Forms. Plato, however, never supposed that reflection upon ourselves as knowers is a condition for the having and certifying of other knowledge claims. No one needs confirmation that his eyes are open when looking directly into the Sun. Knowledge of Forms is like that visual experience: We see them or not. The seeing is so forcible that we do not require, as Descartes supposes, the additional act of self-acquaintance to certify that mind has something before it, something seen as it is.

The issue between Descartes and Plato is a difference of opinion regarding the conditions for knowledge: Is it enough that we see things as they are, or must we be able to certify that our judgements about the things perceived are justified by the evidence? Plato dispenses with this additional requirement for the reason just mentioned; Descartes insists upon it. Mind is to step back from its engagement with the ideas perceived to satisfy itself that our judgements satisfy a criterion for truth, namely, the one of clarity and distinctness. This is the emphasis which diverts attention from the objects of belief, redirecting it to the evidence or reasons for belief. Descartes' *cogito* is for this reason a more complicated agent than Plato's *nous*. *Nous* can be relied upon to grasp its object. The *cogito* must do that while satisfying itself that this seeing meets the evidentiary standards for true belief. This is the difference between a mind first dazzled but then filled by the light of the sun when emerging from a cave, and that other mind so much in control of itself that it will not assent to any idea unless it is satisfied that the idea is clearly and distinctly perceived. Plato's mind knows, as though spontaneously. The mind described by Descartes is more considered, as knowledge achieved differs from the responsibility for citing the reasons which justify true belief.

There is of course a basis for Descartes' caution in the gap which exists between mind with its ideas of other things, and those things themselves. Our ideas are, with the one exception of our self-knowledge, representations. They are placed in us by God, with the guarantee that ideas perceived clearly and distinctly will be true. We need take care that this condition is satisfied before we claim the truth of our ideas, thereby invoking the divine guarantee. This is routine in the case of necessary truth: God might contravene them, says Descartes, but not without violating those conditions for order which God has himself prescribed. The basis for our conviction is all the more fragile when the claims at issue are true contingently, if at all. Here God's intervention will be *ad hoc,* as he defends us from deception in particular circumstances. Establishing the evidentiary basis for our beliefs, their clarity and distinctness, is obligatory if we are to call upon the divine guarantee. No wonder that Descartes is preoccupied by the reasons for belief.

Plato has averted these difficulties by supposing that truth is the identity of knower and known, and not the relationship of an idea or judgement to the object or state of affairs satisfying it. For there is no gap between *nous* and the Forms it knows. Plato would have us consider these two things. On the one side, *nous* is already imprinted with the Forms—i.e., they are innate—this implies that knowledge of the Forms is self-knowledge and that truth is the identity of thinking mind and the ideas thought. On the other side is Plato's insistence that *nous* is active, where its principal task is the one of passing beyond the finitude and perspective of obfuscating body in order that the universal, necessary, and eternal form of things should be disclosed to it. It follows that the ideas within us are not like raisins in pudding, so many discrete and disparate lumps. They are instead the traces of rationality, the evidence of cosmic order as they draw to themselves that bit of world-soul which inhabits this particular body. This is rational intellect as it passes beyond body so that it may discern the Forms in themselves. Descartes' caution would be inappropriate here. Mind need not hesitate to pronounce its judgements true while evaluating the evidence for them, for *nous* has returned to its rational source, seeing things as they incontestably are. Descartes' *cogito* knows that order vicariously, by way of its ideas and judgements. That is his reason for saying that mind should scrutinize its claims so carefully, taking responsibility for affirming its judgements only as there is evidence necessary and sufficient for their truth.

The reciprocity of method and mind implies that this difference of emphasis within intuitionism should express itself in different claims about mind's activities and faculties. We do find that other difference. Plato's *nous* is a universal principle or activity without personality, while Descartes' *cogito* is particular and subjective, wanting confirmation of its judgements about other things, and still more exigently about itself. *Nous* needn't care about itself; first, because its disassociation from the rest of world-soul is temporary and incidental; second, because its only task is the one of exhibiting or perceiving the differentiations and order of the Forms; third, because they fill and articulate it in a way that precludes error. Descartes cannot be so cavalier when the mind he describes lacks all these advantages. He must describe the *cogito* in ways that supply it with all the powers required for establishing that its ideas are faithful representations.

7. Descartes' notion of intuiting mind

What are the structures and behaviors that Descartes ascribes to mind? We expect that the answer will be quickly forthcoming, because Descartes often professes his sensitivity to the reciprocity of method, mind, and ontology. If his intuitionism requires that mind have certain powers, and that the method be applied to certain entities only, then surely Descartes can be relied upon to specify these restrictions. This is a reasonable expectation, but one that leaves us disappointed. Descartes argues in the *Meditations* that two things are so plain as to be certain: namely, *that* I am and *what* I am. Having discovered by self-inspection that we exist, we expect that mind's inspection of its nature will be equally unproblematic: Each of us will apprehend his own mind as it acts, seeing its structures and functions as they are.

> But what then am I? A thinking thing. What is that? It is something doubting, understanding, affirming, denying, wishing for, wishing not, imagining as well, and seeing.[16]

These are the modes of our intuition, but notice that this list says nothing of the properties or design which qualify mind for intuitive thinking. How is it that we formulate a judgement and then stand back from it to satisfy ourselves that our judgement is clear and distinct, only then affirming the judgement? How is mind organized so that it may perform this contemplative doubletake? We expect that intuition will quickly discern its own conditions. We are surprised, and a little confused when the pertinent facts are not immediately visible. Then we remember that intuitionists—from Descartes through Kant, Hegel, Husserl, and Sartre—do not agree about the identity of those activities and faculties that were to be as evident and certain as the fact that I am.

8. A different way of determining mind's features

We avert these disputes about the nature of intuiting mind only if we repudiate intuitionism as our method for discovering the character of intuiting mind. Rather than ask what mind perceives itself to be, we may ask about those acts and faculties which are presupposed but available to inference as mind inspects whatever things different from itself are set before it. Descartes never suggests that we should proceed in this way, as no one committed to the intuitionist method ever should do. Yet we have no alternative to this inferential, nonintuitionist procedure when Descartes is unable to describe the structures of intuiting mind, and when his successors disagree so radically about the properties revealed to self-inspection. I shall argue below that Kant is a vital figure within the intuitionist tradition, though he did not hesitate to choose inference over intuition when he set out to identify the conditions for intuition. I suggest that we apply this Kantian technique while foreswearing certain of the implications that he intended when speaking of these conditions as "transcendental." This word signifies to Kant that the mental conditions for intuition are exempt from every constraint but moral and rational ones; that is they are not subject to the limits imposed by space, time, and causality. If, on the other hand, "transcendental" means only that any mind thinking intuitively need have these conditions within it, then there is nothing objectionable in the word, for its means only that our inferences have universal scope as they apply to every intuiting mind. This is innocuous, as it would be if we were to claim equal universality when inferring from leaky faucets to least conditions that need obtain in all of them. More accurately now, our procedure in identifying these conditions for intuition is hypothetical. Starting from the claims for intuition—e.g., that it provides direct and certain knowledge of the matters set before us—we make hypotheses about the kinds of things that mind need do in order to inspect the matters given to it.

There are, I infer, five mental activities or faculties required for intuitionist thought. First is a sensorium in which ideas or percepts appear before the mind. Second is the mind's "keen vision" for discerning these contents, including their differentiations and relations. Third is a power for resolving (i.e., analyzing) complex and obscure ideas into their simpler parts. Fourth is the synthetic power for constructing, or deducing, complex but clarified ideas from these simples. (These last two considerations are the two sides of judgement, as we affirm that some complex idea has particular constituents, or that a clarified complex is formed by joining particular simples.) Fifth is the reflective act in which mind discerns itself and evaluates its products. Are my judgements well-made? Who and what am I? These are questions falling to this reflexive act. It has the responsibility for assuring both that we have evidence sufficient for making true judgements and for discerning mind's nature and role as the self-certifying foundation for all knowledge claims.

There are of course some presuppositions additional to these five. Descartes emphasizes, for example, that language is required for expressing our judgements, where the applications of logic bear especially upon these sentences. The expressing of judgements is, nevertheless, incidental to judgement, as we prove by remarking the many judgements which are not expressed as sentences. They testify to the various places where language hardly goes, where there are no words adequate to the subject matters considered—e.g., the shifting moods in the face of a friend. These are things that we see and understand, though having no words to express what is seen. There are likely to be many judgements which we formulate and confirm without relying upon language for their expression, so that language, however essential to many judgements having abstract content, is not so universal a consideration as the five listed before it. Will is a more likely candidate. Descartes insists that no judgement be affirmed until its clarity and distinctness is perceived, will being the power for withholding assent while reflection establishes that this condition is satisfied. Where no judgement shows its necessity on its face, we should withhold our assent from every one. Will is, therefore, a sixth act or condition for making true judgements. I reduce this claim to a subsidiary place because will is more a defense against error than a condition for knowledge. Later intuitionists will acknowledge all of the five considerations cited above while denying or ignoring this sixth one: they will deny that will is vital to knowledge.

The inferred character of these principal five conditions for intuitionist knowledge contrasts with the things inspected, including sensory data, ideas, and judgements. These are the cynosure for which mind's inferred acts and structures are the background conditions. We are reminded of that metaphor which directs so much of intuitionist thought: Mind is a theatre where events occurring on stage or screen are set luminously before that witness who observes them. This is the metaphor which comes nearest to expressing these complementary emphases: There are the matters presented for inspection, and the mutual conditioning of thinking subject and the matters thought. Nothing is given if there is no subject to observe it, while no subject is illumined if there is no content to excite that thinker's intuiting powers.

9. Is mind inspectable?

It is not implausible that the conditions for intuition should be uninspectable, with inference as the only method for identifying them. Mind, we might say, is like the eye: it brings the visible world into focus without itself being inspectable. Yet Descartes has so plainly demurred; nothing, he says, is better known to mind than the mind itself. Shouldn't it follow that all five of these consituent conditions are known to mind as it turns upon itself? We may sometimes examine the data or judgements set before us without regard for our method's psychological conditions; but can't we also turn upon ourselves while making distinctions or joining thoughts or words? We expect, if we are intuitionists, that self-reflecting mind may observe its own attitudes and behaviors, as a dancer monitors her posture while moving across a stage. Descartes' failure to elaborate upon these aspects of mind might count against his claims to thoroughness but not against the intuitionist demand that every claim about any matter of fact be certified by an act of inspection. Intuitionism would be free to establish that it does have access to its own conditions, thereby vindicating the claim that this is a universally adequate method. We should be able to say and confirm that mind is a theatre existing in and for itself, requiring only God or its own self-constituting act to secure its existence. Eliminate the reference to God and there remains this inspecting, self-reflecting, and sustaining subject. This is the substance that should be first in knowledge as well as first in being.

This is or ought to be the intuitionist program, so far as method roots itself in the psychology which it presupposes. Yet nothing so tidy is accomplished, because self-reflection does not expose more than evidence for some of the powers listed above. There is, for example, our claim about that sensorium in which ideas and sensory data appear as given. Kant remarked that the unity of consciousness cannot be explained from within consciousness, but only as we appeal to the extraconscious—i.e., "transcendental"—conditions for it. Inspecting mind is equally confounded when asked to account for its own acuity and applications. This is true whether it is the mind's "keen vision," its power for analysis and synthesis, or the ones making it capable of self-reflection. We have the products of thought and sensation, as when an argument is expressed on paper, while the activities themselves and the structures required for performing them are a mystery to self-inspecting mind. Descartes never tries to describe them. Husserl does try; but he fails for a reason endemic to intuitionist method: self-inspecting mind discovers the effects of what is done, to it or within it, not their causes.

This conclusion is the basis for Locke's scepticism about our prospects for knowing the external world, for we cannot be assured that our percepts are like their causes, meaning the things they represent. This same principle should make us dubious about the claim that mental affections are a sufficient basis for assertions about the nature of mental activity. There is no reason for supposing that the effect is like its cause, so that we might discern the structure and activity of mind in the matters inspected. Kantian arguments enforce this point in a somewhat different way, as Kant emphasizes the unity, neccessity, and universality of experience while saying that particularities within the given could not be the basis for these features. Finally, and perhaps most surprising, inspecting mind does not even have a comprehensive view of its content. This is the Kantian and Freudian discovery that organizing ideas and motives are disguised or unknown to us even as they direct thought and action.

These several remarks converge on this one point: intuitionism cannot depend upon the mind's *inspectio* for a comprehensive specification of the mental conditions which make intuition possible. We might hope to identify these conditions inferentially as Kant does in the A Deduction of the First Critique, where apprehension, reproduction, and recognition are said to be conditions for the unity and intelligibility of sensory data. But these are inferences used to identify the conditions which make intuition possible. These inferred conditions are not themselves inspectable, as the mechanisms for integrating percepts, organizing thought and retrieving information from memory are not inspected but only inferred.

A self revealed altogether to itself is, since Descartes, the intuitionist ideal. That these essential conditions for intuition do nevertheless elude inspection is a fact plaguing intuitionism throughout its development. There are two alternatives, one as damning as the other, when the psychological conditions for intuition are not inspectable: Either the method has restricted application, thereby failing to achieve the universality claimed for it; or we have a "universal" method which ignores or denies the conditions for its application—i.e., those conditions are "noumenal," so that questions about them are "meaningless" or "unintelligible." Descartes never espouses either one of these choices. There was no reason for him to do that so long as he supposed that the conditions for intuition are subject to discovery by a self-intuition. But Descartes also fails to tell what these acts and structure might be. Intuition alone could not tell him, so that the reciprocity between his notions of method and mind is incomplete and unsatisfactory.

10. Descartes' intuitionist ontology

There is no comparable embarassment when we consider this method's ontological presuppositions, for Descartes is careful to assure that the domain of things to which the method applies, or part of it at least, is suited to its applications. There are three kinds of entitites to consider: sensations, ideas, and mind itself. Sensations are obscure in two ways: in themselves and in regard to their origins. Their causes have acted upon our bodies, producing nervous reactions which terminate in these effects. These causes would be partially or altogether unknown but for God's guarantee; it justifies our claim that clear and distinct ideas of these sensory data are like their causes. We penetrate the obscurity of the sensations themselves only as we use ideas to think them. We see, for example, the various states of wax, sometimes brittle, other times soft, but we do not understand the stable form expressible in these protean ways until we have discerned the wax's geometrical essence. Only that idea enables us to predict and explain the various sensible appearances. The ideas of essential natures exist originally as ideas in the mind of God. He has placed them in our minds, thereby guaranteeing their fit. Certainly, God's mind and His manner of inspecting ideas is different from our own, as God presumably inspects an essence all at once while we require time for surveying its parts and relations. This is a specific difference, but one that cannot reduce the generic identity of ideas, whether in God's mind or our own. Hence, the fit of God's ideas to His own mind already anticipates the demand that they be suitable for inspection by our minds. The ideas relevant here are the "simple and pure natures"; they are ideas of spiritual or corporeal substance, or of properties which are common to substances of both kinds. So, we think the essential extendedness of material things, as we have a geometry with which to construct and then demonstrate the defining properties of spatial forms. We also have an idea of ourselves as thinking beings, and ideas of the existence, unity, and duration of every material and spiritual being. It follows that every idea is subject to one or both of the things promised by Descartes' method: every idea is inspectable; some ideas are the simples from which more complex ideas are constructed or derived. Ontology is therefore perfectly calibrated to method. We can inspect the pure and simple natures, but also each step of our constructions and derivations, and even sometimes the whole skein of steps.

Is there, however, a contradiction in my account of method's relation to its two presuppositions? For I claim that Descartes' psychology is not adequate to his method: he announces *that* mind is, but he says very little about *what* mind is after remarking that it thinks. Descartes has nothing to say of mind's structures, or their constraining effect on how or what we think. Is this evaluation consistent with my saying that the ontology presupposed by Descartes' method dovetails nicely with it? For thinking substance is one of the simple natures which Descartes would have us inspect. How can Descartes' psychology be inadequate to his method, when the idea of thinking substance is one of the ideas set plainly before us? The answer has two parts. Descartes' ontology complements his method by providing for the ideas which are to be the objects of inspecting mind. Yet this fact does not guarantee the ontological adequacy of ideas which are alleged to be either simple and pure or derivative and complex. So, the idea of thinking substance is that of a luminous consciousness playing upon its content or itself. But this is not the idea of those structures or activities which are pertinent if mind is to be a conscious agent, one that inspects its contents and self while analyzing and synthesizing its ideas. Descartes does make mind available to itself; we do have, he says, an idea of ourselves as thinking substances. But that idea is, in Leibniz's terms, clear and confused. It is not an articulate idea of that structure which mind need have in order to perform as Descartes requires. Descartes' intuitionism is, therefore, incomplete. Inspecting mind requires that mind should have a structure and behaviors that inspecting mind cannot identify or confirm.

11. Does knowledge reach beyond our inspecting minds?

Remember now that the interplay of method, mind, and ontology has knowledge as its aim. Knowledge for Descartes is the certain and evident cognition of essences and their relations. Intuition is to be our method for knowing these things; but then this other question remains: How far does intuition reach? Can it extend beyond mind into the world where the existence and character of things are independent of what we think or say of them?

Knowledge should be cosmic if its objects originate as ideas in the mind of God. It should reach beyond our finite minds to the archetypes from which God creates this and any other actual world. Intuition of the sort which Plato describes promises to disclose these Forms. Intuition as Descartes describes it cannot do that, because the ideas placed in our minds have been modified to suit our finite intellects. We cannot so much as imagine the essences in God's mind, or the differences between them, their material instantiations, and the ideas that were filed and reduced before being placed in our minds. We might start with our ideas, hoping to identify and then substract whatever in them is peculiar to the fact that we entertain them. But there is no way that Cartesian intuition could make this determination, for it does not have information about God's ideas or the material world with which to make comparisons. We are stymied because of being separated from the world by the very ideas that were to supply our access to it. We risk having to say that human knowledge cannot extend past the content of its ideas into the world. We are saved from having to say this by two things. First is the consideration that ideas which are necessary because their negations are contradictory are a reliable basis for claims about the world as it must be. Second is the alleged fact that God's goodness precludes His deception. These necessary and contingent truths are the only reeds on which to base Descartes' assumption that the intuition of matters standing directly before our minds is a sound basis for inferences about the existence and character of things existing independently of us.

This is disappointing. Method was to be the procedure for investigating truth. Now truth's ambit is shrunk to the perimeter of self-inspecting mind. That happens because Descartes' method has been warped by its psychology and ontology until it produces a crippled result. Plato has already described intuiting *nous* as it reaches out, grasping the Forms, prehending things as they are. Descartes has a different psychology: He supposes that Plato's world-soul divides into myriad individual minds, each one a sliver of intellect exhibiting the essences which originate in God's mind. This is a sceptical retreat from Plato's intuitionism, because our knowledge of these essences is passive: Rather than search for essences at their source, we wait for God to place ideas of them within us. We have merely to turn upon ourselves, looking within as God guarantees the applicability of our ideas to the world. But then we are firmly in touch with ourselves while out of touch with the world, with no way to confirm that our ideas are adequate to it. Knowledge extends no further than the ideas we clearly and distinctly perceive. No wonder that God is the linchpin within Descartes' metaphysics, the one factor saving Descartes from psychologism and subjective idealism.

12. God's role in Descartes' theory of knowledge

That so many readers deny the importance of God within Descartes' metaphysics is worth remarking. We should reject this interpretation for the flagrant mistake it is; but then we learn something fundamental of method and theory as we consider the factors which oppose them to one another. For Descartes' claims are animated by two conflicting motives. First is his theory about the universe, and our place within it. Second is Descartes' method, with its associated psychology and ontology. These two are mutually supporting when Descartes affirms that the essences which make the world intelligible are suitable for presentation to inspecting minds. There are other times, however, when metaphysical theory outruns the method. Their opposition is conspicuous when Descartes formulates his notion of God.

We have two things to consider: Descartes' strictures regarding what shall qualify, as an idea, and the demands that his theory makes of God. Method requires that every idea be set before our inspecting minds, where nothing counts as an idea if it is not susceptible to inspection. The only simple ideas, however, are those of mental and corporeal substances, and the ideas of properties common to them— e.g., unity. The idea of God is not one of these simples; but neither is it one of the complex ideas constructed from them. Consequently, we have no idea of God. We are left with the name, but without content for the idea of God's nature. This result subverts Descartes' metaphysics in both of the places where God is essential to it; i.e., to the guarantee that clear and distinct ideas have extramental referents, and to his theory of cause. It is, for example, vital to Descartes' realism that God should guarantee the truth of our clear and distinct ideas, for otherwise most of our knowledge would reach no farther than the ideas themselves. Necessary truths would obtain in every possible world; but there would be no basis for saying that contingent ideas do have objects which are independent of us for their existence and character. Only the assurance of God's perfection, including his existence and incapacity for deception, saves us from scepticism. More obscure but equally vital to him are Descartes' claims that, first, there is no less perfection in a cause than in its effect, second, that we cannot understand the effect if we do not understand its cause, third, that finite effects have an infinite cause, and fourth, that God is the infinite cause from which all else derives. I, for example, am not cause of myself. Nor can I have a comprehensive idea of what I am and how I exist if I do not perceive the manner of my generation by, and continuing dependence upon God. God is perfect and complete. We are the derivative and contingent expressions of His being, so that the clearest ideas of ourselves are incomplete and obscure when formulated in ignorance of Him. This is Descartes' debt to Plotinus for whom God is the One, and source of all differentiated, contingent things. If method precludes our having an idea of this God, then so much the worse for method.

13. The opposition of theory and method

A philosophic method should enable us to conceive and prove everything which our metaphysics affirms; or we should not want to say anything that is not assertible and testable by the standards of our method. The fit between these two is imperfect when theory is leaner than method or when theory would have us say and prove something which is meaningless or undecidable by the lights of our method. Eliminative materialism is an example of the one imbalance, when theory denies the reality of intrasubjective phenomena while we use an empirical method which discovers them. Descartes' own claims are an instance of the other conflict, where theory speaks of the world in ways that method would bar.

There may be several explanations for the fact that a philosopher so eminent as Descartes espouses a method that would deter the formulation of his own metaphysical theory. But one reason is decisive, namely, the failure to think systematically so that method and theory are calibrated, each one reinforcing, neither one precluding the other. Perhaps Descartes is careless about this reciprocity between method and theory because of ignoring the consequences of a fact which he does otherwise acknowledge: a method will have its own psychological and ontological presuppositions. Every method is, because of these associated claims about mind and the world, a metaphysical theory in its own right. The opposition between one's metaphysics and method is, therefore, a conflict between two metaphysical theories, each one motivated by different considerations.

No wonder that some of Descartes' interpretors have argued that God is irrelevant to his metaphysics, as He must be unknown and unthinkable if we have no ideas of Him. Yet God is all the while vital to Descartes' theories of knowledge and being, in the ways summarized above. The dispute over Descartes' "real" beliefs is, apparently, unresolvable. Method alone might turn Descartes to atheism, though method is incompetent to express ideas that are fundamental to his more explicit metaphysical theory.

Which has priority, method or the metaphysical theory it formulates and tests? Method has priority in the respect that it limits the content—hence, the claims—of theories formulated within it, as a method having a severe empiricist meaning requirement prohibits the formulation of claims about God or eternal possibilities. The order of authority is reversed, however, when we emphasize that it is theories which are true or false, and theories with their explicit claims about the world which direct action—e.g., as our notion of cause has regulative force in ordinary practice and experimental science. Where method is only instrumental to formulating theories, we may want to enrich method so that it may serve for expressing and testing them.

Taken together, these contrary views preclude our saying that either one, theory or method, is prior to the other. Yet, there are two bases for accommodation. First is the consideration that no method is plausible if it does not incorporate the logical, psychological, and ontological claims of theories which are believed to be confirmed. Second is the fact that confirmations of a theory are also confirmations of the logic, psychology, and ontology presupposed by the method used to formulate and test it. There is an unspoken conviction within Descartes that method does cohere with his theory in this way. Descartes believes, for example, that his claims about mind's character are directly confirmed, with the result that intuitionist method's psychological assumptions have the truth of independently formulated theoretical claims as evidence for their truth. He also supposes, if only tacitly, that success in using the method redounds to its logical, psychological, and ontological assumptions. If, for example, deduction produces clear and distinct (hence, true) ideas, then our success in confirming their truth speaks for the validity of our logic. These reinforcements—of method by theories confirmed and of credible theories by reliability of the method used for testing them—are an intuitionist ideal. The reinforcements are plainest when the topics of inquiry are similar to the method's presuppositions, as the study of emotions confirms both our claims about them and our assumptions that intuiting mind is available to itself. But reciprocity also obtains when the theory being formulated and tested is one having a subject matter which is remote from the intuitionist method's presuppositions—e.g., geometry. For here too our successful theorizing confirms some claims about logic, mind, and ontology, as proofs relying upon imagined constructions confirm the assumption that mind is able to assemble complexes from the simples set before us. It follows that the method for formulating and testing claims about matters of fact, especially this intuitionist method, is not independent of the theories it tests. There is a convergence, as the factual claims assumed by the method prefigure the ones it tests.

This is a troubling result. We have averted the collision of Descartes' method with his metaphysics by destroying their independence. Method is, however, useless as a test of theory if method already presupposes the truth of the very theory to be tested. This is not a problem when the theory at issue concerns particulars or lower-order generalities, as Descartes requires that anything considered by the mind be a simple or complex of simples. There is nothing in this to anticipate the character of particular simples or the complexes constructed from them. The results are more pernicious when both theory and the presuppositions of our method are very general, for then the circle is very small: Method's presuppositions restrict its applicability, while every thing to which it applies confirms those assumptions. Intuitionist method is like that; it bars us from saying anything which violates its presuppositions, e.g., that no uninspectable things are real, while everything we can say confirms them—as when everything acknowledged as real is inspectable. Much of the power credited to Descartes' intuitionism devolves about this pair of mutually supporting claims. Still, this cannot be the final word about the relation of his theory and method, as one or the other must be ignored if we are to say yes or no to the idea of God.

What should we do when forced to choose between metaphysical theory and method? There is, or seems to be, one answer that is always correct: look beyond method's dispute with theory to the facts themselves. What are they? Some philosophers satisfy this demand for the facts by looking to sensory experience. It is, they suppose, the unimpeachable basis for solving every intellectual dispute. What are the sensible phenomena, they ask, all the while supposing that these and the facts are one. If metaphysical theory and method appeal to different sensory data then both may be sound, though their factual claims are different. If method and theory rely upon the same data, then they agree about the facts, whatever their apparent differences. If one or the other cannot tell what data would settle their dispute, then that one is disqualified as meaningless. Empiricism is to make the evaluation simple and unproblematic, as sometimes it is. Yet, how shall we proceed when the factual disputes between method and theory concern the status of mathematicals or other things whose reality exceeds every possible empirical difference? We realize that this first proposal settles these more difficult cases only by ignoring them. For the appeal to sensory data is only the injunction that we apply a method having an ontology which is explicit but narrowly drawn. Anyone rejecting this ontology, as it identifies factuality with empirical data and their differences, may ignore the claim that empiricism is a neutral ground for adjudicating the disputes between metaphysical theory and method.

A different way of arbitrating these disputes would have us go in the contrary direction. It would locate the facts which settle these disputes by calling on rational intuition. This is the standpoint of Plato in the *Seventh Epistle,* and of the Absolute described in Hegel's *Phenomenology of Spirit.* They reject the contest of method and theory as the symptom of partialities endemic to discourse and its fractured conceptualizations. Clear vision, especially the sight of intuiting reason, is to liberate us from these partial truths and contending points of view. Too bad that this persuasion is only the inverted image of the first one, as rational intuitionism is like empiricism when both suppose that we may withdraw from theory in order to argue from a point of view where truth is assured by our accurate perception of reality. The one looks to ideas, the other to sensory data; but either way, disputes between metaphysical theory and intuitionist method are to be settled by deferring to the facts as seen.

Notice, however, that neither of these appeals to the facts is naive and unproblematic. Both assume that we have direct access to the facts, though this is itself a tacit claim about that method which is to guarantee the truth of our judgements. What method is this? Just that intuitionist method whose ontological assumptions are challenged by such theories as Descartes' metaphysics, with its notion of God. For never mind the difference between empiricism and rational intuitionism. They are merely two expressions of the one method which prescribes that we should decide the truth of our claims by a direct inspection of reality.

Why have we ignored this blatant appeal to intuitionism even as we try to arbitrate intuitionism's conflict with metaphysical theory? Because there is a powerful conviction within us that we might surpass, evade, or settle "merely" theoretical disputes by examining the facts as they are set directly before our intuiting minds. Our appeal to "the facts" speaks to this impatience with theory and speculation.

Every claim about the world might be settled, we hope, by direct inspection. There is also this other consideration to explain this apparently harmless invocation of directly inspectable facts, namely, that method, especially intuitionist method, is not widely understood as having psychological and ontological presuppositions. Method seems innocent and neutral when intuitionism congratulates itself for a minimum of artifice. For isn't method just the directive that we should turn the eye, or the mind's eye, upon whatever things are set before it? Certainly, we are to be rigorous as we examine the given; but it is always the exhaustive inspectability of the things set before us that is fundamental. We ignore the fact that this intuitionist method is complementary to a psychology and an ontology, so that its passion for "the facts" is a function of their demand that everything real must be inspectable.

We had hoped to resolve the dispute between intuitionist method and Descartes' metaphysics by deferring to the facts, but there are no deciding inspectable facts. The conflict will have to be resolved in some other way. What might that be?

A usable answer will have to identify the pertinent, dispute-resolving facts, while acknowledging, first, that we have no direct access to them, and second, that any method appropriate for locating these facts will be constrained by the psychology and ontology it presupposes. There is a method whose ontology does not conflict with any noncontradictory claim formulated within it. That method also provides a way for testing these claims, as we may hypothesize that God exists and then ask what difference would be made if there were to be a God. This difference might be sensible, but then too it might happen that we could only specify it conceptually, as would be true if God were the unperceivable but necessary condition for all sensible, physical reality, or the One. Either way, we could establish the meaningfulness and applicability of our hypotheses by identifying those conditions which would obtain if the hypotheses were true. Descartes' problem could not arise if our metaphysical theories were formulated within this other method, because we would regard both the metaphysics implicit in his method and the one of his explicit theory as hypotheses. Asking then about the difference that would be made to reality if either were true, we would also identify and evaluate the evidence available for deciding between them. The metaphysical applications of this hypothetical method, with its psychological and ontological assumptions, are described in *Hypothesis and the*

Spiral of Reflection. That claim is incidental here, where the method at issue is Descartes' intuitionism and where theoretical claims are to be formulated and tested to its satisfaction. Descartes is embarrassed. He has described the limits upon intuition, and they preclude our having a clear and distinct idea, or any idea whatever, of God—though God is fundamental to Descartes' view about knowledge and being. The conflict of his method and theory is irremediable within the framework of Descartes' own thinking. There is no procedure there for testing these opposed claims about reality.

14. Method's ascendance over theory

A method's conflict with one or more of the theories it tests may have this remarkable consequence. It may intensify our commitment to that method, thereby to the metaphysical theory which is more or less explicit within it. These issues coalesce when Descartes' method-ological rigor asserts itself in the following two ways.

First is the preference for method over any theory it might be used to formulate. Method expresses our faith that the world is know-able, but it is also the hard edge of the demand that our passion for truth should not make us credulous. We are to call true, and believe, only those claims that method can formulate, test, and prove. We become positivists, as Descartes risks becoming, when reverence is diverted from theories and inquiry to the autonomous procedure which constrains our theorizing. Not what we say of the world, but only the routine for approving these sayings: this is our focus when method's applications, and not the various theories tested, are our point of reference. We who cared to be wise about the world learn to settle for the reliability and prudence of our method. Does it keep us from error, deflating the pretensions of those who say more? That is wisdom enough. This emphasis seems justified because of being con-sistent with our philosophic birthright. For the method to be used for testing theories is the one demanding that we open the mind's eye in order that we may see things as they are. This sober act of inspection, always judicious, nothing hidden or disguised, is the high road from *nous* and the terrible eyes of Greek philosophers to the long shadows of our Cartesian afternoon. No, Descartes would not have us look directly on things themselves; but yes, we do retain that inspecting power, and we do turn it critically upon the theories that would lay the world bare. No longer being explorers ourselves, we are to have the fiercest standards for what shall count as seaworthy. Very few metaphysical theories will ever leave port.

The second point is relevant now, for the complementarity of method with mind and ontology has the effect that method stifles theory to the benefit of that metaphysical theory immanent within itself. The favored metaphysical view affirms that the only thinkable reality is the one to which this method gives us access. Ours is to be a world where reality is a function of our being able to think it. Nothing will be real if it is not or cannot be set before and perceived by our inspecting minds. This will be a world having one organized focus, for it will be constituted by those acts of recognition, analysis and synthesis with which mind differentiates and arranges the matters set before it. Method's psychology will begin to intrude upon its ontology to the point of dominating it. For what shall be prior in being: the things inspected, or the mind which entertains them?

We are reminded that mind is the measure, and that mind's responsibility for meaning and truth lodges all the power for constituting a thinkable reality within our minds. We shall decide these two things: first, what thoughts or sentences are to count as meaningful; second, that meaningful thoughts or sentences have satisfied mind's criteria for what is to count as true. Descartes supposes that these criteria have been set within our minds by God, though his intuitionist successors will discount that claim in favor of the view that we decide the criteria both for meaning and truth. Judgements or assertions will be meaningful and true only as they satisfy these stipulations of ours.

Notice that the right to make these stipulations may be so construed as to empower us for determining the domain of things existing. The argument confirming this is straight forward. Let us agree that there is or can be a true sentence signifying anything that is. Conversely, no thing exists if there is not and cannot be a sentence truly affirming it. This last remark puts the burden of existence on true sentences, for something exists only as there is or can be a sentence affirming that it is. Remember now that the criteria for what shall count as true are settled by mind. Remember too that questions about truth cannot even arise until mind has decided the rules for meaning, because meaningful sentences are the only ones that can be true. It follows that snow being white is not an actual or even a possible state of affairs until mind has formulated the rules making this formula, 'Snow is white,' meaningful. Once that is settled we can ask if the sentence satisfies our standards for truth. If it does, then yes, there is the state of affairs, the matter of fact, signified by the sentence. But if not meaningful or true, then this putative state of affairs is annhilated. It falls into limbo with all the referents to our other meaningless sayings.

'Reality' is, apparently, only a word used for signifying in the "material" mode that set of judgements or sentences which are true in the "formal" mode, those which have satisfied minds' criteria for truth. But then all of the things acknowledged in this way will exist contingently, meaning that they exist at mind's pleasure. It has made the rules determining what shall count as meaningful and true, and it may change those rules. No matter then if we distinguish necessary from contingent truths; that is merely a way for distinguishing between the rules for deductive and inductive logic when both of them have no special claim apart from our determination to use the rules constituting them. Only mind itself will exist necessarily, though we need be careful in telling what sort of necessity this is. For my existence is contingent rather than necessary in the respect that I need not be. Yet, I do think, as when I establish the rules for meaning and truth. Then my existence *is* necessary, necessary as a condition for the thinking which creates the domain of other existents.

The special status of my experience is confirmed by the consideration that it does not depend upon the application of these rules, or upon the finding that some thought or sentence is true because of satisfying them. For I confirm my existence by an act of direct inspection. This self-discovery is the fundament on which the existence of every other thing turns. I decide what shall count as meaningful and true, as I discover in self-perception that I have the power for making and unmaking every coherent story about the world. I am the measure of all that is, and is not.

These two factors, a positivist emphasis upon method at cost to theory and the reinforcing of the subjectivism implicit within his intuitionist method, are Descartes' legacy to metaphysics. Descartes' intuitionism murders theory by requiring that every speculative idea should satisfy the demand that its referent be exhaustively inspectable. It cannot be true, or even meaningful, if that condition is not satisfied. The idea of God has been our test case; it must be simple, says Descartes' *Rules,* or the complex constructed from simples. That it is neither entails that we have no idea of God; hence, that God does not exist. What is to happen when other speculative ideas, matter and the uninspectable aspects of mind, for example, have been mutilated to satisfy method's demand that nothing can be real if the idea of it is not exhaustively inspectable? We are to turn upon ourselves, remarking how difficult it is to know other things, celebrating another time that nothing is better known to mind than mind itself. That Descartes' own metaphysical theory carries so far beyond the demands of his method is the example to remember as we consider the variant kinds of intuitionism, and that bias against speculation, in metaphysics or even science, for which they are the source.

Chapter Two

The Dialectical Cycles of Intuitionist Method

1. A privileged sanctuary

P hilosophers have fled from nature as a humbled tribe eludes an enemy by retreating into the bush. Then, as all of nature was claimed for physics and science, we took our stand as the masters of logic, morals, and especially of mind. For surely, I am, I exist each time I pronounce or conceive it. My own mental states are directly inspectable, with no gap between them and me. There is no reason then for commending or inflating the evidence which might justify my claims, for I say of my mind exactly what mind shows itself to be, not more or less. Still, my verbal reports about my mental life are only the expression of my self-knowledge, not that knowing itself. My self-knowledge is not essentially linguistic or even propositional. I know my mind because I am immediately available to self-inspection. The judgements made about me are true, and known to be so because the mind knowing is identical with the mind known. Language merely reports about discoveries which are made within the intimacy of this relation. Mental activity is not a subject for which we need language or science to inform us. The experimental, inferential, and fallible character of scientific method is irrelevant here, where the subject matters are ready to hand and where claims about them are certain. Philosophy is the discipline having title to this domain. Its subject matters are prior to and more assured than any that science can explore. For science is removed from its objects, first collecting evidence, then hypothesizing about those variables which determine that matters should be as we find them. Philosophy, by comparison, is specially privileged. Its judgements are evaluated immediately against data standing directly before the mind's eye. This is true, originally, of our self-knowledge, but it applies as well to logic and morals. Why do they share this authority? Because logic prescribes the operations which mind is to enact when thinking correctly, while morals are the norms which direct the will as mind acts justly. Logic and morals are the two regulative forms of judgement, so that a mind knowing itself would have to know them. These three—mind, logic, and morals—are the subject matters we defend. Scientists are welcome to their inferences. We prefer our knowledge of mind and its rules to their opinions about nature.

The method securing our authority is intuition. Mind has saved itself from the obscurities of nature and the speculations of science by turning upon itself, discovering there a trove of certainties. This emphasis upon mind, as activity and sanctuary, is a constant within intuitionism, despite some variations. Plato's views about intuiting mind have sometimes encouraged the idea that intuition might exceed the boundaries of self-consciousness, as *nous* reaches beyond us to the Forms. But even Plato is usually more cautious. Mind knows the Forms, he says, because of having been seeded with them—i.e., because its ideas of them are innate. Knowledge of the Forms is, therefore, a kind of self-knowledge: knowing them we know something of our selves. We live within the crucible of our minds. Intuition is our light.

Descartes, more than Plato, is surveyor of that place where logic, psychology, and morals are formulated or discovered, and refined. Descartes' ontology becomes our own as we agree that nothing can be real if it is not inspectable. We learn to say with him that the self-reflecting, thinking subject is the central fact of our world, and every other one conceivable; his psychology becomes our metaphysics. Intuitionism is already ancient and mature when he enlivens it; but all of that method's modern variants are reformulations of him. They elaborate what he suggests; or they exaggerate some one or a few of his ideas, perhaps neglecting the rest. We never can ignore Descartes while searching for his roots.

2. Four organizing notions

It is also true that history must not fascinate us to the point where all of intuitionism seems an anticipation of Descartes or a footnote to him. His formulation cannot be our only point of reference if we are to understand the variations of intuitionist thinking and its motives. There are four notions to consider as we describe intuitionism in terms which are somewhat independent of the ones that Descartes used. First is the distinction between content and form. These are distinct emphases within intuitionist thinking, so that a philosopher may dwell on one or the other, while regarding the alternative as derivative. Second is the basis for this difference. I suggest that sensory data are the original content for intuition, while ordinary language is the source for form. Intuitionist thinking evolves as philosophers refine these two beginnings, creating substitute contents and forms. My third point is the shifting emphasis within intuitionism as priority is given to one or the other of a different pair of complementarities: some intuitionists emphasize experience; others prefer to examine mind as it makes and enjoys experience. Fourth is the progression of our justifications for intuitionism. We move from naturalism to representationalism to transcendentalism to practical common sense, then back again to naturalism. This progression moves uneasily in a circle. We are never content with a last justification when issues left unresolved impel us beyond it.

Each of these considerations destabilizes intuitionist thinking, and promotes changes within it. Where intuitionism is the dominant method within the history of philosophy, these bases for change are useful explanatory rubrics for thinking about the greater part of our history. My concern is different. It extends only to the factors which set this history in motion, not to their many expressions. Another disclaimer is also appropriate: I do not suggest that every intuitionist is, or should be, located at the same place as his contemporaries within one or more of these cycles. The state of intuitionist thinking may be thoroughly diverse, with any one thinker in a cycle or cycles very different from those of his contemporaries. Like a choppy sea, there will often be currents and waves moving in several directions. I shall not try to characterize more than a few of the actual historical cycles, and then only for the purpose of illustrating these three dialectical progressions: content and form, mind and experience, and the justifications for intuitionist method.

3. Content and form

We start with the first of these points, that intuitionism can have either of two emphases, one of content, the other of form.

Intuitionisms of content are comprehensive of everything inspectable, including percepts, memories, feelings, and moods. When thought and ideas are assimilated to these more apparently sensible contents, as in Hume, then they too are included among the contents subject to inspection. Intuitionisms of content are drenched in the vigor of experience; the ones of form are spare. They attend to differentiations within phenomena, or to the manner of their organization, especially as these differentia or relations—e.g., color or relative size—are abstracted from the content whose form is exhibited. Foremost here is Plato's idea that mind apprehending the Forms knows the differences which may be present in sensory data. There is also Wittgenstein's claim in the *Tractatus* that the world is intelligible because of the configurations among its constituent objects and knowable because of the configured sentences representing these states of affairs. This emphasis upon intelligibility helps to explain the aprioristic bias of these intuitionisms of form, as we may claim to have inspectable ideas or relations in advance of the content to which they apply. It also helps explain the fact that the intuitionisms of form are more rigorous and abstracted than the ones of content.

3a. Content

The intuitionisms of content have two opposed emphases. First is the bias toward sentience. Second is the contrary emphasis on description. Intuitionisms of this kind move back and forth between self-absorption for enjoyment or reflection, and description.

The method is truest to itself when description is repudiated for discrimination and feeling. That is so because description is always partial, distant, and false to the continuity, resonance, and detail of experience. Intuitionisms of content are always unfaithful to themselves at the moment when they turn discursive, trying to communicate about matters which are imperfectly represented by our descriptions.

The appeal to content unadorned is therefore a frequent test of authenticity, as intuitionists of content return from distorting description to the content described. This call to fidelity is a counterforce to that progression which goes from mute appreciation through lyrical expression to abstract description, and back again to mute fascination. First in the progression are those nominally philosophic claims which are better described as practices. Transcendental meditation and Zen are two examples. Next are the existentialists. They emphasize the novel, ineffable qualities of experience, encouraging action and enjoyment, not reflection and description. Third are those phenomenologists who depart from self-enjoyment only to the point of using language to evoke these same experiences in other people. Phenomenological descriptions of this sort reproduce within us the feelings and discriminations of the person reporting his own experience, so that philosophy in this style is very close to lyric poetry. We are farthest from content when intuitionism passes from expressive to descriptive language. Rather than express the quality of my mood in ways calculated to arouse the feelings in you, I describe what I see so that you may understand it. Your feelings for it are an incidental and unintended effect. Some familiar questions ensue now, with two being fundamental: How much is description distorted because of being selective? Are there a priorisms which shape our description, thereby warping our perception of the given?

Description is selective in three ways: (1) Our vocabulary of descriptive terms is limited to a more or less gross set of differentiations within a qualitative range, as we have few color words and still fewer words for describing the look of a face. (2) There are semantic and syntactic rules to determine what shall count as a well-formed sentence. These rules limit the combinations of words, as 'It is raining numbers' is barred because of being contradictory. 'Thinking machine,' once thought to be contradictory, is now accepted as meaningful. How many of the other nonsense rhymes composed of words that are meaningful in themselves signify possibilities to which we are barred by the combination rules? Also worth remarking is the fact that these rules combine with our limited abilities for interpreting sentences to limit the complexity of possible descriptions. There are, for example, myriad qualifiers which truly designate properties observed within experience; but no sentence having a verb modified by thirty adverbs will be understood. There is furthermore the Chinese-box character of many complex sentences, where grammatical phrases are embedded in successively more comprehensive structures. These sentences confuse us even though their grammar is formally correct. Add now that we have limited resources for signifying the properties and complexities within the content inspected, and we realize that significant features within it may be unrepresented within our descriptions. (3) Descriptions are divisible into sentences, and sentences into phrases and words; but there may be nothing in the content which corresponds to these discrete, linguistic units. Our sentences exaggerate differentiations within experience, making separations where there are only distinctions within that content. Content is resolutely divided into separate packets of information.

We might throw up our hands, despairing that experience might be described, reverting to mute intuitionism and its preference for the simple enjoyment of whatever is given. That would be a misconceiving of philosophy's task, for descriptions are not appraised in the terms appropriate to the experience described. That descriptions are selective, with formal properties of their own, is a symptom characterizing all of thought. No cellist hears the rough edge of his bow on the strings while reading a score. None of us should expect to perceive all the textures of an experience when hearing it described. Description refines the content it represents, ignoring discernible parts of it. The intuitionists of content are forced to choose: we can enjoy content, or describe it. We may do both, though we cannot recreate the content enjoyed, by imagining it, from the description alone.

One other consideration enforces this division: Descriptions contain some *a priori* bias or structure determining the kinds of data to be selected, and the principles for organizing our claims about them. Selectivity has reminded us of the incommensurability between content and description, the one as integrated and whole, the other as a representation having formal—e.g., grammatical—properties of its own. This other point remarks that the language used for describing the world is a specification of the kinds of things we may find there. More than the fact that we have disparate words and independent sentences for representing the continuous weave of experience, this is the fact that language anticipates the kinds and relationships that may be present in the world. Is there anyone who still describes the moon as following him, like a cat, across roof tops? Galileo seems to have known people like that, people ready to interpret the content of experience in ways prescribed by their beliefs.

These beliefs are exhibited in the vocabulary and grammar of what we say and also in the circumstances or manner of our using them. They are most conspicuous in what we say, that there is a moon, for example, moving as we do; and also in the forms used for saying it, as English grammar requires that we should describe the world as though it were constituted of individual things having properties which qualify and distinguish them. Grammar encourages us to assume that its sentences are independent of one another, so that each one is true only as the truth conditions specified within it are satisfied, as 'The snow is white' is true if the snow is white. We infer that the things represented are, like the sentences, free-standing, self-contained, and independent of one another. We may resist describing a situation until one or another of these independent substances are specifiable within it, as though the matters described did not have a character sufficient to justify description until they satisfied our regulative notions about the least standards that things need satisfy in order to count as real. These biases are mutually confirming: Grammar anticipates that the world will be constituted of individuals; our hypotheses identify some of these individuals, thereby validating grammar's claim.

These a priorisms are, with selectivity, the factors subverting intuitionism when it aspires to communicate accurately about content. Intuitionists are wary of these barriers to content so that intuitionism moves nervously between a commitment to mute experience, and the desire to tell others about that experience. The one alternative turns away from theorizing of every sort as we strain to inspect things as they are. The other alternative is already a kind of theorizing, though one that is naive about its assumptions. It prefers to believe that description is never a barrier to content, where every descriptive claim is founded transparently and incontrovertibly in the content described. The intuitionisms of content never can avoid, therefore, the dilemma posed above; they may encourage us to enjoy content or describe it, but the one will be mute and the other selective and distorting. Enjoyment is authentic in its own right without having to call it philosophical. Description mediates our appreciation of content. If description is philosophical, then philosophy is a conceptual refinement, one that alienates us from the continuities and vigor of content. This is an opposition that intuitionists cannot resolve.

3b. Form

We are ready now for the intuitionisms of form. They distinguish between a content to be discerned or organized, and the forms, relations, or rules for differentiating and ordering content. The intuitionisms of form are often more complicated than the ones of content, because there are two things to be done: Form must be discovered or invented, then applied. Discovery is sometimes as easy as listening to a melody in order to hear the order of its notes or searching within visible things for their organizing shapes and relations. These are examples of forms intrinsic to content, where inspection achieves understanding as we identify the differentiating or organizing forms. But there is also that other intuitionist attitude where the relation of form to content is the legislative one of a mind which projects form onto content. We use Platonic-Husserlian ideas or the rules of ordinary language in order to make sensation or behavior intelligible. These forms may be learned, as language is learned, or innate. Either way, the forms used legislatively are *a priori* in the restricted sense that they supply the differentiations or orders with which to think or perceive content.

There is a bias among intuitionists favoring the legislative uses of form, meaning form projected rather than forms seen or heard as they are instantiated in content. Plato and Descartes are paradigmatic. They believed that we have luminous apprehension of Forms or concepts, and that these are used projectively as we impose or discover differentiation and order within sensory data. Ordinary language analysis is their modern counterpart. For what is more familiar than the question, "What could we say of that?" where the saying introduces words that are used to differentiate and understand the matter at issue. No set of distinctions is closer to hand, and none more dependable. These are the distinctions that are made as we act, often successfully, within the world. Language prefigures, we suppose, the differences which may be discovered there. Ordinary language analysts would convince us that the linguistic sources of form were already familiar to the Greeks; and this is true. Plato's views about the Forms derive partly at least from the fixed meanings of words. Aristotle's claims about the physics of primary substances are reinforced by the subject-predicates forms of Greek. This intuitionist use of language persists through modern times, as when 'I,' 'me,' 'my,' and 'myself' appear dozens of times in Descartes' *Meditations* before that paragraph where Descartes confirms what language has anticipated, that "I am, I exist." There is also Kant's derivation of the transcendental categories from the table of judgements, a table of ordinary sentential forms. Ordinary language, used in these several ways, is commonly the source of philosophic genius.

The intuitionism and a priorism of the conceptual analyst's procedure is apparent. For we decide what to say of the world not by interrogating nature then hypothesizing about the variables which generate the behaviors observed, but rather by turning within ourselves, asking as before "What would we say of that?" Whom do we ask? Not children; they might be uncertain, incoherent or incomplete in the stories they tell. We ask the fluent adult. He will know the rules and nuances with full command of that universe prefigured in them.

Quite a different intuitionism of form is the one which insists that the rules of ordinary language are too loose, that the world made articulate within ordinary speech is vague. Intuitionists of this sort require that the semantical riches of ordinary language be subordinated to the rigor of a constructed, syntactic framework, where individual terms are "introduced" by rules which fix their signification. Our understanding of the world will be accurate and articulate, they say, only if knowledge claims are reconstituted as statements which meet the standards of this improved language. This claim elevates mind to a position where it has total control over the things it understands. For mind will have arrayed before it those structures which were designed to suit mind's own requirements for understanding. Surveying these structures, mind will see the world under forms which it has prescribed. Plato's *nous* could not have a more commanding view, though with greater modesty Plato supposed that mind would have to discover the world as it is, not as mind formulates it. Still, Plato might have liked these reconstructions, all spare and lucid, their information visible immediately to an inspecting mind.

There is a familiar epigram for these prescriptivist claims about linguistic form. It is Wittgenstein's remark that "The limits of my language mean the limits of my world."[1] Language is to exhibit the forms which make the world thinkable. There is, for example, *The Structure of Appearance,* where Nelson Goodman tells us how to use a system of formally related sentences for the ordering and interpreting of sensory data; and also that cousin to Goodman's view, the idea

that our world might be represented most perspicuously by axiomitized sciences, with physics at the apex of a pyramid where all
the other sciences are derived from it by entailment relations and
bridge principles. A more remote expression of Wittgenstein's dictum
is Thomas Kuhn's idea of "normal science," the claim that we think
about the world within a conceptual paradigm, using it as a kind of
miner's lamp to prefigure the domain being investigated.[2] The idea of
normal science is Hegel's claim that thought and history exhibit, at
any particular time, one or more controlling ideas. But then all these
intuitionisms of form, Hegel included, are expressions of the assumption that the world is intelligible, thinkable, and knowable by way of
those conceptualizations which specify or exhibit the world's form.

Notice the order of priority in these examples, and in Wittgenstein's remarks: We are to believe that the possible differentiations
and orders available to our world are founded in the thought or language used for conceiving or talking about it. This says that the properties possible in our world originate in thought or language, as
distinctions available to self-inspecting mind. Imagine Plato extolling
mind's power as it exhibits and thinks those archetypes which may
be projected onto sensory experience, and discerned there. Content
nearly disappears, as we say that all of its intelligibility derives from
the forms used to think it; they differentiate content, or supply the
relations for organizing it. Yet, form is intrinsic to content, so that an
emphasis on one to the exclusion of the other is flagrantly partial.
This is the point of Kant's remark that intuitions without concepts
are blind, while concepts without intuitions are empty. We needn't
endorse Kant's view about transcendental synthesis to agree that each
of these two, content and form, implies the other. A plausible intuitionism will provide for both of them. It is perplexing, therefore, that
intuitionists are so quick to exaggerate one at cost to the other. Why
this happens is my next topic.

4. The dialectical refinements of content and form

Intuitionism leans to one or the other: to content as it includes
differentiations and relations, or to form as these two are represented
or prescribed. Neither one is obscure or remote. They are as natural
and familiar as sensory data and ordinary language. These two are

autonomous but complementary, the one as content, the other as form. No other resources are closer to hand, and no others are more reliable for understanding and practice. We use and enjoy them unself-consciously. They are, or seem to be, close to the reality of things. We depend on them for reliable information about the world and our place within it. Intuitionist reflection always starts with one or the other of these resources, however refined its later claims. This is true historically, as claims about ideal languages are elaborations of the syntax discovered in natural languages. We see it too within the reflection of individual thinkers, as Plato's Forms may be abstractions from the semantics of ordinary Greek. There are many intuitionists who test their abstract claims against the evidence of sensory content or ordinary language, as Parmenidean and Plotinian claims about the One may have been tested against the directly experienced unity of our self-consciousness. Ordinary language and sensory experience, including self-consciousness, carry this authority because each of them assures that intuition shall have a true-to-the-world, and nearly inexhaustible, subject matter. But then intuitionism makes an apparently capricious choice: Rather than accept these two as equally fundamental and complementary, it emphasizes one at cost to the other. Why this emphasis?

The answer seems to be that one or the other is regarded as fundamental, and the other as derivative. I do not mean that the ability for using a language might seem to derive from sensory experience; but rather that many distinctions in ordinary language are apparent already in sensory experience; or conversely, that the differentiations and relations within sensory phenomena are prefigured in the ways we speak. The intuitionist distortion of these resources begins here, where sensory data or ordinary language is given priority so that proving the derivability of its complement becomes an objective for philosophic reflection. Distortion is magnified when the real character of experience or language is misdescribed or ignored in order that we may redescribe it in ways suitable to the program for deriving one from the other. Why do intuitionists deny their equality in order to insist that one should be derived from the other? First, because one and its derivative are logically simpler than two, each independent of the other; second, because the mere correlation of distinctions in experience to those of language seems adventitious until we have established that the one is foundational and the other one derivative; third, because an unconsidered preference for content or form makes us quick to suppose that one should be the measure of the other.

This third point is decisive, for measure is prescriptive, not merely descriptive. Content or form will be the source for intelligibility, hence, comprehensible in itself. The other, its complement, will be intelligible because differentiation and order are inherited from or projected onto it. Remember that philosophers are not always satisfied to be describing things as they are. We often prefer the ideal to the real, sometimes insisting that nothing less than the ideal can be real. This urge to ideality is common among intuitionists as they prescribe exquisite refinements for sensory data or ordinary language. We are to believe that these refinements are not distortions; they are, intuitionists say, the obscured but essential core of the content or form being redescribed. We remark, for example, that sensory experience is opaque to the welter of kinship relations. We introduce the words signifying these relationships, 'third cousin, twice removed,' in order to project, then discern these relationships within the things perceived. We notice, on the other side, that there are many more plastic shapes than are signified by our language. Faces are an example. We introduce proper names, to signify them.

Are there some philosophically interesting properties which are discovered in content or form, then projected onto its derivative? There are. Consider, for example, the normative relations which pervade ordinary language, though they are absent from sensory data. We are to see the world differently as we use these normative concepts for thinking and speaking about it, seeing a red light as reason to stop. Even more tantalizing to philosophic instincts are the cases where some set of relations or distinctions credited to form or content is to be devalued or erased because no basis is found for it within its complement. There is, for example, Hume's devaluation of ordinary language talk about causality. We interpret the words literally, believing that they imply the reality of causal powers and necessary causal relations. But then we find that there are no percepts of these powers and relations, so that the realist bias of our language is to be suppressed.

Ideality takes an additional turn when this ground within language or experience is itself redescribed in ways that justify the redescription of its derivative partner. Hume's views about the erroneous implications of causal language is still a useful example.

For Hume cannot prescribe changes in our ordinary talk about causes with sensory experience as his ground until sensory experience is itself refined in ways that support his revisionist interpretation of ordinary language. Consider, for example, the potter making a bowl. We see him shaping the clay as the convex form of the bowl fits the concavity of his hands. This does seem to be empirical evidence for the truth of Aristotelian claims about causal efficacy, especially as Aristotle has written of formal, material, and efficient causes. Hume will have to support his revisionary claims about ordinary causal language by stripping experience of all the evidence that would support the Aristotelian notions still prominent in ordinary language. He does that by insisting that sensations are atomic, where the separability of everything distinguishable is a required principle for interpreting sensory data. The apparent continuity of perceived causal processes, of hands shaping clay, is now disclosed as an illusion, with those continuities redescribed as a sequence of discrete events. Only now can we insist, first, that events previously perceived as causal are merely sequential, and second, that ordinary usage be revised to express this difference.

There are parallel reformulations on the side of form, as when the moral implications of ordinary discourse seem diffuse or contradictory. Intuitionists respond by introducing a set of higher-order principles for organizing and focusing the implications of ordinary language. This second example exhibits the same pattern as the one before: where content or form is ground and the other is its derivative, we refine the ground as we discover that previous formulations of it are deficient as bases for whatever claim we are projecting on to the derivative. Sensory data are refined until we are justified in purging ordinary language of a mistaken theory of cause and effect; moral language is refined until we can use it for projecting moral imperatives into experience.

4a. Naive beginnings

The dialectic of philosophic history is often the elaboration of successive refinements, whether ascetic or baroque, in ordinary language or sensory data. We project intelligibility into contexts where it is lacking, or we reformulate the ground for intelligibility so that differentiation and order may be projected onto its deficient complement. There is, however, a cost: We ignore the real character of the thing being "improved" until we can no longer discern anything of that substantive ground in our refinements. The result is more and more sublimed, less and less in touch with the materials giving life to the abstractions. Successive refinements leach intuitionist subject matters of credible or workable materials, so that philosophic renewal is often a return to the familiarities of sensory data and ordinary language. William James and J.L. Austin are examples, the one as he discounted the Humean refinements of sensory experience, the other as he reacted to the logicist denaturing of ordinary language. Each of them is a naif compared to the views he displaces; but we hear the authenticity of their demands: Renounce abstraction and refinement; restore the substance of intuitionist content and form.

But is it true that these two are intuitionists? Let me show that James and Austin, together with their refining successors, are intuitionists, before returning to some last remarks about the dialectical counterpoint of sensory experience as content and ordinary language as form.

4ai. JAMES

We start with James, and especially his neutral monism. I ignore just now his doubts about the reality of a conscious agent, the transcendental ego. James, as much as Hume, doubted that introspection discovers a subject who organizes and inspects the given. There is only the overflowing, many-dimensional, infinitely differentiated tide of experience. There are, he says, two poles within it, one of content, the other of organizing intention.[3] Content includes relations so that form is already intrinsic to it; but then intention adds those additional forms of organization, plans of action for example, which serve our human interests. Experience is the laminate of the two: the content given, and our human ways, particular or generic, for organizing it. James is an intuitionist for three reasons. Phenomena are, using the words of art, (1) presented or given, and (2) inspected or perceived. (3) Reality is constituted only of the things given: *esse es percipi,* where *percipi* signifies every mode of apprehension but principally sensory perception and conceptualization. James would insist that we use 'perceive' with a special emphasis, one that allows for perceiving without a perceiver. This is an important claim below as we consider the intuitionist psychology; but it is incidental here, where the sufficient condition for intuitionism is an emphasis upon the given and its perception, together with the ontological claim that reality is constituted or made intelligible just because of being given and perceived.

4aii. AUSTIN

There may be no intuitionist of content more devoted than James to the unimproved phenomena, but J.L. Austin is his peer as an intuitionist of form. For Austin does not tell us what the words should say, but only what the words are used to say and imply. He describes his method in this way:

> In view of the prevalence of the slogan 'ordinary language,' and of such names as 'linguistic' or 'analytic' philosophy or 'the analysis of language,' one thing needs specially emphasizing to counter misunderstandings. When we examine what we should say when, what words we should use in what situations, we are looking again not merely at words or meanings whatever they may be, but also at the realities we use the words to talk about: we are using a sharpened awareness of words to sharpen our perception of, though not as the final arbiter of the phenomena. For this reason I think it might be better to use, for this way of doing philosophy, some less misleading name than those given above—for instance 'linguistic phenomenology,' only that is rather a mouthful.[4]

Linguistic phenomenology is the practice of surveying a word's uses in order to learn the rules which govern its use. These rules determine the range of uses which are grammatically correct, those considered "meaningful." This survey might begin with a good dictionary; but it never ends there. For the dictionary definition is at once too simplistic and too abstract. It could only be our starting point for an examination of a word's diverse uses, each use colored somewhat by its context. The faculty required for making this inquiry is imagination, as we imagine disparate circumstances, many of them never experienced, where the words might be used in specific ways. It is the montage of these uses, some of them familiar, many of them rare, which exhibits the logical form of the word. Only here, quite late in the investigation, can the linguistic phenomenologist step back from particular uses to regard the "logical geography" of a word. He is to see the complex of rules for using this word, each one exhibited in its common and limiting applications.

The ordinary language analysis has started with the most familiar materials, as nothing is closer to hand and better known than the words we speak. This starting point is transfigured, however, by our objectives, for we are very close to Plato's idea that *nous* regarding the Forms knows the differences which may be present in sensory data—i.e., in content. As Austin puts it, "our common stock of words embodies all the distinctions men have found worth marking, in the lifetime of many generations."[5] This notion of language is, on the face of it, much weaker than the prescriptivist role that Plato claimed for thought. For Austin is conservative; the study of linguistic usage is not to specify all the possible distinctions and orders which are available for instantiation in any possible world. This is to be an inventory of only those differences which are assertible in our language, hence, within our "universe of discourse." Still, ordinary language analysis does promise an anticipatory illumination quite the equal of *nous* as it examines the Forms. For Austin would have us believe that the only possible worlds that we might think and know are the ones formulable within our language. Ordinary language analysts are the surveyors of this, more limited range of possible worlds, and they do promise an *a priori* inspection of all the differences and relations, all the forms, which might be credited to our world.

Someone who demurs may be thinking of that cautionary phrase in the longer paragraph quoted above; we are considering not only words, says Austin, but also the realities they signify, where the words sharpen our perceptions of phenomena without being the final arbiter of their properties. This does imply that we should press inquiry beyond our words to the things they signify, though Austin himself never does what he seems to recommend. He never looks beyond words to their objects, sometimes correcting language if our ways of speaking about the world are not adequate to the phenomena discovered there. For language is the only resource considered when Austin looks for access to the world. His encounters with it are always mediated, so far as his papers reveal, by words. Phenomena are never considered except as they are revealed by the words used for talking about them. All his discoveries of important differences within the world are founded in the observation that there is some word or phrase signifying these otherwise neglected things or relations. Facts, other minds, capacities and excuses: Austin writes confidently about all of them, always supposing that analyzing our use of words is the sufficient basis for our claims about them.

There were three factors important to the intuitionism of William James. All of them are conspicuous in Austin: (1) There is a given. It is comprised of words and their uses, then of the rules exemplified by these uses. We might sometimes consider the uses of words as they appear in books or are heard in conversations; but more often, their use is imagined. That imagining, and the variations it produces, is the act essential to entertaining the given, whatever the provocation to analysis. Imagining is conceptual rather than figurative, as we imagine what might be said without having to imagine either the words printed or uttered, or the possible states of affairs they signify. (2) The given is perceived, where perceiving like the given itself is conceptual rather than sensible. We are to think the possible uses, discerning the pertinent rules. Analysis terminates as we survey a word's many uses and the complex of rules which they exhibit. We discern this word's "logical geography," all of it set coherently before our inspecting minds. (3) Intuitionists of content typically suppose that reality is comprised of the matters inspected. Intuitionists of form are only slightly more restrained. They suppose that the forms inspected are the necessary and sufficient conditions for all that is intelligible within reality. All its differentiations, all its relations originate here in the array of those differences and relations with which we think or talk about the world. Nothing is for us, and in that regard nothing is, if it cannot be thought under the rubric of these words.

4b. Refinements of form

The dialectic of content and form typically begins when ordinary language or sensory experience is endorsed as the touchstone for understanding: one or the other is to supply the distinctions and relations which make reality intelligible. Either one, content or form, may be primary, the other one derivative. That starting point is refined as we strain to express those features which are projected from the ground onto its complement. The examples that follow illustrate this dialectic. They show the elaboration of content or form as either is said to be thought's ground and the other its derivative. Notice however this anomaly in my examples: Some of them are careless of historical order, as ordinary language is the naive ground for numerous variations and refinements, though Austin is later than Carnap and Plato. This is a tolerable discrepancy if we suppose that ordinary language is a kind of permanent resource, available from the beginnings of philosophic reflection as the paradigm for form. It is merely accidental then if the historical order of philosophers having views about form or content is not the logical order of development, as the refinements of Carnap and Plato come before Austin's phenomenological linguistics.

Deferring content and starting with form, let us consider its development beyond the discoveries of ordinary language analysis. Analysis will have shown that ordinary language embodies one or, more likely, several different and opposed "theories" about all the world or its parts. It will have discovered these systematic commitments by running down the implications of individual words, as 'motion' implies 'matter,' then 'space,' 'time,' and 'cause.' Taking up different constellations of words, mentalistic or aesthetic ones for example, we might expect to discover categorial claims that are independent of these materialist ones, and maybe incompatible with them. Still, it might be true that our various "theoretical" commitments can be made to cohere with one another, thereby confirming that ordinary language expresses a unitary if complex view of the world.

That is not likely, so that anyone wanting to express a coherent view of the world will have to choose his own words from among all those which are available, expressing thereby a consistent view of the world and our place within it. This is the real-life practice of formulating theories, not hoping to discover them, like old Rome, half-revealed in the routinized uses of everyday language. For it never was plausible to expect that ordinary language analysis would save us the trouble of formulating our own theories by recovering the elemental commitments of our language. How could we wait for it to do that when no one claims to have finished the analysis of any single word? There is anyway the risk of too much zeal in locating all the theories intimated there, when the theories we want are just the ones that are valid in our world. Who can say that most or even half the suggestions of ordinary language do have application here? Austin said that they do: how else should we explain the fact that the rules for using our current words have been shaped by centuries of use? This is no argument at all, if we do not believe in satyrs and ghosts though having the words that signify them.

4bi. GADAMER

We dare to move beyond the analysis of individual words. Rather than inherit one or another theory from the bone yard of established usage, we invent our own. Large parts of the theory may derive from the categorial implications of established usage; but this will be our theory, the one that we create for making the world thinkable. To Wittgenstein's remark, "The limits of my language are the limits of my world," we add this one from Hans-Georg Gadamer:

> Language is not just one of man's possessions in the world, but on it depends the fact that man has a world at all. For man the world exists as world in a way that no other being in the world experiences. But this world is linguistic in nature. This is the heart of Humboldt's assertion, which he intended quite differently, that languages are views of the world. By this Humboldt means that language maintains a kind of independent life over against the individual member of a linguistic community and introduces him, as he grows into it, to a particular attitude and relationship to the world as well. . . . Not only is the world 'world' only insofar as it comes into language, but language, too, has its real being only in the fact that the world is represented within it. Thus the original humanity of language means at the same time the fundamental linguistic quality of man's being-in-the-world.[6]

Gadamer encourages this move beyond the resources of language,[7] as a cook might be addled by the people who never get around to cooking because of their reverence for the implements.

> To sum up, I would say that the basic misunderstanding concerning the linguistic character of our understanding is one of language, as if language were an existing whole composed of words and phrases, concepts, points of view and opinions. In reality, language is the single word whose virtuality opens up the infinity of discourse, of discourse with others, and of the freedom of 'speaking oneself' and of 'allowing oneself to be spoken.' Language is not its elaborate conventionalism, nor the burden of pre-schematisation with which it loads us, but the generative and creative power unceasingly to make this whole fluid.[8]

Gadamer would have us use language for making interpretations: "the primary thing is application."[9] The matters to be interpreted are texts, history, works of art or nature. But always they address us with a character or sense of their own.

We can, then, bring out as what is truly common to all forms of hermeneutics the fact that the sense to be understood finds its concrete and perfect form only in interpretation, but that this interpretive work is wholly committed to the meaning of the text. Neither jurist nor theologian regards the work of application as making free with the text.[10]

There is, however, a reason for doubting that the things interpreted do have an integrity which stands apart from our interpretations, for what is that intrinsic order or sense, and how could it be known apart from our interpretations of it? This is a place where the authority of the ground must be reaffirmed against the pretensions of its derivative complement. Form dictates to content.

[T]he linguistic world in which we live is not a barrier that prevents knowledge of being in itself, but fundamentally embraces everything in which our insight can be enlarged and deepened. . . . This is of fundamental importance, for it makes the use of the expression 'world in itself' problematical. The criterion for the continuing expansion of our world-picture is not given by a 'world in itself' that lies beyond all language. Rather, the infinite perfectibility of the human experience of the world means that, whatever language we use, we never achieve anything but an ever more extended aspect, a 'view' of the world. Those views of the world are not relative in the sense that one could set them against the 'world in itself,' as if the right view from some possible position outside the human, linguistic world, could discover it in its being-in-itself. No one questions that the world can exist without man and perhaps will do so. This is part of the meaning in which every human, linguistically constituted view of the world lives. In every view of the world the existence of the world-in-itself is implied. It is the whole to which the linguistically schematised experience is referred. The variety of these views of the world does not involve any relativisation of the 'world.' Rather, what the world is is not different from the views in which it presents itself.[11]

One cannot read this without thinking of Kant: The world stands before us as a never completed manifold; that which is subjective because of having been created by mind as it thinks the given is nevertheless called objective because we cannot help but think of it as standing apart from us.

In all of this, interpretation satisfies the purposes of intuitionist method.

[T]hat which people like to call 'intuition' in the nineteenth and twentieth centuries is brought back to its metaphysical foundation: that is to the structure of living, organic being, of being the whole in each individual.[12]

[A]ssimilation is no mere repetition of the text that has been handed down, but is a new creation of understanding. If emphasis has been—rightly—placed on the fact that all meaning is related to the 'I,' this means, as far as the hermeneutical experience is concerned, that all the meaning of what is handed down to us finds its concretion, in which it is understood, in the relation to the understanding 'I.'[13]

Language succeeds in returning all of thinkable being to the living 'I' because of tracing its origins and power to divine creation: "In the beginning was the Word." The words used for interpreting the given are the light with which our human minds create a thinkable world.

The light that causes everything to emerge in such a way that it is manifest and comprehensible in itself is the light of the word.[14]

Language, quite ordinary language, is our instrument as we approximate, though never achieving, God's own perfection.[15]

[T]he universality of the hermeneutical experience could not be available to an infinite mind, for it develops out of itself all meaning, all noeton, and thinks all that can be thought in the perfect contemplation of itself.[16]

What is this difference between us and God? Is it only that God, the infinite mind, would create his own forms as the means for objectifying then reflecting upon himself, while we are obliged to use the resources of our everyday language?

This would explain those lyrical passages where Gadamer emphasizes the work of art, and especially the poem, as the purest expressions of hermeneutics.[17] In them, interpretation is not the reading of an alien text, but rather the God-like creation of a thinkable world. Like God, the poet creates meaning out of himself, even when using the rough words of ordinary language. Having done that, he reposes within the world he has made. It stands before him, or he lives and thinks within it, every difference and relation visible to him in the words he has used to create it.

But is this true to Gadamer? Hasn't he said that jurists and theologians must respect the integrity of the texts they read? Isn't it true that every single interpretation strains and tears because of being unable to accommodate everything important to its text? We read the book another time, exposing those presuppositions which blinded us the last time to this book's motives and themes. Doesn't this succession of interpretations speak for the priority of interpretation, the act, over any particular reading? Isn't the emphasis upon this activity a reason for saying that texts such as nature are separate from us, while forever obliging us to recast our thinking about them?

This is a reading more congenial to Dewey than to Gadamer. Consider the jurist. He is not a scientist trying to identify the variables generating some phenomenon he observes but has not made. He is, to the contrary, a maker of the law. He starts within a tradition he has not made. But then his interpretations of the law are expressed in his rulings. They are the law. There is also the poet. He uses the forms of his tradition, but the poems are his own. He may struggle to discover the presuppositions within one of his poems, for they obscure the world that is expressed there. This annoys and confounds the poet, because he cannot see deeply enough into the world he has made. No wonder that he reworks this poem or writes other ones, always hoping like Hegel's Absolute that he may think "all that can be thought in the perfect contemplation" of himself.

There is only this one result to fear: the world created by our interpretations has no security apart from our determination to persist in the interpretations which create it. That security is precarious, for it will not be difficult to prove that every interpretation is motivated by interests which are personal and maybe disreputable. There are, for example, the interpretations having no foundation beyond our desire for making the world safe for ourselves. This motive, possibly unknown to us, may be discovered by those other thinkers who have been taught to live within the world of our self-interested interpretation. We are not surprised when these other interpreters "deconstruct" our world merely by revealing our motives.

This is horrific if the only world known to us is the one made intelligible by our interpretations, for then we are faced with two awful choices: Use discredited interpretations or confront the world without them—seeing it as nothing because of having repudiated the only sources for whatever was intelligible within it. There will be only this one consolation: We may divert ourselves by recapitulating the history of our deception or by comparing the various discredited interpretations. Where none of them is any longer accepted as true, we may nevertheless compare their styles, marveling at the many strategies for deceiving us. This can only be a diversion, for we shall have to replace these old interpretations if the world is not to stand before us as an unthinkable void. We shall have to practice a combination of amnesia and bad faith, forgetting that every interpretation is the expression of private motives and power, while knowing all along that we are deceived in the name of a saving intelligibility.

This is one result of moving beyond ordinary language analysis in order to achieve those forms which are usable for thinking about content. Austin is passive to whatever theoretical discoveries he makes within ordinary language, as though it were sufficient to expose any and every articulation within our universe of discourse. But why believe that the logical grammar of some few, disparate words will have more than incidental utility for making comprehensive sense of our circumstances, as though the logical geography of 'sick' might be useful to someone suddenly taken to a hospital? Gadamer has demanded that the forms used for interpreting content should be more systematic and cogent. If his interpretations are not always so practical as this last example implies they should be, they may nevertheless be powerful enough for making sense of whatever practical circumstances do confront us. Still, Gadamer is like Austin in supposing that ordinary language makes the distinctions which are important to the life-world. He knows that science chooses an improved language, but he discounts that preference because of believing that science is oblivious to essential human needs. It is, he says, merely the instrument for subordinating nature to the demands of consumption and production.[18] Gadamer ignores this other possibility: that language may be amended or replaced in circumstances where it lacks the resources for clarifying experience in ways that thought requires. This is the justification when intuitionists of form reconsider their ground, altering natural languages so that improved languages may express those differences and relations which are to be projected onto sensory data.

4bii. CARNAP

Rudolf Carnap is a philosopher of this other sort. He describes his program in this way:

> . . . the reduction of 'reality' to the 'given' has in recent time been considered an important task and has been partially accom-

plished. . . . The present study is an attempt to apply the theory of relations to the task of analyzing reality. This is done to formulate the logical requirements which must be fulfilled by a constructional system of concepts, to bring into clearer focus the basis of the system, and to demonstrate by actually producing such a system . . . that it can be constructed on the indicated basis and within the indicated logical framework.[19]

The elements of these constructional systems are to be concepts and relations. The principal relations are the ones specified by Russell and Whitehead in *Principia Mathematica*—e.g., 'and,' 'or,' and 'if-then.' The more remote sources for these relations are mathematics and ordinary language. Similarly, the concepts to be reconstructed may have been discovered within scientific theory; but most of them have originated, like 'atom,' 'force,' and 'field,' within ordinary language, however simple or crude their formulation there.

Ordinary language analysts suppose that clarity regarding a word's many uses is a sufficient basis for using it to project form onto the world. The tissue of our various words maps our universe of discourse—hence, reality—for everyone schooled in the language. Carnap, however, is not happy with ordinary language. He dislikes the equivocations within ordinary language concepts and the obscure relations of sentences within those sciences which are expressed in ordinary language. His reconstructions displace ordinary language in the ways that Descartes' *Rules* substitute the relations of simples to complexes for the obscurities of ordinary discourse.

> By a constructional system we mean a step-by-step ordering of objects in such a way that the objects of each level are constructed from those of the lower levels. Because of the transitivity of reducibility, all objects of the constructional system are thus indirectly constructed from the objects of the first level. These basic objects form the basis of the system.[20]

The use of these reconstructions is also powerfully Cartesian, for Carnap is an intuitionist of form, one who supposes that his constructions are the source for whatever intelligibility is projected onto, then discovered within, reality.

> [T]he reduction of higher level concepts to lower level ones cannot always take the form of explicit definitions; generally more liberal forms of conception in reduction must be used. Actually, without

clearly realizing it, I already went beyond the limits of explicit definition in the construction of the physical world.[21]

In a remark partly clarifying this last phrase, Carnap writes that

> construction theory employs a natural language and maintains that
> objects are neither 'created' nor 'apprehended' but *constructed.*[22]

Reality, we may suppose, is only the complex of these objects and
their relations. No wonder then if it is the "physical world," and not
merely "objects," which is constructed.

Kant has insisted that concepts without intuitions are empty.
Carnap too will need something additional to his conceptual reconstructions if he is to "construct" the physical world. That other com-
ponent is sensory data. With the constructional system serving as
form, they are content. Differentiations and relations expressed in the
constructional system are projected onto them, though sensory data
never achieve more than the secondary role which Carnap assigned
to them when he emphasized form as the ground for intelligibility.
We see this bias in the claim that sensory data confound us by their
diversity if we address them without the advantage of mediating concepts.

> In choosing as basic elements the elementary experiences, we do not
> assume that the stream of experience is composed of determinate dis-
> crete elements. We only presuppose that statements can be made
> about certain places in the stream of experience, to the effect that one
> such place stands in a certain relation to another place, etc. But we do
> not assert that the stream of experience can be uniquely analyzed into
> such places.[23]

This remark is explained in a preceding paragraph.

> After deciding to choose an autopsychological basis for our system
> (i.e., the acts of consciousness or experiences of the self), we still
> must determine which entities from this general domain are to serve
> as basic elements . . . (W)e realize that in this case we do not take the
> given as it is, but abstractions from it (i.e., something that is epistemi-
> cally secondary) as basic elements. It must be understood that con-
> structional systems which proceed from such basic elements are as
> much justified and practicable as, for example, systems with a physi-
> cal basis. However, since we wish to require of our constructional

system that it should agree with the epistemic order of the objects, we have to proceed from that which is epistemically primary, that is to say, from the 'given,' i.e., from experiences themselves in their totality and undivided unity. The above-mentioned constituents, down to the last elements, are derived from these experiences by relating them to one another and comparing them (i.e., through abstraction). The more simple steps of this abstraction are carried out intuitively in pre-scientific thought already, so that we quite commonly speak, for example, of visual perceptions and simultaneous auditory perceptions, as if they were two different constituents of the same experience. The familiarity of such divisions which are carried out in daily life should not deceive us about the fact that abstraction is already involved in the procedure. This applies a fortiori to elements which are discovered only through scientific analysis. The basic elements, that is, the experiences of the self as units . . . we call *elementary experiences*.[24]

This remark is equivocal. For what is primary, the stream of experience, or that differentiated totality which is produced when experience is schematized—i.e., when categories or concepts are applied to it? Which of these two is the "given"? Carnap may have Kantian reasons for saying that each is prior in the respect appropriate to it. But then his drift is plain: Conceptualizations expressing the differences formulated within the constructional system are the basis for whatever differentiations and relations are credited to the given. Form is projected onto content, thereby making it thinkable. But these are not the crude distinctions of ordinary language. Differences that were obscure there are clarified here. All the logical relations and implications of our various claims are perspicuously expressed. Form has been reconstructed and purified.

Carnap is like Kant in supposing that mind will first make its objects, then regard them. Carnap does, of course, express this point in a somewhat different way. Objects, he has said, are neither created nor apprehended but constructed. The following claim speaks to the use of science for generating the objects which science, itself, will then regard by way of its true statements about them:

We have repeatedly pointed out that the formulation of the constructional system as a whole is the task of unified science . . . How should we determine the aim of unified science from the viewpoint of construction theory? The aim of science consists in finding and ordering the true statements about the objects of cognition . . . In order to be able to approach this aim, that is in order to be able to make statements about objects at all, we must be able to construct these objects . . . Thus, the formation of the constructional system is the first aim of science."[25]

We use the constructional system in order to synthesize the objects in its domain. These are the objects which satisfy its sentences, making them true. We then plead a kind of amnesia; forgetting that we have made the things represented, we remark that the conceptual system is a good representation of them.

There are several steps to this idealist result. First is the inventing of a constructional system. Second is our concern for differentiating the stream of experience. Third, objects are created when the differentiations and relations of the system are used to organize the sensory data. I mean that sentences of the theory reformulated within the system project its predicates onto the sensory stream, while satisfying the system's coherentist requirements for truth. These are requirements founded in our purposes: the sentences are true if they tell a coherent story adequate to our personal or social interests. Fourth, we regard our conceptual constructions as representations of their domains, so that fifth, we may see our sentences and concepts satisfied by the objects to which they apply. This is mind's progression as it moves from a transcendental and prescriptive attitude to one that is naturalistic and empirical. The intuitionism of form is, however, mind's overriding bias and objective: We are to make and inspect conceptual systems, using them to project differentiations and relations onto sensory content. Mind makes and inspects its forms, using them to create a world of intelligible objects.

If we are asked the reasons for describing Carnap as an intuitionist, there are the three factors confirmed already in Austin and James: (1) something is given, in this case a system of reconstructed concepts; (2) that system is perceived and applied; (3) all the differentiations and relations credited to reality are founded within this conceptual given. When these concepts are applied to sensory data, than their product too, namely experience, is a thinkable given. These schematized data are, indeed, all that we could mean by reality. This claim is almost explicit in the following remark:

> The concept of reality (in the sense of independence from the cognizing consciousness) does not belong with (rational) science, but within metaphysics.[26]

Claims about a reality that is independent of mind for its existence and character are metaphysical, hence meaningless. Responsible claims about reality are left to Carnap's "rational" science, meaning those constructional systems which are to be used for making sensory data thinkable. These are the systems making reality safe for intuition.

Carnap does allude to intuition, but always for the purpose of repudiating one version of it: ". . . intuitive understanding is replaced by discursive reasoning."[27] This passage is reminiscent of the one quoted from Heidegger in the Introduction. It rejects that narrower idea of intuition which supposes that the matters inspected are presented without an intervening conceptualization. Husserl and Hume are intuitionists of this naive sort, but no Kantian is or can be. There is, however, nothing to preclude the inspection of schematized sensory data. They too are presentations, even when mediated by the objectifying apparatus of the constructional system. We should also wonder about the conceptual system: isn't our thinking about it unmediated in exactly the way that Carnap repudiates when saying that we have no intuitive access to sensory data? This is a point that will be considered again in Chapter Three when we take up the "myth" of the given. We note just now that Carnap espouses a kind of rational intuition each time that he uses the word *erkennen*. That is the word he uses when implying that mind inspects and grasps the differentiations and relations articulated within his constructional systems.

It is my thesis in this section that these systems are the refinements of notions which originate in ordinary language. Carnap ignores that derivation for two reasons. One reason is his admiration for the deductivist reconstructions of Descartes' *Rules*. Origins and motivations are disguised or forgotten when these reconstructions emphasize logical simples rather than historical sources—e.g., the elementary predicates of a reconstructed language rather than the ordinary language distinctions from which these predicates are refined. The other reason is the obscurity of these origins. For there will be many predicates in our reconstructions which are not easily traced to ordinary language, 'charge' and 'mass' for example. Their source is physics, not ordinary English, French, Italian, or German. The claimed derivation of every more refined intuitionism of form from ordinary language is therefore bogus.

This second point is the one to challenge if we care to insist, as I do, that the intuitionist elaborations of form do inevitably start from the observation that ordinary language is deficient in some way as the system for projecting order onto sensory experience. Let us agree that many of the concepts that would be vital to Carnap's reconstructions do not originate in ordinary language. Finding allusive substitutes there for notions which are better expressed in a theory's mathematical language is often difficult. But all of that is incidental to this more general claim: There is a dialectical relation between the intuitionisms of content and form, a relation that begins where content is sensory data and form is ordinary language. This proposal does not require that all the refinements of content or form should originate in sensory data or natural languages. It supposes only that these two are the naive starting points for intuitionist reflection, where the use of either one as ground and the other as derivative complement requires that intuitionists should promise to locate intelligibility in that ground in order to show how it is inherited by or projected onto the complement. Nothing in this bars the intuitionist from refining, purifying, or reconstructing his ground in ways that alter the refinement until its sources in ordinary language or sensory content are unrecognizable.

There might have been, in principle, a total breach between ordinary language and one of Carnap's reconstructions, with nothing common to them, though each was used to bestow intelligibility on content. That discontinuity would be surprising; and it does not obtain. Most of the concepts that Carnap will reconstruct originate in ordinary language. This includes all or most of the words used for signifying elementary differences among sensory data, for example, 'red,' 'darker,' 'larger,' 'square,' many of the theoretical words such as 'energy,' 'force,' 'momentum,' and many or all of the most general, categorial words such as 'space,' 'time,' 'cause,' 'thing.' Intuitionists of form do often surpass ordinary language as they establish a basis for intelligibility within a reformed language, or set of concepts. We may also anticipate the day when form has been elaborated to the point where little or nothing of ordinary language survives within it. But we might still want to trace the origins of this ground to that set of differentiations and relations prefigured within ordinary language. Why should we bother to do that? Because those are the forms to which intuitionists first turn, the forms they revise, and the forms to which they more or less explicitly revert when successive refinement has leached all sense from the ground that was their source.

4c. Refinements of content

What happens when we turn the tables so that content rather than form is the ground for intelligibility? Are there intuitionists who have elaborated or purified the content of experience, leaving others to enjoy its raw diversity? James is already an advance toward refinement from the mute appreciation of sensible content. His distinction between the objective and subjective poles of experience testifies to that. Still, James is very close to the vigor of things. Intuitionists refining content beyond this point should be easy to find, as there are scores of artists who refine our pleasure in color, shape, size, and contrast. We are surprised to find that there are not so many of these content-purifying intuitionists, many fewer than the ones of form. Why? Because the dominant philosophic instinct is the one for form. We take content and the world for granted. They are the given, the provocation to reflection. We make ourselves responsible for describing or explaining them. We do that by elaborating the systems of words, concepts, or Forms which are to exemplify or represent the differences in content. These conceptual systems are to be the basis for intelligibility, where all the differentiation and order within content derive from them. There are, accordingly, fewer intuitionists of content than of form.

4ci. HUME

Hume is one of the exceptions. His insistent "empiricism" is just the intuitionist demand that all the contents of every idea should derive from impressions which are or can be set before our inspecting minds. The force of his intuitionism is apparent in many places. Here are two of them, then an application of Hume's intuitionism.

First is the claim that

> All the perceptions of the human mind resolve themselves into two distinct kinds, which I shall call *Impressions* and *Ideas.* The difference betwixt these consists in the degrees of force and liveliness with which they strike upon the mind and make their way into our thought or consciousness.[28]

Remember now that existence is only the force and vivacity of our impressions, so that Hume identifies reality with the things inspected.

Second is the intuitionist bias in Hume's explication of his "philosophical relations."

> It appears, therefore, that of these seven philosophical relations, there remain only four, which depending solely upon ideas, can be the objects of knowledge and certainty. These four are *resemblance, contrariety, degrees in quality,* and *proportions in quality or number* . . . (T)his decision we always pronounce at first sight, without any enquiry or reasoning.[29]

Reasoning would be extraneous, because we see these relations as they are.

The best known application for these intuitionist views is Hume's justification for denying that "whatever begins to exist, must have a cause of existence."[30] This principle is not true, he says, because it cannot be shown to be either "intuitively or demonstrably certain."[31] The difference between these two criteria seems to be as follows. The causal principle would be intuitively certain if we could test it as we do the claim that 'This is red,' inspecting the datum which makes it true. The principle would be demonstrably certain if its negation were a contradiction. Two considerations are pertinent here, and intuition is fundamental to both of them. On the one side, we might hope to demonstrate that the negation of the causal principle is a contradiction. The argument would advance in steps, each one perceived as necessary as we move to the conclusion that the denial of this principle requires that something should both exist and not exist, that being the only sort of contrariety which Hume acknowledges as a basis for contradiction. Ideally, the proof would be short, so that we could comprehend the entire argument in a single glance, seeing it as certain and self-evident. The second consideration is relevant here, for there is no contradiction in saying that something might exist without a cause. We prove that by imagining the alleged effect. Existence, we remember, is only the force and vivacity of impressions, so that this imagined datum misses only some degree of that vivacity. Anything conceivable can exist, Hume says, meaning that the things imagined could also have that added vivacity. Each one of the things imagined would then be perceived, as it was imagined, without an antecedent. It would exist without a cause.

This argument, together with Hume's claims about impressions, ideas, relations, and existence, help to confirm that his "empiricism" is only intuitionism. There are other kinds of empiricism, including the view that existence is independent of our perceiving, though every existing thing does or can make an empirical difference, and also the view that hypotheses prove their applicability to the world by entailing differences which would be perceivable if the hypotheses were true.

Hume's account is different from either of these two, because it locates all of reality within the domain of impressions, while requiring that every principle used for thinking about them should be susceptible to an immediately confirming perception. This Humean "empiricism" is not any kind of naturalism. It has no affinities to the view which locates us within the world so that our interactions with it may be the basis for testing our hypotheses about it. This view of Hume's is only a more spartan version of Descartes' intuitionism, one that rejects innate ideas while reducing the ideas we do have to copies of impressions.

Hume is, however, less naive than James, for he regards content with an armory of analytical devices, each one calculated to identify the elemental features of content as it is presented and inspected. We are told that everything inspectable is either an impression or an idea, that every idea is the copy of some impression because mind has no power for creating ideas, and that everything distinguishable is separable. Our comprehensive application of these rules produces a post-reflective content. It differs from the naive content of immediate experience, as the mingled and mutually penetrating phenomena which James describes differ from the sensory atoms described by Hume.

Notice that Hume has located form within content. Form as differentiation is explained as the difference that is common to phenomena seen as "same again." We may have a word to signify this class of similar particulars, as 'red' signifies red data, but the word is merely a token marking a difference already observed. We provide in a similar way for form as organization by remarking the spatial and temporal relations among sensory data, but here too the organizing features of content are perceived within it. The forms are merely an extraction from content. Content is the ground; form is derivative. Content has had to be refined beyond the tumultuous sensory given of intermingled colors, shapes and the rest so that we may justify our claims about form by citing some aspect of its reformulated ground. We say that there is no causal necessity after resolutely atomizing the sensory given. Only now is it plausible to say that all of reality is like a pointillist painting, every spot of color compossible with every other one.

4cii. HUSSERL

Are there other intuitionists who surpass even Hume in refining our naive appreciation for content? Husserl is an intuitionist of that sort, one who refines content in order to provide for form. Here are some passages from that section in the *Cartesian Meditations* where he writes of eidetic analysis:

> [W]e must bring to bear a fundamental methodological insight, which, once it is grasped, pervades the whole phenomenological method. . . . The method of eidetic description . . . signifies a transfer of all empirical descriptions into a new and fundamental dimension. . . . By the method of transcendental reduction each of us, as Cartesian meditator, was led back to his transcendental ego—naturally with its concrete-monadic contents as this de facto ego, the one and only absolute ego. When I keep on meditating, I, as this ego, find descriptively formulable, intentionally explicatable types.[32]

These "types" are the more or less complex qualitative differences discovered within experience, the difference between tables and chairs being an example.

> Let us make this clear to ourselves, and then fruitful for our method. Starting from this table-perception as an example, we vary the perceptual object, table, with a completely free optionalness, yet in such a manner that we keep perception fixed as perception of something, no matter what. Perhaps we begin by fictively changing the shape or the color of the object quite arbitrarily, keeping identical only its perceptual appearing. In other words: Abstaining from acceptance of its being, we change the fact of this perception into a pure possibility, one among other quite 'optional' pure possibilities—but possibilities that are possible perceptions. We, so to speak, shift the actual perception into the realm of non-actualities, the realm of the as-if, which supplies us with 'pure' possibilities, pure of everything that restricts to this fact or to any fact whatever. . . . The variation being meant as an evident one, accordingly as presenting in pure intuition the possibilities themselves as possibilities, its correlate is an intuitive and apodictic consciousness of something universal. The eidos itself is a beheld or

beholdable universal, one that is pure 'unconditioned'—that is to say:
according to its own intuitional sense, a universal not conditioned by
any fact. It is prior to all 'concepts,' in the sense of verbal significa-
tions; indeed as pure concepts, these must be made to fit the
eidos . . . each singly selected type is thus elevated from its milieu
within the empirically factual transcendental ego into the pure eidetic
sphere.[33]

Husserl's example gives the impression that the only forms important
to him are the ones of type, as table is an essence. But this is a mis-
reading, for Husserl would apply the same mode of analysis to the
relations responsible for order. This is apparent when a geometer
discovers the constitutive ordering principles within figures by proceeding in this way: He varies the relations until the figure and its
properties are transformed because of being altered beyond those tolerances which fix its identity. Forms of both kinds—i.e., differentiating types and organizing relations—are, says Husserl, founded in
content, then refined in eidetic reflection.

Mind uses these ideas of essence to prefigure all those differences
and relations which may be present within sensory experience, as I
know what to look for in particular chairs if I know the essence of
chair. This is, however, so much a version of Plato's and Descartes'
realism, and of their theories of perception, as to make us doubtful
that Husserl might have credited mind with the power for creating
refined ideas by reflecting upon its sensory data. Yet, they must be
acquired in that way if these ideas are not innate. If some of our
geometrical ideas originate as qualifications within an innate spatial
sense, like the geometry founded in Kant's forms of intuition, these
qualitative ideas do not. They are acquired as we reflect upon our
sensory data. Only later do we regard every table with the wisdom of
knowing what tables must essentially be.

Still, Husserl's ideas of essence are very refined. We need only
compare them to the ideas which Hume describes as being copies of
impressions. Why not say that Husserl is, like Plato and Descartes, an
intuitionist of form, not one of content? Certainly, he uses the ideas
as they do, to project form onto sensory content. Yet there is the
difference mentioned before. Plato and Descartes never doubt that
ideas of Form or essence, however qualitative their contents, are innate. Husserl doesn't agree that they are innate. How do we acquire
them? Only by refining these ideas from an original sensory content.

Mind has never had to learn the possibility of the phenomenological reduction. It has always started its reflections by turning upon the content provided by its sensory data. The progression to eidetic reflection is the last refinement of ideas that are first extracted there.

These examples, i.e., Austin, Gadamer, and Carnap on the side of form, James, Hume, and Husserl on the side of content, exhibit the traditional assumption that content or form will be the ground, while form or content, is derivative. Each of these biases has an impulse of its own, as the chosen ground is successively reworked in order that it may be more effective as the source for whatever is ascribed to its complement. Yet, all the vitality is leached from content when the differentiating and organizing principles have been extracted from the data perceived. These Husserlian ideas may be more adequate as refinements of content, hence, as vehicles for thinking the forms discovered within content; but they lack the sensuosity and detail that first draws us to content. Carnap, in a parallel way, loses the thinkable forms in the technicalities and abstractions of those constructional systems which he would have us use for thinking the sensory given. The forms introduced by theories which are too complex and obscure defeat intuitionist understanding, inviting the return of those ordinary language distinctions which are, says Austin, "all the distinctions men have found worth making, in the lifetime of many generations."

4d. *The parity of content and form*

Could we avert these two dialectical cycles, each one moving beyond then returning to its ground, by renouncing the alleged priority within each one of content or form? Rather than describe one as ground and the other as its derivative, could we affirm instead that neither one is prior, that these two are distinguishable but not separable, coequal and complementary? The bearing of each one upon the other might then prevent us from refining either one beyond the place where it is applicable to the other. This resolution seems unlikely because the history of intuitionist thinking so often prefers the dialectical cycle where one term is ground and the other is its derivative complement. Yet there is an important exception. Hegel supposes that content and form are equally fundamental, as differentiation and order are intrinsic to content but also the condition of its intelligibility. We may emphasize the sensuosity of content, or the differentia-

tions and relations, i.e., the concrete universals, which make it
thinkable: but this is an expression of our interest, not the claim that
one is ground and the other its derivative. This distorting interest is
corrected as we acknowledge the parity of content and form, each
one a condition for the other: it is content that is thinkable but only
as informed, and form that exists only as it differentiates and orders
some content. Hegel would have insisted on the parity of content and
form while acknowledging the useful dialectic between them. For he
might have agreed that the successive reformulations of content or
form do supply ever more powerful bases for the description of its
allegedly derivative complement. What Hegel would not have liked
are those refinements which purify and reformulate the original starting point until content and form are denatured. For intuitionist reflection will know the given by discerning it more accurately, not by
reconstructing the given in ways that misrepresent it. Every succession of dialectical revisions, whether of content or form, is likely to
have this distorting outcome, so that intuitionists who take up the
dialectic late in its cycle may deplore the aridity of these later formulations. Technical virtuosity or caricature will have often displaced
the form or content that were to be refined, though the motive for
these refinements is long forgotten. Why not terminate the dreary
history by returning to authentic content and form as they are known
to a naive mind turned freshly upon them and itself? Why not return
to sensory data or ordinary language as they are perceived, reliably
and concretely? This is the cycle as intuitionist reflection renews itself in these most familiar of contents and forms.

5. The reciprocity of mind and experience

One aspect of the movement between content and form is a clue
to a second and distinctive kind of intuitionist dialectic. This other
dialectic is implicit in Hegel's resolution of the priority claimed for
content or form. In themselves these two have parity; it is our attitude, our emphasis upon one or the other which establishes its priority in the order of interest. Notice what this assumes. On one side is
experience with differentiated, organized sensory and conceptual
data as its substance. On the other side is mind as it regards or makes
this experience. Intuitionists may devote themselves to experience,
never looking for or finding the inspecting subject; or they may turn

upon themselves, each one regarding himself or herself directly, or catching his reflection in the things he does.

Here, as in the dialectic of content and form, there is a relation between the two sides and a motive for correcting and elaborating what is said of one or the other. For suppose that we credit the given with a certain complexity. Aren't we provoked to discover those mental activities and structures which enable us to make or appreciate these aspects of experience? Shouldn't we test the discovery of one or another mental power by looking for the difference that it makes to the phenomena thought or perceived? Either way, we imply a certain parity and reciprocity between these two, where neither one is available to inspection if it is not joined to the other.

It is this reciprocity and mutual dependence which impel a spiral of elaborations. For suppose that we make the contrary assumption. We regard mind and experience as separable or even singular. We agree with Hume that there are impressions and ideas, but no mind; or we say in the manner of Kant's ethics that a mind turned upon itself may have a direct view of its structure and activities without regard for the phenomena to which these acts apply. Suppose too that we seem to have an inspectable content which justifies and confirms this claim to separability. These are examples of the methodological point that an intuitionist may prefer to examine one or the other side of this reciprocity while ignoring the other side. But then it is vital that the characterization of either side be tested for its coherence with the other one. Why? Because every characterization of intuitionist experience or intuiting mind looks forward, however tacitly, to the support of its complement, namely mind or experience.

There are differing resolutions for this complementarity, as Plato, Descartes, Locke and Kant differ in their characterizations of mind and experience. Each of these resolutions is unbalanced, so that the dialectic begins, if either side of a reciprocity is redescribed in a way so consequential that it forces a redescription of the other side.

Suppose we have assumed that inspection reveals a diversity of shapes and colors but no relations stronger than contiguity and repetition. These are, we say, sensory atoms related only in the ways that Hume described. They are connected in space and time, more or less regular in their associations and more or less similar. We credit mind with no powers beyond the ones required for discerning the character of the data set before it. But then someone else, Kant for example, discovers that these phenomena cohere in a way for which Hume cannot provide—there are geometrical necessities which are unexplained by the contiguities, regularities, and similarities which Hume remarks. Finding nothing that would explain these necessities within the data themselves, we ask if they might be explained by something that mind is doing. Following Kant, we specify the "transcendental" conditions for the unity of space and time, and the necessity of their internal relations. This characterization of mind's activity identifies the source for that difference first noted within experience; but it is, furthermore, the basis for additional anticipations regarding experience. So, Hume has said that our expectations for the future are the consequence of habit; but he has not identified the conditions for our having an experienceable future. It is Kant who elaborates upon mind's power for making experience to the point where he can locate the generative ground for that future; transcendental ego, he says, synthesizes time as well as space. This succession of claims is an example of the movement from experience to mind and back again, as we describe and then redescribe one or another, finding the basis for our redescription in some discovery made within its complement.

Here is another example. Suppose that our inspection shows the world to be rich in every way but one; we regard the diversity of phenomena, remarking their spatial, temporal, and dynamic relations but finding no evidence of their value for one another or themselves. Mind is only the careful observer. Self-inspection reveals, however, that the value of things is critical for us. We discover that mind never recognizes anything without regarding it as more or less significant for some purpose or plan of our own, or as that thing affects the things about it. That we may have regarded and described experience without concern for these attitudes and values seem inexplicable, except as we have wanted to describe things as they are, not as we appraise them. But even this much is too sober, too spartan. Recognition of our own valuing nature sensitizes us to the values already present within the world inspected. We look again, seeing that it too is suffused with value, as everything present there is consequential for some others. This example is like the one before; a discovery on either side of mind's relation to experience initiates a sequence of discoveries which move back and forth between these two.

Intuitionists suppose that the reciprocity of mind and experience is symbiotic; nothing happens in experience unless there is some mental act anticipating, registering, or constituting it, while every one of mind's acts is discernible within experience. It is this reciprocity which moves intuitionists through a succession of reformulations. No characterization, whether of mind or experience, can be taken as fixed so long as a new discovery in either one may require that we amend our claims about the other. This dialectic may enrich our appreciation of both mind and experience without producing the arid, overly technical or abstracted results of the form-content dialectic. Indeed, the later inspections of mind and experience should be all the more sensitive to real differences and dependencies within them.

There are, however, two risks. One is an excess of subtlety. We risk losing the forest for the trees as happens when every difference on one side is traced to the other side and back again. We lose the unity that intuitionism claims for self-inspecting mind in this excess of subtlety. Compare Sartre's nuanced account of being-for-itself in *Being and Nothingness* to Descartes' thumbnail sketch of the *cogito* in his second *Meditation*. Successive elaborations of mind's relation to experience have produced a result that is sometimes too dense. We recover our bearings by invoking that simpler but constraining archetype. The other, more dangerous, risk is the one of subjective idealism. This is the implication when mind claims responsibility for every difference within the given, even if we can say on the other side that all of mind is revealed in the experience it has made. Rather than a given set independently before us, we have an experience whose every differentiation and relation is claimed as an expression of mind's activity. What is there within intuitionism to avert this closure? Only Descartes' remark that mind does not seem to have made all of the given. Nor does the reciprocity of mind and experience demand this subordination of one by the other. We can renounce a complementarity so perfect that it denies the independent existence and character of the world known to experience.

5a. Sartre

We need some examples of this relation, its dialectic, and its pathology. Here are some passages where Sartre describes it:

Modern thought has realized considerable progress by reducing the existent to the series of appearances which manifest it.[34]

The appearance is not supported by any existent different from itself; it has its own *being*.[35]

All consciousness . . . is consciousness of something.[36]

(Self-consciousness) is the only mode of existence which is possible for a consciousness of something.[37]

Thus we have attained the ontological foundation of knowledge, the first being to whom all other appearances appear, the absolute in relation to which every phenomenon is relative.[38]

There is only intuitive knowledge. Deduction and discursive argument, incorrectly called examples of knowing, are only instruments which lead to intuition. When intuition is reached, methods utilized to attain it are effaced before it; in cases where it is not attained, reason and argument remains as indicating signs which point toward an intuition beyond reach; finally, if it has been attained but is not a present mode of my consciousness, the precepts which I use remain as the results of operations formerly effected, like what Descartes called the 'memories of ideas.' If someone asks for a definition of intuition, Husserl will reply, in agreement with the majority of philosophers, that it is the presence of the thing (*Sache*) 'in person' to consciousness.[39]

Sartre is concerned that the world should be directly available to inspecting mind. He establishes its availability by saying that the world is comprised of that "series of appearances" which is set before our intuiting minds. Self-conscious mind is to be, reciprocally, the ontological foundation for all of being. Now the dialectic begins, for this is an alteration of our belief that the world is knowable though largely independent of our thinking for its existence and character. Sartre and those intuitionists who agree with him must rework their characterizations of mind and experience until each of the two is calibrated to the other in ways that satisfy the demand for perfect disclosure.

5b. Heidegger

We are reminded of Heidegger, and especially of that extended section in *Being and Time* where he writes of truth and reality. Heidegger has been arguing that the Aristotelian notion of truth, "that the essence of truth lies in the 'agreement' of the judgement with its object"[40] is secondary to the more elementary fact that truth is *disclosure*. " 'Being-true' (truth) means Being-uncovering," he says. Truth is achieved when nothing remains hidden in the phenomena inspected, when things are seen as they are. What is the ontological status of the things disclosed: Are they independent of mind though available to it, or is their reality conditional upon the fact that they are experienced as ready-to-hand or present-at-hand?

> Of course only as long as Dasein is (that is, only as long as an understanding of Being is ontically possible), "is there" Being. When Dasein does not exist, "independence" "is" not either, nor "is" the "in-itself." In such a case this sort of thing can be neither understood nor not understood. In such a case even entities within-the-world can neither be discovered nor lie hidden. *In such a case* it cannot be said that entities are, nor can it be said that they are not. But *now,* as long as there is an understanding of Being and therefore an understanding of presence-at-hand, it can indeed be said that in this case entities will still continue to be.[41]

Heidegger has also written, in the sentence immediately before the paragraph just quoted, that

> the fact that Reality is ontologically grounded in the Being of Dasein, does not signify that only when Dasein exists and as long as Dasein exists, can the Real be as that which in itself is.[42]

This acknowledgment of things undisclosed is all-important to the dialectic of mind and experience, hence, to questions about the reality of things uninspected; but then Heidegger says nothing more to detail or confirm it. Relevant too is the fact that this last quoted sentence comes after the place where Heidegger has expressed his preference for idealism. Idealism, he has argued, is superior in principle to realism so long as it is grounded in the existential-ontological features of Dasein, hence, in Being itself.

This most fundamental grounding joins reality to truth, for that disclosure which is prior logically to every other one is the revelation of Dasein to itself.

> Being-true as Being-uncovering, is a way of Being for Dasein. What makes this very uncovering possible must necessarily be called "true" in a still more primordial sense. *The most primordial phenomenon of truth is first shown by the existential-ontological foundations of uncovering.* Uncovering is a way of Being for Being-in-the-world. Circumspective concern, or even that concern in which we tarry and look at something, uncovers entities within-the-world. These entities become that which has been uncovered. They are "true" in a second sense. What is primarily "true"—that is, uncovering—is Dasein. "Truth" in the second sense does not mean Being-uncovering (uncovering), but Being-uncovered (uncoveredness).[43]

This is Descartes' *cogito* as Being, where everything else *is* only because of being disclosed to inspecting mind, and where the principal
difference from Descartes is the existential emphasis upon a Being-in-
the-world, a Being thrown among and fallen within the things disclosed to it. I shall be arguing in Chapter Six that intuitionism has its
beginnings in Parmenides. It is good therefore to have Heidegger's
remark that "Parmenides was the first to discover the Being of entities, and he 'identified' Being with the perceptive understanding of
Being,"[44] that is to say with a mind conscious of all its affections,
hence, with itself. Heidegger recapitulates, in this way, the themes
discovered already in each of the preceding intuitionists. All of them
insist that there is a given, that it is perceived, and that all of reality
turns about this dyad, as the only reality is either the thinkable given,
or mind as it thinks the given.

This is a decisive moment for the dialectic of mind and experience. For Heidegger, like Sartre, has moved beyond the claim that
there is a world available to inspecting mind. This world exists, he
says, only as it is disclosed to Dasein. Heidegger has reduced his
argument to a very small circle. Being, he says, is Being-in-the-world,
where Being-in-the-world is the complex phenomenon or act which
includes all the phenomena disclosed together with that being who is
their self-inspecting witness: "within-the-worldness is based upon
the phenomenon of the *world*, which, for its part, as an essential
item in the structure of Being-in-the-world, belongs to the basic constitution of Dasein."[45] This is an oblique way of saying that the dialectic of mind and experience completes itself in a comprehensive
idealism where nothing is to count as real if it is not set before a
"perceptive understanding." This condition and test for reality is to
apply, I assume, as much to mind's reality as to the reality of the
world experienced; nothing is real if it does not satisfy the demand
that it be disclosed, hence, inspectable and "true." There is still the
further possibility that the given exists not merely as a qualification
of Being-in-the-world, but rather because Dasein has created its own
experience as Kant's transcendental ego synthesizes an experience for
itself. Still, Heidegger has already said enough to confirm his idealism: reality exists as a qualification of that primordial Being to whom
it is disclosed.

This is the all but final step in a dialectic which secures mind's
access to the world by reducing it to those appearances which are set

before, and qualify, the mind itself. Realists might ask that mind loosen its grip, allowing the world its independence in order that we might think again about the conditions for mind's access to it. Perhaps there is some other way of knowing the world, one that leaves its character and existence independent of the fact that we think about it—e.g., as we may represent every possible state of affairs without reducing these possibilities, or the actualities instantiating them, to states of mind. Intuitionists will reject this other way of considering the issue, because only the representations, not their objects are inspectable. Hypotheses about those objects would be speculative in the way that intuitionism deplores, so that intuitionists who reject the perfect idealism of Sartre or Heidegger will prefer to start again within the familiar intuitionist problematic: the world, they will say, is available to mind without being its qualification or product, though we know the world only as we inspect it. It will not be long before the given is appropriated another time, to the same idealist effect. Why this should happen perpetually within intuitionism is left to Chapter Four, and the discussion of intuitionism's psychocentric ontology.

6. Providing for content and form, mind and experience

There is one additional consideration before we turn away from the dialectical cycle of mind and experience. For this second dialectic joins easily with the one of content and form to produce the complex intuitionist views familiar to us. There are intuitionists of content who suppose that mind enjoys and sometimes reports about the content set before it, and intuitionists of form who say that all of the order and differentiation within experience is a consequence of the ways we think or talk about it. Most intuitionist theories make some claim about the relation of content and form, and then another claim, superimposed on this first one, about the relation of mind and experience. Millenia of intuitionist thinking have taught us to expect that a comprehensive intuitionism will provide for both of these dialectics. Anything less is incomplete. Hume and James provoke that uneasiness when they write amply enough about content and form, but not about mind. We satisfy ourselves that their theories are sufficiently complex only as we remark that they do acknowledge experience and do give reasons for otherwise ignoring mind—e.g., it is uninspectable. But then we do carry on thinking within the framework of this second dialectic, reaching for the mind they cannot find.

Is there a rule or formula laying down the possible combinations of these two dialectics, and also the development from any one position to its successor? There does not seem to be a rule of that sort. All that we do have is a reliable development from the naive to the critical, from the stance of a mind passively regarding content or form to the attitude of thought as it claims responsibility for making content or imposing form. This line of development usually passes beyond a concern for the world experienced to an ever more elaborate regard for mind itself. We go from attention to the contingencies affecting us through a specification of the necessities and universals suffusing that experience to a characterization of mind as primordial ground. All of this is characteristic of intuitionist thinking in our culture. Some other cultures value passivity more than action. In them, the dialectical cycle might be reversed. They might go from an overvalued emphasis upon engagement and responsibility to the cooler, more detached attitude of a mind stepping back from an experience it observes but does not make. Variations like this one are consistent with the intuitionist demand that nothing be said about mind or experience, content or form, if it cannot be confirmed by inspection. With fidelity to this principle as their only constraint, intuitionists are free to explore the four poles of these two oppositions in any order they can justify.

We have the history of Western philosophy as evidence that our intuitionists have no interest in some of the combinations and developments available to them, as no one affirms, then renounces, mind's responsibility for a differentiated and unified given. Our intuitionists prefer the cycles established among us. They are forever drawing the world into mind by way of language or experience, insisting all the while that inspecting mind is "existentially-ontologically" prior. Science or practice may divert intuitionist attention, suggesting for example that some aspect of the things claimed as given or mind itself is uninspectable. Intuitionists then strain in either direction, alleging that these things are inspectable or that they do not exist. But these are situational, historical episodes. They may temporarily redirect, but they do not alter the abiding rhythms of content and form, mind and experience.

7. The justifications for intuitionist method

Each of the dialectical cycles considered above is fundamental to the statement and development of intuitionist positions, as every intuitionist theory makes some claim about the relation of content and form, mind and experience. There is also a third dialectic, one that is different from the other two because of turning from the particular claims and subject matters of intuitionist theory to the justification for intuitionist method. Intuitionists may say that nothing is real if it cannot be perceived or thought. They may emphasize that mind's own reality is the fundament on which every other reality stands. But this is not enough. Intuitionists are obliged to explain what they do and why they do it. This third dialectic is the progression of their justifying self-interpretations.

It might seem that intuitionism requires no defense. The promise of knowledge, meaning certainty about matters of fact, should be reason enough for espousing it. But what is it that we know? How far does the given extend beyond inspecting mind into a mind-independent world? Intuitionists may answer this question while thinking of mind as a theatre where the things known are set before our inspecting minds. They should observe that the knowledge they promise may not reach beyond the given into the world. Certainty will be easy but cheap if the things known go no deeper into the world than mind itself. It is this tension, between mind-centered experience and the world beyond, which generates the dialectic of alternative justifications for intuitionist method. Intuitionists should be able to justify our saying that their inspection of the given reaches as deeply into the world as there are differences to observe. But how deep is that? How far beyond our minds might the world stretch? How accessible is the world? This third dialectical progression supplies the justifications for saying, alternately, that intuition's reach is shallow or deep. These four justifications—naive realism, representationalism, transcendentalism, and common sense—mark the steps from realism to idealism and back again.

7a. Naive realism

Naive realism supposes that the given we inspect is just the world itself. In Plato, this is the world of Forms, where inspecting mind is the active principle which reaches out to grasp the Forms, becoming in that moment identical with them. Our idea is the same, though its applications are different, when we say that vision is a kind of beam, searching out and illuminating the colors and shapes of the substances before us. Either way, whether vision is rational or perceptual, we are to see things as they are. Of course, too many of us never have rational intuitions like the ones Plato describes; and we stumble occasionally among the perceptual illusions which confound this theory of perception. We come to doubt that the world is or can be accessible to us in the direct way that it proposes. Still, naive realism has a simple genius. There is, it says, a mind-independent world which is intelligible in itself and accessible to knowledge. That world is to be the *telos* of inspecting mind, with no barrier between it and ourselves. Nothing is to mediate as we search for differentiation and order within the world as it lies about and before us.

7b. Representationalism

This is justification by exposition. We make the idea plausible by telling what it requires of knowledge and the world, then by reminding ourselves of the good motives for proclaiming it. Yet, naive realism disintegrates when too many illusions and false beliefs convince us that something does mediate between the world and our knowledge of it. Putting a good face on this intrusion, we say that the mediator is nearly transparent. It is form, shaping our minds as it shapes the matter of the things represented. We who entertain these forms understand everything that is intelligible within the matters formed, even though we never see them directly but only think them by way of these forms, their natural signs.

Aristotle is the best exponent of this notion. The world is composed, he says, of substances having matter and form as their constituents. What is more, a substance interacting with some other one may alter it, as a ring affects hot wax, by leaving its form upon it. Our knowledge of these substances, hence, of the world, is secured by the fact that mind relates to the world somewhat as wax relates to the ring. There are, Aristotle supposes, these three bases for our knowledge of the world, all of them converging upon the realization within our minds of those forms which are already present in the things known. First is perception, as the things seen and heard press their form upon our minds. Second is thought, as it abstracts from one or a succession of percepts in order that it may reflect upon the universals exhibited within them. Third are the subject-predicate forms of Greek grammar. They are already an abstraction from, and representation of, the categorial differences present within the world. These three, words, thoughts, and percepts, are such good representations that we never do or should stop to consider that the matters immediately before the mind's eye are only representations, not the things they signify.

We are vulnerable, however, to the suspicion that these representations may not be good surrogates for the things known, for how could we establish that the things represented are like their signs? Where is the perspective, independent of language and experience, from which to compare them to the things they represent? There is no vantage point of this sort, so that claims about the representational force of thought and perception are merely speculative. We may believe that our thoughts and percepts are like the things they signify, but we cannot prove it. We lose our confidence in the transparency of these mediating representations. Rather than being an open window onto the world, they are a barrier to the direct inspection of the things represented. These signs, whether natural or conventional, have displaced the world to which they were to give us access. For it is only these representations, not the world, that mind inspects and knows.

This story, that form in the world is identical with form in perception, thought and language, was dubious from the start. For there are many languages used for representing matters of fact, and they vary considerably from one another, even as they are used to represent and communicate about any one state of affairs. The differentiations and orders projected by each of these languages makes some contact with differences and orders in the world; but not to the point of our being able to say that sentences are pictures of the things they represent. We may have supposed that thought is more accurate a representation than language, perhaps because of assuming that thoughts are images of the things represented. It is pertinent, therefore, that images are frequently inaccurate as representations, as a red percept is not like the wave lengths producing that image in us. If thoughts are not images, then we need ask what basis there is for supposing them to be like the things they represent, as 'second cousin twice removed' is a notion correctly used sometimes, though it is not at all like the thing represented. Aristotle merely assumes that language, thought, and perception supply accurate likenesses of things which are not otherwise directly inspectable; we are to know these things by inspecting representations which are presumed to be like them. This argument is defenseless against the sceptical charge that we know the representations but nothing of their objects. Intuitionists demand certainty. They prefer that we restrict our attention to the representations themselves, withdrawing our commitment to their objects, if this will save us from hypotheses which intuitionism is unable to confirm.

Naive realism and representationalism are behind us now. Transcendental prescriptivism, then its variant, transcendental constructivism, are just ahead. For we have abandoned our hope of knowing the world in itself, either directly or as represented in perception, thought, and language. We are on the verge of losing the world for all the purposes of knowledge. There is something given for inspection, as language, thought and perception are given. But how shall we account for whatever is intelligible in them when their sources and objects in a world beyond us are renounced? Can we turn the other way, finding the necessary and sufficient conditions for everything intelligible within the mind itself? For why not say with Protagorus that man is the measure of all that is that it is, and of all that is not that it is not? We do not know or need anything of an ulterior world, one that is disguised, mediated, or hidden altogether. Naive realism was right to insist upon the immediacy and accessibility of the world. It erred in supposing that the world's reality has its origins beyond us, as if the existence and character of the world were independent of the ways we think about it. For reality is always indeterminate, waiting for us to decide the exact character of the things present there. Indeed, the world as given has no properties except the ones that we ascribe to it. It is, so far as we can know, only as we see and report it, where the only appeal from one consistent interpretation of the world is a different interpretation. This third justification renders the world safe for intuition by purging reality of everything that might stand apart from the intuitionist given. Representationalism was happy to populate the world with anything that might be known by way of its representations. This third justification, so sceptical of the link from representations to their objects, would ignore or obliterate them. It turns representations into realities, calling objective what is subjective, controlling, even creating the given.

Mind's attitude toward itself is transformed. Naive realism was passive, with forms impressed upon it by the things which are thought or perceived. Even representationalism waited for perception to supply some of the phenomena which it would use as signs, as our percepts are the natural signs of their causes. Representationalism allows that mind be active when creating linguistic signs, but even this activity is sometimes reactive, as we say of the world whatever the sensory data show it to be. In all of this, mind presumes to know its place within the world. Mind registers the world's effects upon it, and then reports about them, confident that our representations are a mediated but correct reading of the world. Scepticism has poisoned this conviction. In its first moment, we are baffled: there is a world intimating itself to us, though we cannot know it as it is. Now, in a further moment, we begin to doubt the very existence of a mind-independent constraint upon the given: why repeat that the given is a representation if we never do or can have independent confirmation for the claim that something is represented? The very existence of a world beyond us might be only the fantasy that mind contrives as a defense against the realization of its own responsibility for everything occurring with experience. Our humility in the face of the world, common to naive realism and representationalism, becomes an embarrassment. We recover, and react with aggressive self-confidence. For if the given is not a message from beyond, then it does not merit too deferential a regard from us. Rather than register and attend to it, we may alter the given as we please, with only consistency and coherence to restrain us. No longer self-effacing as we survey and report about the given, we make our own demands of it; reality will exhibit those differences and relations which we prescribe. The focus of command is now turned 180°. Rather than defer to the given, worrying that our reports are accurate to it, we require that the given should exhibit the distinctions which we have projected onto it. The given is inspectable as before, but with the difference that we have prescribed its form.

7c. *Transcendentalism*

This third justification for intuitionist method is the one of prescriptivist a priorism. Mind lays down the only distinctions that may be employed, as thought and experience are formulated. This was Plato's view as he argued that Forms are present in mind as the ideas with which we think the sensible world. Descartes' version is equally powerful: No property which is not first entertained as a clear and distinct idea is intelligible; no idea which has not first been certified as clear and distinct can have application within the world. Hence nothing of the world is knowable if it is not already founded within a clear and distinct idea. For Descartes, as for Plato, ideas function projectively. We see differentiations and order within the given to the extent that we regard its features as the instances of our ideas. But then the ideas too are inspectable. They are like the experience that is rendered intelligible by their application; both of them satisfy the intuitionist demand that nothing is real if it is not inspectable.

I have been supposing that the given has no character in advance of the time when differentiations are projected onto it; but there are two views about this. The less radical claim holds that we impose definition and order upon a given which is otherwise uncertain and determinable, or that the given overwhelms us with its diversity until we have used a spartan set of predicates for marking differentiations within it. These positions agree that the given has some intrinsic character of its own, though too little or too much. The more radical formulation insists that the given has no intrinsic differentiations of its own, nothing that might be articulated or emphasized by the distinctions that we introduce as we think it. The properties and structures we apprehend within the given are, therefore, only the ones that we have projected onto it. Nelson Goodman sometimes endorses this second, more radical view, though his prescriptivism then entails that mind has created every intelligible difference within the matters it thinks or describes.[46] Kant, though no realist himself, repudiated Fichte for just this romantic excess, for this is the step beyond prescriptivism to constructivism, where thinking an intelligible world passes over into inventing then projecting every difference that makes the given thinkable. It is, however, this constructivist heresy that is closer to the demands of intuitionist purism. For this third intuitionist justification prefers that nothing claimed for knowledge should be vulnerable to sceptical arguments. Phenomena which are already more or less intelligible in themselves will have to be discerned. Couldn't we be mistaken about them? Isn't mind saved from the possibility of error if it prescribes the identity of every least quality or relation discerned within the given? Constructivist a priorism invites the charge of comprehensive idealism as it claims this responsibility for intuiting mind.

I have been describing this third justification as an a priorist and prescriptivist or constructivist one. We may also describe it as "transcendental." This title is earned because of mind's relation to the world it thinks: this is a mind set apart, one that transcends the world rendered thinkable by its rules or ideas. We may think especially of Kant as he introduced this notion to characterize those acts and concepts which impose least conditions for differentiation and order among sensuous intuitions. But Plato's Forms, Descartes' clear and distinct ideas, and all the distinctions of ordinary language analysis are also entitled to this characterization. Each of them is alleged to be the origin for whatever is intelligible within experience. It is these "transcendentals" which make experience thinkable, hence, inspectable. They clarify or impose those differentiations and orders which are its form.

There is, we know, a difference of opinion when intuitionists consider the inspectability of the transcendentals. Kant usually says that they are not inspectable in themselves, but only as they are exhibited within the experience they organize. Husserl, after Plato and Descartes, demurs. His ideas are the lure for reflection. We look past the data of sensory experience to their eidetic paradigms, turning back again to the sensory data in order to see the paradigm realized in them. Experience, Husserl implies, is more than either reflection upon essences or the insubstantial broth of sensory data. It is sensation enriched by intellect. Its first condition is our inspection of essences. The second one is our projection of them onto the data which are otherwise insufficiently differentiated and structured. In all of this, Husserl supposes that mind will be turned upon itself, so that its efficacy in creating an intelligible experience will be seen. This is his way of assuring that intuitionism will not lose on the side of mind all of the autonomy it has won on the side of the given. For if we cannot be satisfied with a world inaccessible except for its mediating representations, then we should not be satisfied either with a mind whose access to itself is mediated by its product, that is, by experience. The intuitionism which succeeds naive realism and representationalism fears scepticism more keenly than anything else. It secures itself from that threat by identifying reality with the given and by demanding total control of both the given and itself. Mind, like the world, will be real to the extent that it is inspectable. Any part of mind that is exempt from inspection loses its claim to reality. Husserl tries, more insistently than anyone before him, to bring all of transcendental mind within the orbit of inspectability. That he fails, and then affirms mind's partial inaccessibility, should not distract us from the purity of his aim; nothing that is real can be hidden, not in mind or the world. A mind that is transparent to itself as it makes experience is our surest defense against the claim that anything real might escape inspection.

It may seem that the progression beyond naive realism and representationalism to prescriptivism and constructivism is irrelevant to our time, when very few intuitionists are idealists of the sort just described. Nothing could be farther from the truth. Twentieth-century philosophy is awash in idealism, just because intuitionism demands that mind be the measure of a thinkable reality. We have Carnap's reconstructions and his dictum against "external questions," Husserl's eidetic reduction, ordinary language analysis as it surveys our "universe of discourse," and hermeneutics as it regards all reality as a text where every difference is prefigured by our "interpretation" or "reading." Each of these philosophic attitudes is an idealism founded in the intuitionist requirement that mind is to be the source for whatever is intelligible, hence, thinkable, in reality. That most of these philosophers prefer words to ideas testifies to our intuitionist concern for the difficulty of verifying intrapsychic events—e.g., ideas—and to our assurance that words and the rules for using them are not subject to the same sceptical disputes. In the beginning were Words, words so clear and distinct as to be unmistakable in the minds entertaining and applying them. It is from words that Plato, Descartes, and Husserl have inferred to ideas, and with words that we think and say the forms which make the world differentiated and ordered. Words are mind's instruments as it controls, or creates, a thinkable world.

This is the moment within the dialectic of intuitionist justifications when Protagoras is vindicated, the moment when mind does seem to be the measure of all that is and is not. But this prescriptivist cure is deadlier than the representationalist disease. For error and the world's opposition to our plans is evidence sufficient to prove that the world does have a form independent of anything we may think or say of it. What is it that makes us forgetful of error, while inspiring the prescriptivist idea that reality is unintelligible in itself, acquiring order and form only as mind thinks it? Could this persuasion originate in a mistaken appraisal of the activities directed by successful plans? It may seem that a plan unopposed by the world is the very source of the world's form, for it connects otherwise disparate parts of the world by laying down the sequence of behaviors which carry us forward to an objective. Perhaps we misinterpret the fact that the differentiations and orders projected by our plan are the ones first imagined, then encountered as we move through the world. Could it be that the egoistic power so explicit in prescriptivism is the exaggerated expression of the power we feel in a plan that works? Though some plans do misfire as form in the world resists and defeats our aims. Failure, disappointment, and wasted energy remind us that the world does have a form of its own. Intuitionism hopes to defend itself from scepticism by controlling or creating the given. But this given is only a tiny part of reality. Most of the rest is independent of what we think and say of it. We accomodate ourselves to that implacable fact. We are obliged, however grudgingly, to dismantle or ignore all the apparatus of this third justification for intuitionist method.

7d. Common sense

What remains to intuitionists when prescriptivism has collapsed from the weight of its pretensions? Our only conspicuous resources are the ones required for making our way in the world. These include sensory experience, including hands and feet, and the rules and procedures that mind employs for organizing its thoughts before acting to achieve its aims. These are the resources of common sense, the fourth justification for intuition. Embarrassed and repelled by the grandiosity of our previous attitude, we are scrupulously agnostic about the issues which divide idealists from realists. We resist being drawn to either side of their argument as we concentrate upon the practical things that need doing if we are to secure and satisfy ourselves and those others to whom we are responsible. Intuition, meaning direct inspection, discloses all the details of our practical lives, including needs, circumstances, and resources. It makes us transparent to ourselves as we prepare, enact, and revise our plans. Troubled or bemused, but always sober, we tell who, what, and where we are or seem to be.

There might seem to be a chasm separating Hegel from G.E. Moore; but what is Moore's common sense philosophy but a spare version of the self-discovery and self-realization which Hegel describes as the aim of every consciousness turned upon itself. This activity is morally strenuous because of obliging us to be honest as we describe our circumstances, motives, and aims. It also enforces humility, as we understand that our resources are inadequate though our needs are urgent and our situation precarious. Common sense does not indulge us by pretending that our powers for world-making will save us from reality. Its aim is modest: We are to inspect and report the circumstances, ideas, rules, and practices which supply the content and direction of our lives. We may dig the garden, start a business, or write a book; doing these things or some others, we enact the forms which we have inherited and learned to apply. We may alter these forms until they suit us better, as we also build safe houses; but we never do prescribe the world's form.

7e. The cycle repeats

Common sense is the last of intuitionism's four justifications. That is plain when common sense is superseded, almost immediately, by naive realism. This happens when the emphasis on practice encourages us to ask about the objective conditions for effective action. How must the world be and what must we do within it if behavior is to succeed? There is no place here for a merely phenomenological account of technology and practice, one describing the look and feel of our tools, and the quality of our experience as we accomodate to the world as it requires their use. The phenomenological descriptions of this experience might satisfy our aesthetic sensibilities without supplying the knowledge or power for controlling our circumstances. The inquiry required now is different from that, because of having to determine the character of the things themselves. How are they to be used; what are their tolerances and effects? Common sense is superseded when inquiry drives beyond the small circle of effective self-concern to identify those things in the world which are important to our aims. First supposing that we see the things themselves, then renouncing naive realism for representationalism, we start the cycle another time. These are the justifications, the recurring attitudes, almost the moods, of a subject who is alternately realistic, grandiose and prudent. Resting nowhere for long, intuitionists move perpetually within this cycle.

8. Conclusions

There are, I have been saying, three dialectics active within intuitionist thought: the ones of content and form, mind and experience, and these four justifications for intuitionist method. Every intuitionist feels their separate demands, though he may emphasize just one or two of them. Do intuitionists favor some one or few of the positions generated by these dialectics, or do we find them dispersed throughout the range of possible views? The answer seems to be that we have both circumstances at once; there is a dominant bias, even a vortex, within the exuberant anarchy of independent thinkers, each one developing a position of his or her own. In our time, intuitionism speaks for form as prior to content, and for mind as it prescribes the possible forms of experience. This intuitionism assumes a transcendental stance to justify its prescriptivist assumptions. Ordinary language analysts, Husserl, Carnap, and the philosophers of hermeneutics all speak in its voice. They resonate with the authority of Plato, Descartes, and Kant. The other intuitionists are more diverse, with as many kinds of intuitionism as there are possibilities prefigured by these three dialectics. Their diversity is historically incidental; it is a kind of white noise expressing indifferently the myriad alternatives established by the dialectics. The dominant emphasis on form, mind, and transcendental prescription is more significant. For this is the position that intuitionists assume when they declare that philosophic knowledge is prior to knowledge of every other sort. This is originally the view that philosophy is foundational, that philosophers have discovered and now occupy that ground from which every other sort of knowledge derives. Why say this? Because these transcendental prescriptivists suppose that they have identified the power of mind as it creates an intelligible world. No wonder then if prescriptivism is the ascendant intuitionism of our time. This is the weapon for defending our prerogatives from the authority of empirical science. It is not surprising, we say, that science proves the effectiveness of its methods by its descriptions and explanations. Science is only one expression of mind as it legislates meaning and intelligibility. That power is known first and best to philosophy. We locate it within our inspecting, self-inspecting minds. The logic used for thinking the world, the values used for appraising it, and mind as known to itself are, all of them, subject matters that are prior to, because conditions for, the ones of science. Staring down the scientific onslaught, we turn it aside. Intuiting mind is prior in knowledge and first in Being. Every difference and order originates there.

We know that the flagrant idealism of this view is not obligatory, even for intuitionists. For all of them, except the prescriptivists and constructivists, agree that the existence and character of the world are known to, but not created by, our minds. Still, the problem is more severe than the one of diverting intuitionism from its emphatic idealism. That will likely pass as intuitionism moves through its cycle. The problem is deeper, because we shall have to escape altogether from the grasp of intuiting mind if we are to have an ontology which does not limit reality to mind and those things which are set before, or created by, it. Intuitionists must defend their ontology, especially its psycho-centric theory of Being. Their psycho-centrism is described more carefully in Chapter Four. Chapter Three is a summary of some matters explicit, or implied, in this chapter. Having considered the dialectical cycles within intuitionist thought, we list its defining characteristics.

Chapter Three

Intuitionist Method's Defining Properties

W hat distinguishes intuitionist method, whether it stresses content or form, mind or experience? Here are six factors to consider. Each of them is common to every intuitionist, or a point of dispute among them.

1. The given

1. Intuitionists of all kinds restrict philosophic attention to data which are assumed to be given. The matters given may be sensory phenomena, including colors, pains and moods, or Humean ideas, moral qualities and laws, the rules of ordinary language, logical systems, the structure of space and time, a Carnapian or Cartesian reconstruction, Husserlian noema and Platonic Forms, or thought and will in a Cartesian subject. There is almost nothing interesting to philosophers which has not been claimed as given.

The differences among these candidates for given are considerable. Some data—e.g., percepts—are ephemeral, while others—e.g., Plato's Forms—are eternal. Sometimes the given is so forcible that it compels our attention, pain being an example. Other subjects, such as logic, are so abstract as to require that mind be specially cultivated for discerning them. Some matters given are peculiar to their subjects, as the shading of a desire or mood is distinctive of the person having it. Other givens are common and repeatable, as all the members of a community use and reflect upon the rules of their language. The given is sometimes learned or received, though other times we make it.

These four oppositions—i.e., ephemeral-eternal, immediate-remote, idiosyncratic-common, constructed-received—help to explain the different claims that are made when philosophers choose one or another given as their starting point. Little more is required to explain the dissimilarities among intuitionists as each of them elaborates on the collateral assumptions that are required when one or another of these givens is emphasized. Where this difference animates all the rest of their views, it is only passingly significant that, say, Plato and Sartre are both intuitionists. I am not concerned, however, with these contrasts among the various kinds of given, or with the variety of doctrines warranted by them. It is only the shared method that is relevant now. For intuitionist method limits the views which result from its applications, irrespective of the data to which it applies. Intuitionism has that effect when it supposes that every subject matter is given to inspecting mind, where the appreciation, accurate description or construction of a thinkable given is our one philosophic task.

1a. Attention compelling properties

This is a plausible objective only as the given has certain properties which compel our inspection. There are three such properties: (a) The given is a luminous presentation. Its articulations are visible and impelling, as sunlight draws the eye. (b) The given is the source of intelligibility, and its standard. No distinction is thinkable if it does not originate as a difference or relation exhibited within the given. (c) The given is the test of truth, no judgement being true if it is not (i) a report about the existence or character of something which is, or could be, present within the given; or (ii) a thought or sentence seen to cohere with other thoughts or sentences.

These factors together explain the fixation which ensues when a philosopher has chosen one of the possible givens as the "real" given. He supposes that this chosen subject matter stands perspicuously before our inspecting minds, that its articulations dominate our attention to the exclusion of all others. These are the distinctions which words are to signify, or thoughts express. These are the "facts" against which philosophic and empirical judgements are to be evaluated. The given, now meaning this chosen given, is to be our point of reference for all thinkable differences and the ground for truth. Every other subject matter, including all of the rejected candidates for given, are unintelligible if they are not derivable from, or discoverable within, this preferred given.

Hume's empiricism is a notable example. He asserts, without argument, that experience is comprised of impressions and ideas, ideas being less vivacious copies of impressions. Both impressions and ideas satisfy the first of the three requirements listed above, that matters given be visible in themselves, thereby drawing the attention of inspecting mind. This Humean given is to be, second, our standard for intelligibility, no idea being significant if it does not have a corresponding impression to supply its content. This given is, third, the test of truth where no judgement is true if there is no impression or complex of them corresponding to the ideas that are affirmed or denied. So, "This is red" is true if there is a red datum. "Nothing here is red" is true if none of our impressions are red. The only exceptions to this account are tautologies, meaning thoughts or sentences which are true for semantical or grammatical reasons, irrespective of the data. For the other cases, Hume would have us examine our impressions to see that they conform to the idea or ideas affirmed or denied. These tautologies require that we inspect our complex ideas, establishing that they satisfy a "precise standard,"[1] or a rule. But surely, this standard, like ideas, impressions, and the judgement being appraised, is inspectable. Hume's "empiricism" is, more exactly, an intuitionism for which all of these things are given.

The subject matters are different but the design of the argument is the same when Plato argues that it is Forms which are given to *nous*. Here again, intelligibility and truth are fixed by distinctions apparent to the mind's eye. Plato agrees with Hume that nothing is intelligible if it does not stand perspicuously before the mind, where every word and thought is meaningful only as it signifies one of these perceivable differences.

Notice, with these two examples as evidence, that the intuitionist is an imperialist, arguing that other possible givens are to be subsumed under, or derived from, his own. Hume supposes that ideas derive from impressions; Plato has said that the differences within sensory data are discernible only as we have ideas of Forms. Here are Plato and Hume in thrall to the same assumption, each one presuming that the other's given is unintelligible, because unperceivable or unthinkable, unless regarded from the standpoint of his own.

Plato's deference to the given is paradigmatic for his every intuitionist successor. The given is to inspecting mind, he says, as the Sun is to the eye. Each given is a luminous presence, one that compels our attention. Where the Sun gives life and visibility to natural things, the given illumines distinctions which are already present within, or derivable from, itself. Inspecting mind is drawn to them as the eye turns to sunlight. We cannot help but see the Good, and then use it for discerning whatever there is of difference and order within other forms and sensory data. Plato's figure is misleading only because of locating the source of illumination outside us.

Most intuitionists place that source within us. This is true even of Plato when he writes that the Forms are present within mind as innate ideas. Descartes is all the more insistent when he locates that attention compelling light within us: Mind is to understand differences available for instantiation in the world after first turning upon and inspecting itself. The *cogito* will be our primary given. The world will be intelligible, because I am self-intelligible, exhibiting within myself such distinctions and forms of order as God may duplicate within the material world. Every intuitionist accomplishes this same result, bringing the given home, discovering and appropriating the distinctions which are constitutive of meaning, merging self with the given until the world's intelligibility is our self-intelligibility.

1b. Mind as given to itself

Mind's appropriation of the given has this additional, perhaps unanticipated effect: mind inevitably turns upon itself, each one taking himself or herself as the given. This is the place where mind discovers first that it is, then what it is. We repeat some version of this progression from Descartes through Kant to Sartre, as mind thinks upon itself, infers to some additional conditions for thinking, then tries another time to discern these inferred powers within itself. The effect of this self-inspection is a kind of psychic closure. We have supposed in the beginning that the given is an alien, unassimilated presentation, something that looms before us. We come to appropriate this given, realizing that we may have constructed it, as semantical frameworks, paradigms and hypothetico-deductive systems are constructed. Still, the incorporation into selfhood is plainer when the matters given are experience, moral principles, or the rules of logic. These are things less alien and opaque. They are present in us as sensible content, or as rules forming thought or the will. Their interest is our own. Knowing them, we know ourselves.

This reflection of self upon itself assures that the given will have these two constituents: (a) it will include sensory data, ideas, or linguistic structures; and (b) it will include mind, as it thinks about and incorporates these things. There will often be a certain tension between these two, as one or the other is universal while the other is particular. We expect after Descartes that it is selfhood which will be particular, even unique as "I am, I exist." Hume also enforces that singularity, because of identifying selfhood with the particular array of one mind's impressions and ideas. Singularity evaporates, however, when it is Platonic Forms, the rules of ordinary language or the universal moral law that is given. So, ordinary language analysts insist that we discover the boundaries of meaning, hence intelligibility, by reflecting upon ordinary usage. Every mature language user knows many of the rules for using words, and he applies them on demand when asked to imagine, "What would you say if . . .?" There is no private language and no private self, say these intuitionists. To know ourselves is to know the array of distinctions which are constitutive of our universe of discourse. We who share this world are interchangeable, and, in that respect, indistinguishable. This is close to the idea of the metaphysical subject in Wittgenstein's *Tractatus,* and to Plato's *nous*. But it leaves the issue unsettled. Can there be a singular mind given to itself when its other contents are universals? Plato and Wittgenstein infer from the universality of content to the universality of the knower. But that is by no means the only possible result. Selfhood may have two poles, one singular, the other universal, where singularity is founded in the acts of the individual as he or she thinks the universals.

1c. The "myth" of the given

I have been assuming that the constituents of this complex given are seen as they are, with no "transcendental" activities to be performed behind the scene as the condition for their being as we see them. Sensory data are, for example, presented to us, and seen as they are. Even the mind's own activities and their products—e.g., Carnap's reconstructions—are assumed to be directly inspectable, with nothing hidden. There is, however, the view common to the *Theatetus* and Kant, that nothing is given to a naively and variously determinable sensorium. Mind, it says, is never altogether passive, when every phenomenon inspected has already been conceptualized or schematized. Wilfrid Sellars' phrase, "the myth of the given,"[2] summarizes this point. The boldest reading of Sellars' phrase, one stronger than he intended, is the one of Peirce, for whom nothing is inspectable. There is, Peirce says, no internal object set before the mind; mind has no power for inspection.[3] I shall return to Peirce's views below.

Just now, we need consider the weaker interpretation which Sellars favors; namely, that the data which mind apprehends have already been classified or ordered by us in the moment before we turn upon and inspect them. Plato and Descartes say this when they argue that mind uses clarifying ideas to appraise its sensory data. There is also Kant's argument that sensory presentations have been subjected to the categories of the transcendental ego; it has created a sensory manifold from atomistic sensory data. These are writers who agree that the matters presented for inspection would not be inspectable if these things had not been altered or created before being inspected.

Intuitionists have several possible responses. They may deny the objection, saying that there is no evidence, nothing inspectable, that sensory data are taken up and transformed in some way before being set before the mind as a thinkable given. They may cede the point, all the while insisting that the process of conceptualization is itself inspectable: mind may be said to apprehend first the raw materials, then its conceptualizing of them, and finally the synthesized product, namely, a differentiated and ordered given.

The first response is question begging, because conceptualization may be uninspectable. The second one seems to be empirically false; we do not observe ourselves creating a presentable given from unschematized data. There is, however, a third and better intuitionist argument. Let us agree for the moment that sensory data are not thinkable or even perceivable until conceptualized. No one suggests that any other candidate for given must be differentiated and ordered by thought before being inspected. Certainly Forms, moral laws, and the rules of ordinary language are not held to the demand that they be subjected to a prior conceptualization. The reason is plain: these things already satisfy the requirements for intelligibility, being themselves the point of reference for the intelligibility of sensory data. Selfhood is a sometimes ambiguous, intermediate case. Is it self-intelligible without the benefit of a prior conceptualization? Augustine and Descartes thought so, though Kant and Hegel require that mind should have a self-conceptualization in order that it be self-inspecting. Therefore, Hume—and Descartes, as he thinks the *cogito*—may fall to Sellars' claim that an unconceptualized given is a myth. Plato, Descartes as he assays his percepts, and all the twentieth-century intuitionists of linguistic form are exempt from the charge. The matters they inspect are already suffused with thinkable form.

Sellars' objection to an unschematized given does not fault the intuitionist assumption that something is, finally, given and inspected. No matter that some things are schematized before being set before our inspecting minds, while other things given are already intelligible in themselves; intuiting mind will have, even on Sellars' telling, a choice of inspectable contents. There are two bases for this intuitionist claim. First is the empirical fact that there are inspectable data. Whether the matters perceived are Forms, impressions, or the *cogito,* we have only to open the mind's eye in order to perceive these things. A second reason for claiming them as given is dialectical; intuitionists have reduced knowledge to inspection. Nothing will be known if it is not given. Everything that might be known will have to be brought before our inspecting minds. If there are operations which mind performs as it brings otherwise deficient data past the threshold where they are inspectable, then these too must be perceived. Anything else concedes that mind as a theatre, everything arrayed before it, is incomplete. Intuitionists must avoid having to say that uninspectable mental activities are necessary for the constitution of inspectable phenomena. They cannot betray their own method by conceding that there is some other—i.e., inferential—method that might identify these mental activities. Everything that might be known will be known only as it is set before our inspecting minds. But then something must be given, or there will be nothing at all, meaning nothing to know and nothing that is.

This is a heavy responsibility, more than the given can bear. Anyone objecting to it must do so for reasons that cut deeper than the ones of Sellars. It is not enough to say, in the tradition of Plato, Descartes, and Kant, that nothing unschematized is given. We must go farther, attacking the notion that mind might have, and report about an inspectable content. Is mind like a theatre, with the given set before us? We shall have to reformulate every claim about an inspectable given if this metaphor is rejected. Peirce did that, because

of understanding that intuitionism commits us to the psycho-centric
ontology which is described in the next chapter. But how do we avert
this subjectivist outcome without rejecting what seems irrefutable,
that the matters thought or perceived are vividly discerned and accurately reported? Some reductionist behaviorists and materialists deny
that we have these experiences.[4] Peirce was not one of them. He
agreed that experience is real. It is only the metaphor of mind as a
theatre that is so problematic. How can we acknowledge both experience and our facility for discriminating among our thoughts and sensory data without having to suppose that experience is spread before
mind's discerning eye?

1d. Discourse and behavior as given

We need take care before answering, so that an assortment of
intuitionist views do not escape the question because of finding no
trace of this theatre metaphor within themselves. Suppose, for example, that the given is comprised of the words used for making coherent discourse, or by our actions as we make ourselves intelligible to
one another. It may seem that the theatre metaphor is irrelevant to
views of this sort, as certainly we can think about language and behavior without being intuitionists. Yet, the metaphor is appropriate to
anyone who interprets discourse or behavior in ways that satisfy intuitionist objectives. Those aims are served wherever it is supposed that
we create, by our speech or actions, an intelligible world. This may
not be a world we "see" in any visual sense; but neither do we see
Plato's Forms, Descartes' *cogito,* or the rules of ordinary language.
The metaphor of the theatre is already extended when we speak of
"seeing" any of them. We ask this same right as we say that discourse
or behavior is the source for whatever is differentiated and unified
within the world. We only revise the metaphor, speaking of a motion
picture house rather than a theatre. The significant difference is the
projector which creates a differentiated experience. Mind will have
that role, though we needn't suppose that mind is always making
itself conspicuous as it directs or regards the things that are done. It
may seem to withdraw, as happens when we play a game or perform
any ritualized behavior. For then, it is apparently the rules, not a
world-creating mind, which determine what we do. Wittgenstein argues for this view in the *Philosophical Investigations.*[5] His positive
claim is the rule-governed character of our linguistic behavior. His

negative claim is the irrelevance of directing mind. But this is a kind of delusion. For it is only mind that has made or learned the rules, only mind which regulates behavior so that it observes the rules, and especially mind which enjoys participation in the game, and the spectacle of seeing it played. Wittgenstein is obsessive about eliminating every vestige of this directing, observing mind. Remembering the *Tractatus,* and the essential role assigned there to an observing "metaphysical subject,"[6] I wonder if Wittgenstein was convinced that he had scoured all the traces of his own intuitionism.

Wittgenstein's progress from the passivity of the *Tractatus* to the activitism of the *Philosophical Investigations* is characteristic of intuitionism in our century, as it also moves from Husserl to Heidegger. Discourse and behavior encourage this change, as we make a thinkable world by the words we use and by acting in ways that are comprehensible to other people and ourselves. The play-worlds of drama or film now become our examples of world-making; or we use language, like a Homeric poet, to enlarge the span of our ordinary lives. Either way, in the stories we tell or the language-games we play, discourse is the common foundation for our world-making. Heidegger is somewhat cryptic, but this does seem to be his point,

> [D]iscourse expresses itself for the most part in language, and speaks proximally in the way of addressing itself to the "environment" by talking about things concernfully; because of this, making-present has, of course, a privileged constitutive function.[7]

The things constituted by our discourse are made-present to Dasien as it uses the language which creates them. We are not very far from Kant's transcendental ego, as it makes a thinkable experience in order to inspect it. Heidegger is more obscure than Kant only because of suppressing the difference between first- and second-order thinking. World-making discourse is second-order, leaving first-order awareness to regard the created world as though it were a diaphonous presence—i.e., present without mediation.

The idea of something given, whether observed or created by the mind which intends it, is emphatically the archetypal notion of intuitionist method. This is the eternal dyad, meaning thought or perception as it addresses the things before it. The intuitionist given is, therefore, a plausible target for anyone wanting to replace intuitionist method, its psychology and ontology.

1e. Peirce's rejection of the given

That was Peirce's aim when he argued that thought is a sign process, where every datum is a sign requiring an "interpretant" to construe it.[8] A sign's object may be a previous sign, or some extramental state of affairs, as a percept is the sign of its cause. The interpretant is not a mind—i.e., not an interpreter—but only one additional act in the sign process. It may become the sign and object for later moments in the progression where signs are generated and interpreted. These ideas are difficult to apply, even one hundred years after their formulation, when machines think without having to incorporate intuiting minds. Still, the direction of Peirce's thinking is apparent. We are to acknowledge all the content of sensible experience, telling how it enters into thought and action without conceding that these phenomena are presented for inspection like actors on a stage or film on a screen.

This is the motive for saying that Sellars' objection to the given is too weak. The more important target is the intuitionist model of mind as it affirms that content, of every sort, is known to a directing, inspecting thinker. It is this beam of mental light and the content exposed or created by it that is fundamental to intuitionists, but dubious as a claim about knowledge and mind.

Here, where our task is the one of identifying intuitionism's defining properties, not yet the one of replacing this method with a different one, we can summarize these intuitionist claims about the given. There are three points: (a) The given is composed of whatever things are presented for inspection, whether sensible or conceptual; (b) The given is a complex of phenomena first presented, then schematized—as Kant described experience—or it is an array of phenomena which do not require conceptualization because of being intelligible in themselves—e.g., the Forms; (c) The given is the source and measure for every difference and relation that may be ascribed to the world, so that there is no appeal beyond it as we test our claims about reality.

2. Contingency and necessity

The second feature common to intuitionist theories is not independent of the first one. It deserves a place of its own, because of being fundamental to most intuitionist inquiries. This is the difference between *contingencies* and *necessities.* Intuitionists typically suppose that the given embodies one or more structures whose necessary relations are a matrix for the expression of contingencies, as it is necessary that colored patches be extended, necessary that consciousness be the relation of an intending subject and its object, and necessary that correct uses of "am thinking" should presuppose the truth of "am thinking about something." Contingencies give determinate, manifest expression to these structural relations, as a particular color patch is red or yellow, round or square. One might try to minimize these necessities by saying that they are empty, as tautologies are, but that would be mistaken. These necessary relations are the grid within which the contingencies are effusions of diversity and chance. They shape and limit the relations among contingencies, as in the examples above. Any particular array of contingencies might endure for a while, never recurring. The necessary relations are different. They are regulative and essential, hence, universal, as color must always and everywhere be extended. Does every given have both determinate contingencies and determinable necessities? A final answer is impossible when philosophers are ever ingenious at finding something new to count as given, and where there is no evidence that the necessities we know are—in an *a priori,* Kantian way—the conditions for any experience. However, all the subject matters commonly taken as given do exhibit necessities and contingencies. The examples cited above suggest this, and everyone surveying the various, alternative givens will confirm it for himself; both are present in sensory data, ordinary language, Plato's Forms, space and time, and syntactic structures.

2a. The complementarity of contingency and necessity within the given

There is something deep about the reciprocity of these two within every given, as we discover when we try to imagine that all the given's features are only necessary or only contingent. So, a logical argument might be circular, every sentence following from its antecedents. But the individual sentences will be materially true or false, hence, contingent. If we eliminate contingency by saying that each of the sentences is a tautology, the contingency will force itself upon us in another place. That happens as we consider the argument as a whole, asking if it is true or false of something beyond itself. This mix of necessities and contingencies also prevails on the other side, as when a given that is replete with contingencies—e.g., sensations— also embodies some ineliminable necessities—e.g., that color and sound presuppose extention and duration. The pertinent generalization is an easy step from these examples: We never have a given where there is only contingency or only necessity.

There is, however, a difficulty in locating necessities. Intuitionalism requires that everything credited to the given be visible there. Necessities which are not inspectable within the given cannot be present within it. Kantians deny this, saying that experience has necessary conditions which are known to inference, but not inspection. These views about the efficacy of uninspectable, "transcendental" conditions for experience are, however, contrary to the intuitionist principle that anything real must be discernible within the given, not merely inferred as its conditions. Kant's position within the intuitionist tradition is equivocal, as Chapter Six will tell. Ignoring his views just now, we ask again: Are the necessities ascribed to the given inspectable there?

2b. Finding the necessities: two procedures

This is problematic, for reasons having to do with the character of necessity. Let us suppose that the necessities acting as constraints within the given are saved from the limbo where every necessity is dismissed as a tautology. Consider, for example, the necessity that a lock should open to a key of complementary shape if only their geometry is at issue. Neither lock and key, nor a diagram of their geometry exhibits this necessity as one of its parts or relations. How can it be true, therefore, that the necessity within relationships like this one is visible to inspecting minds? The intuitionist answer requires that we distinguish the constraint perceived from these two things: First, from the recognition that this is a necessity; second, from the operation which shows it to be one. How do intuitionists confirm that a relationship suspected of being necessary is necessary? The answer varies with the character of the relationship to which necessity is ascribed. Here are two procedures to which intuitionists resort.

2bi. THE FIRST PROCEDURE: IMAGINED VARIATION

One technique is applied to such cases as the complementarity of lock and key, the obligation for keeping promises, and the requirement that colored things be extended. We test the constraining force of these relations by varying one or both of their terms, each time holding constant the original assumptions. Does the lock open to keys of a different shape; is a promise made when I do not accept, in the moment of making it, some determination of my future conduct; could the spot of red be so small as to occupy no space. We are to discover, through the course of these variations, whatever necessary constraints there are within them. The test is conducted within the imagination, whether figurative or conceptual, so that nothing which is affirmed on the basis of the test should exceed the matters given within it. We are to observe the constraints within an imagined example as we might see the point where stretching a rubber band just a little more would break it.

2bii. THE STRUCTURE OF THE *COGITO* AS REVEALED BY IMAGINED VARIATION

One application of this procedure is fundamental to intuitionist method. That is Descartes' use of it for proving the necessity of his own existence. My existence is certain and necessary, he says, each time that I think or pronounce it.

Descartes would have us distinguish between the fact that I am and what I am. So, I am to look past the manner of my current thinking to perceive that I am. No matter then if I am doubting or dreaming. Either way, I see that I am. What is it that I see? Just the vivacity and act of my being, as dreaming and doubting are acts. I am certain that these self-perceptions are accurate, with two considerations to justify my assurance. One is the fact that nothing is hidden: I see the given as it is. The other consideration explains this first one: there is no gap between knower and known, no occasion for a failure of memory or the obscurities of distance, hence, no basis for error. My certainty is founded and justified by the immediacy of mind's relation to itself.

Notice, however, that my certainty in affirming these claims about myself is not to be confused with the necessity that I exist. Necessity is ascribed to my existence, not merely to the assurance with which I testify about it. What additional evidence is there for saying that my existence is necessary?

Descartes' answer is implicit in his characterization of mind's structure. So, I do see myself existing, as I observe that I doubt or dream. However, the necessity of my existence lies not in the fact that

I doubt or dream, but rather in the fact that I would not be able to see myself doing either thing if I did not already exist. There must be a second-order consciousness testifying to the existence of first-order consciousness. This account of mind's self-reflecting structure is implied in a passage from the *Meditations:*

> I am, I exist; it is certain. For how long however? Well, for as long as I think, for perhaps it could even happen that, were I to stop thinking, I would with that completely cease to be.[9]

The obvious interpretation for this remark is that I exist so long as I think, e.g., doubt or dream. Ceasing to think, I cease to exist. This is true if mind's existence is identical with this act of thinking. This is, however, too simple. Descartes' starting point is not the one of having to identify the conditions for existence, but rather the one of having to specify the conditions for our knowledge of things existing. It is not sufficient, therefore, that he locate the basis for his existence in the act of his doubting or dreaming. Every Thomist could be expected to know that existence is an act, and that every act exists. This first interpretation of the passage is, therefore, a commonplace of scholastic thought. More to the point, it does not solve Descartes' problem. That problem has two parts: first, to discover the evidence for saying that I am; second, to put my existence beyond the possibility of doubt by establishing that I must necessarily exist.

Descartes accomplishes both objectives within the more general program which requires that nothing shall be said to exist if there is not sufficient evidence for declaring that it exists. We have provided for part of that evidence by saying that there is no gap between knower and known as we examine ourselves, seeing that we are as we seem to be. This is one part of the solution, but not all of it. Descartes requires that the evidence of my existence should be registered and appraised. Who is there to appraise it? Only myself. The fact of my existence is my discovery, the discovery to which I testify. *Esse es percipi.* I exist when doubting or dreaming as I have seen that I do. Yet, this doubting or dreaming is not all of me, because the seeing of first-order thinking has presupposed my second-order thinking. If dreaming exists because of being seen, then so must we affirm the existence of that second-order thinking which has perceived it. The necessity of my existence is just here in the fact that first-order consciousness presupposes second-order consciousness as its necessary condition. Second-order consciousness is necessary as the condition for affirming and confirming what is true, namely that doubting or dreaming does exist.

There is, apparently, a difficulty in this claim about self-confirming acts of intuition. Must we also confirm the existence of the second-order act in a third-order perceiving, thereby implying an infinite regress? Descartes would have hoped to avoid this difficulty, perhaps by saying that self-reflection is comprehensive as mind glimpses itself while regarding the first-order act. This is not so vain a hope as it might first seem, for the one distinction vital to the structure of a self-confirming mind is the one distinguishing naive, unreflected awareness from the act which assays that first-order act and its object. Descartes is happy to assume that this second-order act unproblematically confirms itself. We can ignore this issue in favor of the one that is more cogent here: I have remarked my own existence as I dreamed or doubted, I must necessarily exist if I have perceived myself as existing.

This confirms that the proof of my necessary existence is an application of the technique which calls for imagined variation of the given. Its utility is apparent when varying the relation of first- and second-order awareness quickly reveals the necessary constraint between them. We alter their relation by eliminating the second-order act. Now the constraint is exposed, for we cannot eliminate the one without losing the other. I mean that the first-order act exists only as it is seen to exist by that second-order act whose existence we have just denied. Their relation embodies necessity, as the second-order act is presupposed by the first-order awareness. But equally, we can vary their relation in another way to reveal a second necessity; we eliminate the first-order act, thereby losing the second-order awareness when it is extinguished because of having no object on which to reflect. Each of these two orders of awareness is a necessary condition for the other one.

2biii. TWO KINDS OF NECESSITY EXPOSED BY IMAGINED VARIATION

Imagined variation reveals two kinds of necessity within the relationships it tests. In some cases, necessity endures if one of the related factors is held constant, whether or not the other one varies within the boundaries established by their necessary relation. So, the shade and size of a color patch are incidental to the fact that every color patch is extended. Nor does it matter that I am doubting or dreaming; my second-order awareness necessarily exists if either one of these first-order activities is seen to occur. Necessities of this first sort are founded in the relation of a condition to the class of those differences which it conditions. The condition is presupposed when any one of the differences is realized. Regretting the confusion this introduces, but hobbled by having to use the one word, 'condition' and its variants, I call these necessities *unconditioned.* This term signifies that these necessities are unaffected by diversity in the values of the conditioned variable, as the character of extension is not affected by the particular shades of extended color patches. The other necessities discovered by imagined variation are *conditional.* In them, the necessity of a relation does depend upon the specific values of all the factors related, as it is only specific shapes that are complementary. It is a lock of specific configuration which opens necessarily, in a space purged of all but geometrical factors, to the key of complementary shape. Change either one of the variables, and the necessity is lost.

2biv. THE SECOND PROCEDURE: DEDUCTION

Do these two kinds of necessity carry over when we take up the second of the two procedures for establishing necessity within the given? They do, in a different but telling way. This other procedure is one that Descartes describes in the *Rules.* We often characterize his method as *deduction,* though deduction is only a specific application of the principles recommended there. For Descartes' way of proving necessity is the one of *construction:* We are to construct complexes from simples, using specifiable rules for establishing that any particular complex has been constructed from its simples in accord with these rules. Geometrical figures and proofs may be constructed in this way, but so did Seurat and Signac construct their paintings in the way that Descartes prescribed to science. There are, however, no necessities created as the aggregated dabs of color create figures and scenes, because the pointilist construction rules are loose and permissive by deductivist standards. Knowledge demands more rigorous principles because, as Descartes would have said, its truths should be necessary and certain. We achieve that rigor when the construction is deductive, for then our justification for any next line in a proof satisfies one or the other of these three requirements: that next line is identical with a preceding line; it is a part of a prior line, having been detached from it in accord with one of the inference rules; or it is a complex of lines or parts of lines having been constructed in accord with the rules. These rules include only the principles of identity, contradiction, excluded middle (usually), and their derivatives. The construction produced by their application is, in effect, a single, extended thought or sentence whose necessary truth is confirmed when we regard it as a truth function; meaning that it is true for every consistent substitution of truth values for its propositional variables.

This characterization uses the modern language of propositional logic, though Descartes' own account stresses that complexes are constructed from the ideas of qualitative simples—e.g., extention or shape—not from propositional variables. The predicate calculus would be more accurate for expressing the constructions recommended in his *Rules*. The procedure for generating these complexes is, however, the same, whether we use the propositional or the predicate calculus, so that the idea of necessity appropriate to one is also appropriate to the other. That common necessity has these two senses. First, each next step in a construction is operationally necessary if it satisfies the construction rules—i.e., the rules of inference. Second, the construction as a whole is necessary after the completion of every step because of being a tautology—i.e., it is true for every consistent substitution of truth values for its variables.

2bv. The necessities exposed by deduction

This deductivist procedure is like imagined variation in the respect that it does provide for some, at least, of the necessities which might be credited to the given. In particular, it gives perspicuous— i.e., inspectable—expression to the conditional and unconditioned necessities described above. So, a proof exhibits conditional necessity in the relation of its last line to the antecedent ones, for this particular necessity lapses if either factor is varied. The changes we make may produce some different proof, as altering lock and key may create a different complementarity; but this consideration is incidental when it is a specific proof or some particular lock which concerns us. Suppose now that we regard this same proof in a different way, caring only that its conclusion be entailed by its antecedents and not at all about their particular content and form. The necessary relation between this last line and its antecedents is then unconditioned for the reason that it does not depend upon their particular character. How could this be true when we have already acknowledged that this final line is entailed by them, hence, conditioned by them? It is true in just this restricted sense; there are an infinity of sets of thoughts or sentences so arranged that they entail this last one. This, their common conclusion, is unconditioned in the respect established above where the notion of unconditioned necessities is introduced; this final line is stable throughout the range of variation in the antecedents from which it derives.

2bvi. IS ONE OF THE TWO PROCEDURES FUNDAMENTAL, THE OTHER DERIVATIVE?

How shall we rank these two procedures for establishing that there are necessities within the given? Is there some principled basis for choosing between them? Those who favor the deductivist test will likely say that the method of imagined variation is never more than suggestive, because it never does prove the alleged necessity. Deductivists will insist that every necessity ascribed to the given be reformulated and confirmed in their terms. This instinct is not shared by every intuitionist. Deduction, some would say, is only a rigidly constrained application of imagined variation, as we vary the terms of deduction within the constraints laid down by our rules of inference. It is only the length of some proofs which obliges us to express them as ordered sentences transcribed onto paper, where the variations that might have been considered in imagination are suppressed.

The prototypic deduction, and the best evidence that deduction is an instance of imagined variation, is the construction of a three-line syllogism. Suppose that we have a conclusion but not its premises. Imagining various candidates, we try to construct a syllogism having this conclusion. We formulate a succession of proposed assumptions as we construct a proof. The deduction created is a product of imagined variation. Descartes would have likely agreed that deduction is only a limiting case of imagined variation. For the problem to which his *Rules* are a solution is the one of reformulating some complex idea in order to identify its constituent simples and the relations for combining them. With this complex as our conclusion, we are to reformulate the premises from which it is deduced. Here, as in the case of the syllogism, we use imagined variation to identify the simples and relations of which the complex is made.

The elision of these two procedures may seem to be a way of disguising their most important difference; namely, that imagined variation reveals the necessities within a complex of thoughts, sentences or phenomena. It supplies an insight into the internal constraints within a complex, while deduction is a procedure for making complexes. This is a claim having two important assumptions, one that supports it and another which subverts it because of being mistaken.

The first assumption is that the elements of a deduction are its sentences, where the meaning and truth conditions for any one of them may be independent of the meanings and truth conditions for all the others. This fact does encourage the idea that the relations among sentences within a deduction are external, while the ones claimed for the phenomena susceptible to imagined variation are internal.

The other assumption is that the conclusions to deductive arguments follow in some tacitly decided way, that is "mechanically," from their axioms. But there is always room for invention—i.e., for variation. We make this point by supposing again that the deduction is complete, reflecting then upon the correctness of its several steps. Could any of them have been different? Could we derive this same conclusion from a different set of assumptions? We discover that there are degrees of tolerance within a proof, that we could prove the same result using different steps and even different assumptions.

A deductive proof is, therefore, like any other given. We can use imagined variation to expose the constraints within it. Deduction is, however, different in the way that is formulated in the first of these two assumptions: Deduction creates necessary relations among sentences that may otherwise be independent of one another, while imagined variation is more often devoted to discovering the intrinsic necessities within a complex whose parts are related in some more essential way.

We provide for this diversity of considerations by saying that imagined variation is applicable to different kinds of phenomena. Some of them do contain intrinsic necessary relations. Other times, the method is used for constructing deductive arguments where the necessities are a consequence of the inference rules, not because of intrinsic relations among the sentences ordered within the deduction.

2bvii. ONE MISAPPLICATION OF THE DEDUCTIVIST TEST

The confusion between relations internal to phenomena and the sentences organized within a deduction is the basis for one formulation well-known in our time. This is the claim that there are no necessities within nature, though we may think of nature as though it does have necessities within it because of entailment relations among the sentences of our well-confirmed, formalized theories. Suppose, for example, that we have a theory about combustion, and that we interpret the formalized expression of this theory as if it ascribed necessities to the things it represents—e.g., we say that smoke could not fail to occur if certain things are set afire. We need to be careful that we do not overinterpret the information acquired from our theory, for it seems to imply that certain phenomena are necessarily related to one another, though necessity is only a syntactic property of the formalization used for expressing the theory. We should not suppose that necessities created within a complex of sentences do represent necessities intrinsic to complex events. This is the view of Nagel, Braithwaite and Hempel; but their proposal is dubious. Consider its applications to geometry. Is it plausible that there are no necessary relations within the figures and relationships which it describes, but only in the proofs used for representing them? This is not credible when, for example, it is necessary that the internal angles of a triangle in a plane of no curvature are equal to 180°. This necessity may be represented by a deduction, though this relationship, including the necessity intrinsic to it, does not depend in any way upon the deduction. Many scientific laws, as against law statements, are founded in the geometry of space-time. Necessities which are intrinsic to space-time will be fundamental to nature. This intuitionist rendering of necessity, where a relation within nature is reduced to a property of inspectable syntactic systems, is therefore mistaken.

2bviii. DO THESE PROCEDURES CONFIRM THAT NECESSITY IS INSPECTABLE?

Have we established now that necessity, whatever its origins and role within the given, is inspectable? These two procedures—i.e., imagined variation and deduction—do make it inspectable in this limited way at least: We discern or apply some necessary constraints. This much is established when we use either procedure for marking the difference between conditional and unconditioned necessities. Can we also use these procedures for distinguishing some other, still more important necessities—i.e., for distinguishing existential necessities from necessities of form, and universal from parochial necessities?

2bix. SOME OTHER KINDS OF NECESSITY FOR WHICH TO PROVIDE WITHIN THE GIVEN

Existential necessity is founded in the material conditions for cause and effect relations, then analogized to circumstances where the existence of a thinker is a condition for the existence of the things known. Interacting causes are the simpler example. They are necessary conditions for the changes which occur in one or more of them, as a smashed fender presupposes the fender. This is an instance of existential dependency, the necessity that changes in some thing presuppose that thing. The second-order consciousness of Descartes' *cogito* is a more difficult example. The very existence of first-order thinking and its objects presupposes this higher-order act of awareness to confirm it. For things of which we are not certain may not exist. *Necessities of form* are no less familiar than these existential ones. They include the necessary relations within geometry, hence, the necessities intrinsic to a geometrized space-time. *Universal necessities* are the ones obtaining in every possible world, the universality of the laws of logic being an example. *Parochial necessities* include the truths of Euclidean geometry, as they apply only to the space they represent. Still more parochial is the fact that promising entails an obligation to future behavior, where the manners of any tribe may have no application beyond it. Can we distinguish between these two pairs of necessity, using either of the two intuitionist procedures?

The answer seems to be that we can make both distinctions, using either deduction or imagined variation. So, we can identify the constraining force of existential necessity either by trying to imagine a broken glass without imagining the glass or by using a deductive argument having the form of a *reductio* to prove that no change can occur if those things which produce and bear the change do not exist. Similarly, imagined variation enables us to expose the necessities of form by testing a relationship for its tolerances. How far, we ask, can we alter a figure while preserving some property or relation within it? Deduction enables us to identify these same constraints, though here, as before, we may be dubious about a procedure which reduces a necessity intrinsic to a geometrical structure to the entailment relations of the sentences representing it.

The distinction between parochial and universal necessities seems to be equally available to inspection, whether we use imagined variation or deduction. We easily imagine that there might be tribes with rules different from our own. It is necessary here that promises be kept; but there, circumstances are chaotic and unpredictable, so that promising carries no obligation for the future. Imagination is adequate to this and any number of variations. What we cannot imagine is a possible world in which the principles of identity and contradiction do not obtain. This inconceivability is the test of universality. We express these necessities deductively by formalizing the implications of promising, and by way of a *reductio* which shows that there could not be a thinkable world in which the laws of logic are suspended. There is only the minor difficulty that comes when deduction seems to imply that promising entails keeping ones promises in every possible world. Deduction, I mean to say, can be misconstrued as universalizing our parochial necessities beyond their natural boundaries. We counter that reading of it by remembering that axioms for the deduction are parochial. They do not apply within every culture, let alone every possible world.

2bx. WHERE THE TWO PROCEDURES FAIL

It should follow from these considerations that the distinction between contingency and necessity is no obstacle to intuitionist method; intuitionists do regularly distinguish these two aspects of the given. This is, however, a dubious claim when the two procedures exhibit necessity as a constraint on thought or practice while failing to reveal the core of its sense in a way that might be visible to inspecting mind. Consider, for example, the necessity that there be no contradictions. How is this exhibited by either of the two intuitionist procedures? We do have an operational definition for contradictions: they are false for all consistent substitutions of truth values for their variables. This is not yet the inspectable reason we want, for why is it necessary that contradictions be false? We may answer that this is so because of the rules for identifying contradictions and tautologies;

we have stipulated what shall count as the one or the other. This is, however, a solution that makes necessity uninspectable, because of founding it in something uninspectable—i.e., in the conventionality of our logical rules. Inspectability is not better secured if we say that contradictions are barred necessarily because of being precluded by the law of identity, where nothing can be both itself and not itself. For here too, the explanation for necessity refers us to something that is not inspectable, namely the law of identity. Deduction fails, therefore, as a procedure for exposing the origins and sense of necessity to inspecting mind. It is all the more incidental to formulating an adequate idea of contingency.

Imagined variation is also useless as a procedure for explicating whatever is fundamental to necessity. For consider again the necessity that there be no contradictions. This is an issue for which this procedure must have nothing to say when the necessity that contradictions not occur bars us from imagining them. Contradictory sentences and thoughts do occur, but they are expressions of a merely vicarious sort of contradiction, as it is the states of affairs they represent which could not coexist. So powerful is this constraint against thinking contradictions as to exempt us from having to worry about it. They never can exist, and we never can think them. It is only half-satisfactory, therefore, that imagined variation brings us very close to the essence of contingency by exhibiting it in the variability of the things imagined. We still lack what intuition cannot supply. We have no inspectable evidence of necessity as it is in itself, with its origins in the principle of identity.[10] All that we do have are the operationalist notions which derive from these two procedures. We can distinguish most of the differences that are important to necessity and contingency by using them. But conditional and unconditioned necessities, existential necessities and the necessities of form, parochial and universal necessities, are merely specific differences. They are diverse exhibitions of necessity without being its essential core. The specification of that sense and its origin exceeds anything that intuition can provide. Intuitionism can only use its two procedures to measure necessity's constraining effects.

2c. Possibility is uninspectable

This deficiency is characteristic of intuitionist limitations in treating the modalities. It is equally apparent when intuitionists characterize possibility. There too the procedure is operational, as deduction or imagined variation is used to show the possible implications of something alleged or perceived. It is possible, for example, that someone who is four feet tall will yet be six feet tall. We are able to construct a theory from which it follows that he would reach six feet under specified conditions. We can easily imagine him doing that. But this imagining, like the use of counterfactual conditionals in a formalized theory about the future, presupposes that there are or may be possibilities in real things—e.g., in the child who will grow. It does that without telling how these possibilities can be present in a thing. For what is the character of these powers? What is a dispositional property? Neither of the two intuitionist procedures can tell us, as both of them are useful for considering the consequences of having dispositions, but not the dispositions themselves.

There is, of course, the difference between material and eternal possibilities.[11] Material possibilities are events that may occur because there are things disposed for having these effects. Eternal possibilities are properties or their complexes existing as possibles. Intuitionism cannot think these possibilities because they are not actual. The one solution is to say that we think the possibles indirectly, by way of their instantiations. So, Husserl writes of eternal possibilities, but he has only *eidos* appearing before an inspecting mind as evidence for them. He does not, and cannot refer beyond these ideas to the independently existing possibles which they instantiate. Possibilities not instantiated as *eidos* are not considered by Husserl in any way, though he might have referred to them by using the words that signify them. That he invariably looks within the given for the objects signified by his words assures that Husserl will satisfy his confirmationalist, intuitionist scruples. But then it also guarantees that he will never consider possibilities as they exist, uninspectably, in themselves.

Necessity rather than possibility is the modality that has concerned us in the greater part of this section. But these two modalities are equally vital to intuitionists, the one as it supplies the matrix of constant form through which contingencies are suffused, the other as it qualifies any current given for future variation. Both modalities are constraints operating upon or within the given. Intuitionism wants to acknowledges both them, but it cannot locate the origins for either one.

3. The given is inspected

3a. *Four attitudes to the given*

Intuitionists of all persuasions agree that the given is "seen," "grasped," "discerned," "apprehended," "perceived," and "inspected." They also say that the given is "presented," and that mind is "acquainted" with it. Each of these words, together with "intuition" itself, signifies the naive attitude of a mind observing and enjoying the given. This is for some intuitionists the original and abiding attitude. Others suppose that this posture is not achieved until mind has created an inspectable given. For there are these four alternatives: (a) The given may be seen and enjoyed, (b) we may describe it, (c) we may prescribe its differentiations and order, or (d) we may construct it from content and form supplied by mind alone. Description is consistent with our saying that the given is seen but not altered. Prescription and construction require that mind should produce an inspectable given before attending to it.

Notice that these alternatives are indifferent to the richness of the given; the sparest, no less than the most complex, given is consistent with all four of them. So, Hume and Kant address the same given, with the difference that Hume discovers it while Kant is the constructivist who argues that we have supplied some of its least conditions. Equally, our given might be the "life-world," where Heidegger is sometimes the careful pre-Socratic observer, regarding it naively without the use of mediating, distorting theory. This leaves Sartre to argue that our participation in the world is conditional upon the use of organizing theories and plans. We have these examples to prove that nothing is implied about the content of the given when an intuitionist endorses one or the other of these four attitudes. Here is a summary description for each one, starting with the simplest.

3ai. THE GIVEN IS THOUGHT OR PERCEIVED

Naive acquaintance is often thought to be the appropriate attitude as we discover the character of things we have not made. The world commands our attention, leaving discrimination and quiet pleasure or distress as our most suitable attitudes. It might be our circumstances, other people, music, Forms, or geometry which are observed; but always the one imperative is our desire to perceive things as they are. A mind in this attitude is patient; it waits for things to reveal themselves. But mind can be more active without violating the given, as we observe it systematically, wanting to see more or all of it while making no difference to it. The use of imagined variation for locating necessities within the given is an example of this more active but still observant and respectful posture.

3aii. THE GIVEN IS DESCRIBED

Description marks an important change. It need not be intrusive, as some novelists are marvelous observers without seeming to impose themselves between us and the things of which they write. Their descriptions are a record and stimulus to later recall, in the way of a diary; or they are a way of telling others about the things perceived, allowing them an intimation of the given. The mechanics of recognition and description are, however, quickly turned against this naive and reportorial use of words. The given is safe from the affects of description only so long as we insist that recognition is prior to, hence, independent of, our descriptions. The assignment of words is then a kind of labeling, one that is incidental to understanding. Suppose, however, that spoken and written words are only the expressions of ideas, and that mind needs ideas in order to recognize the given. Description will then be the evidence that the given has satisfied the conditions imposed by inspecting mind.

Compare Hume to Plato and Descartes. He supposed that mind easily remarks the differences among its percepts, without having to resort to either the ideas which are their copies or the words associated by habit to impressions and ideas. Description is, therefore, no evidence whatever that the use of ideas is a condition for discerning the given. Plato and Descartes join the sensory data to ideas and words in this more intimate way: They say that percepts are insufficiently differentiated until clarified by our innate ideas. We may be unable to describe the given in any but the most elementary way, only remarking "Something here," until these ideas are applied to it. Only then can the data be described in more richly nuanced ways. Description is, in these circumstances, the evidence that mind has used its ideas to produce an inspectable given.

3aiii. FORM IS PRESCRIBED TO THE GIVEN

We expect that a mind equipped with innate ideas will do more than open itself, naively, to the given. It will likely search the given, proving the cogency of its ideas by finding the data which can be differentiated in ways that satisfy its anticipations. The further development of this notion, intermediate between naive acquaintance and construction, is *prescriptivism*. Prescriptivists do not search the given. Instead, they use ideas that are learned or innate to project differentiations and order onto it. They do this with the conviction that nothing within the given is intelligible if it does not accord with our ideas. Nothing unintelligible can be conceived, so that the given shrinks to the character prescribed by these ideas. This fact has two, somewhat opposed effects. On the one side, little or nothing is perceived unless differentiated by the ideas used for inspecting it. On the other side, some of what is differentiated and seen is discounted, as color, shape, and size are only significant as a medium for exhibiting the projected ideas of wax and the Sun.

It becomes important now that our ideas be related systematically to one another, lest the given be incoherent because of being unintegrated. Plato is a prescriptivist who cares too little about the integration of ideas. The perpetual risk of disintegration within the flux is one consequence. Intuitionists of language do better, especially as the words used for differentiating the given are organized as a theory. This may be the loose and implicit theory of ordinary language or the explicitly systematic theories of science. Everything thinkable will have a place within this fabric; nothing will be given if it cannot be differentiated and integrated as theory prescribes.

3aiv. THE GIVEN IS CONSTRUCTED

We begin to wonder if there is anything about the given for which mind is not responsible. Prescriptivism hears that challenge and replies defensively. The final responsibility for differentiating and integrating the given falls to mind, it says; but the given, especially the sensory given, is a content which mind does not create. This disclaimer is feeble when prescriptivism realizes its dominating impulse by transforming itself into constructivism. Plato and Descartes were prescriptivists. Kant takes a first step beyond them into constructivism when he argues that mind has supplied the necessary conditions for unifying the sensory manifold. Sensory data are received atomistically, he assumes, though experience is unified. Something must have happened to create this unity, and Kant locates that cause in the unifying transcendental ego. He never suggests, of course, that these data have their original source within the mind; they are presented to us adventitiously, having some unspecifiable relation to the noumenal, uninspectable, world.

There are, however, two ways to proceed if one is a determined constructivist. We can emphasize the sensory content differentiated and integrated by our concepts while saying that these data have their source within mind's own imagination; or we can say that sensory data have no constraining effect on the applications of our conceptual systems, where it is only these ideas and theories which account for all that is intelligible and inspectable within the given. Fichte and Hegel's Absolute are constructivists of the first sort. Carnap and Goodman are very close to being constructivists of the other kind. The object of naive enjoyment, is for all of them that sensible world which mind itself has made.

If we survey the progression from naive acquaintance through description and prescription to construction, two issues so far implied but ignored are conspicuous. One is the transformation occurring in the intuitionist notion of judgement. The other is intuitionism's insistent claim that intentionality is defined in the terms of mind's attitude toward the given.

3b. Judgement

Judgement is an equivocal word. More than sagacity, discretion, or good sense, it signifies the act with which mind approves or rejects, affirms or denies, some thought or sentence. This sense is prominent when intuitionists enjoy the given while remarking the differentiations and relations within it. Yes, I see: these are swallows careening above me. My judgement is wordless and mute, only a mental nod to signify my recognition of the matters given. Descriptions of the given are judgements of a more complicated sort. They are affirmed and denied, but only after we have been judicious in selecting the words to use, what to emphasize, what to ignore.

The difference between description and recognition confirms

that *judgement* is a word having several distinct meanings for intuitionists. There is, however, nothing in the difference between them to prepare us for this word as prescriptivists use it. Remember Descartes' *cogito* as it considers the wax during his thought experiment in the Second Meditation. We are to regard the several transformations of the wax while trying to determine its stable and defining properties. None of them is apparent through the sequence of changes which Descartes describes. Mind as it thinks the wax is not merely affirming or denying some claim about an independent state of affairs. Instead, this judgement—i.e., "Wax!"—construes these diverse perceivings as the expressions of an identity-fixing type. This is judgement as it unifies a diversity of appearances under the form prescribed by an idea. Kant applies this sense of judgement without extending it, when he writes that the unification of the sensory manifold in space and time is an act of judgement. Phenomena are made spatial and temporal in the way that those other appearances are seen to be the various expressions of wax.

Constructivist judgements differ from the prescriptivist sort in only this way: Prescriptivist judgement imposes form; constructivist judgement creates its objects. "Thinking doesn't make it so," we say to people more hopeful than realistic. Hegel's Absolute never risks that disappointment. The Absolute is archetypal wherever constructivist judgement presumes to make or unmake the things about which we judge. There are very few absolute idealists among us; but we see the expressions of constructivist judgement in other places. Are there physical objects, or merely phenomenal events? That depends, say Carnap, Goodman, and Quine, on the sort of language we adopt. Are its fundamental predicates physical-object words, or phenomenal-event words? Things occurring in the world created by our use of this language will be one or the other, depending only upon our choice of predicates.

Notice that constructivists will have made judgements of several kinds as they produce and then enjoy this result. First and second will have been the choice of elementary predicates for a conceptual system, and then the use of the system for creating, by thinking, the objects it prefigures. Third, we shall have come full-circle, returning to the satisfactions of simple acquaintance as we regard and enjoy both the structure and economies of our language, and that thinkable world created by its use. This is, of course, a familiar progression; it is just the movement of inspecting mind from acquaintance through description and prescription to construction, then back again to acquaintance and enjoyment.

3c. Intentionality

The other point to notice in this progression of mental attitudes is the hope that intentionality may be defined ostensively as mind regards itself while attending to the given. Intuitionists of every inflection suppose that our awareness is intentional, where thought is always a thinking of something present to or produced by it.[12] Brentano, Husserl, and Sartre are encyclopedic as they describe mind in its diverse moods and attitudes, attending to the given or searching for itself. A more careful specification of the structure which they discover, or merely presuppose, is left to Chapter Four.

3d. Some intuitionists who disclaim the method while using it

It is worth remarking before we leave this topic that many philosophers would deny out of hand that they espouse this intuitionist notion of inspecting mind. These are philosophers who often devote themselves to reformulating our claims about mental activity so as to avoid the Cartesian emphasis upon an inspecting and self-inspecting mind. Very often, they are philosophers of language who suppose that traditional views about conscious intending might be subverted by the careful analysis of intentional idioms—e.g., "I believe (hope, desire). . . ." Some of the analysts who propose these clarifications are "logical behaviorists." Intentions, they say, are exhibited in what we do, where careful analysis of mental words shows that nothing intrapsychic is implied by them. The rules of their use require only that we have evidence that someone has acted in appropriate ways. So, a pianist is not called "intelligent" for anything happening in a private, inaccessible place, but only because he plays in a certain way, where his playing is a public behavior that anyone might observe.

There is, however, a certain anomaly discovered when we compare these claims about the essentially public character of mental activity with the method used for making them. For how should we describe the method which would have us withdraw to a seminar room or study to recall a word's uses, searching for its nuances by way of imagined variation before surveying the "logical geography" of its several uses? This is not behavioral research of the kind familiar to social scientists as they observe human or animal behavior. Nor is this philosophic activity understood by the philosophers prescribing it as the one of tapping into a memory bank, then reading the information recalled, as a machine can report the contents of its memory without our having to describe what it does as Cartesian introspection. Philosophers committed to revising our intentional language rarely if ever explain what they are doing in this cognitivist way. Wittgenstein and Ryle scorned it. They hoped to cure us of Cartesian misconceptions by describing the public criteria for correctly using an array of mentalistic words. But they did that by using no other resource than the one of recalling the words, imagining the circumstances of their correct use—i.e., the relevant "word games"—then generalizing about a correct rule of use. They did all of that by generating, then describing, and sometimes prescribing to, an intellectual given, namely the words and circumstances remembered and imagined. It is, therefore, no defense against the charge of intuitionism if one deplores intuitionist locutions—e.g., "conscious of it," "thinking about it," while using the intuitionist method for identifying and reinterpreting these expressions. Wittgenstein's *Philosophical Investigations* and Ryle's *The Concept of Mind* are the most familiar examples of anti-intuitionist views having this incorrigibly intuitionist foundation.

4. Analysis and Synthesis

Intuitionism is impelled by two contrary but complementary interests as it regards the given: It is discriminating, hence, analytic, but also synthetic and unifying. We may regard either of these as derivative and the other as fundamental, as unity is only the aggregate of matters that have been discriminated then related, while things discriminated presuppose a network of unifying relations as they are coordinated to one another. There is, however, a danger to the claim that either side is fundamental and the other one derivative. Here, as in the dialectic of content and form, or mind and experience, we may lose the complementarity of these two sides as we try to establish that one is generated from the other. We also risk the error of refining our alleged ground to that degree of self-parody where there is no way to generate the other side from it. Hume's sensory atomism and

Kant's transcendental unity of apperception are two examples at this extreme; unity is as incidental to the one as differentiation is to the other. We need be careful, therefore, that we consider these two impulses in ways that avert this imbalance. Where analysis and synthesis are equally vital within a comprehensive intuitionism, I suggest that discussion is more coherent if we begin by identifying some possible grounds for the unity of the given. These are the subject matters which invite analysis.

4a. Eight bases for unity within the given

There are at least eight respects in which the given may be unified. (a It may be unified as a presentation, all of it cohering as a manifold of data which are visible at once or over a span of time, like the differentiated notes of a musical chord. (b It may cohere because of binding internal relations, as cause and effect are seen to cohere for reasons internal to the given. (c It may cohere because of its spatial and temporal relations, as the parts of a jig-saw puzzle are interlocked. (d It may cohere because of being presented within a unitary or unifying act of consciousness. (e It may be unified because we use a set of integrated conceptualizations, a theory or plan for example, for thinking it. (f It may be unified because we use the linguistic expression for a theory or plan to describe or explain the manifold to which they apply. (g The matters differentiated may cohere because we use a set of integrated values for ranking them. (h These many differences are the objects of my diverse attendings so that all of them may be related to one another within my self-awareness. They may all be integrated as qualifications of me.

There may be some other bases for intuitionist unity, as all the things to be unified might fall to the demands of my will and power or to the sympathy which gathers and binds them. These two examples are, however, only the more concrete expressions of the fourth and eighth of the rubrics above, namely, the matters unified because of a unifying perception or because of being experienced as my affections. There might be some other rubrics independent of these eight; but all the principal ones do seem to be included here. Let us consider, therefore, the subject matters which we should anticipate, and do find, when intuitionists turn analytic. The order of consideration follows the sequence of the eight topics just cited.

4b. Analysis of the eight unities

4bi. THE ANALYSIS OF PRESENTATIONS

(a) A presentation may be analyzed to identify its constituents, as phenomenalists divide the phenomenal fields from one another before looking for elementary distinctions within each of them. Hume's account of sensory data is analytic in this way, though Hume proclaims his atomism with the demand that we should accept his analysis as a substitute for the experience analyzed. This is odd because of being too much like the suggestion that we might be able to do without bodies so long as we have anatomy books. Hume's attitude is, however, characteristic among analysts. They claim to identify the essential content of the given so that analysis is only the more perspicuous rendering of its constituent elements. This implies that we should be able to reconstitute the given using only the elements and relations cited by the analysis.

4bii. THE ANALYSIS OF INTERNAL RELATIONS

(b) The analysis of cause and effect relations may only extend to the distinguishing of causes from their effects, as we say that effects are changes occurring in one or more of a set of interacting causes. But then we may go on to say with Hume that everything distinguishable is separable. This principle is a potent analytic instrument, for it implies that effects imagined without their causes may also exist when the causes do not. The continuity of cause and effect relations, and the existential necessities of effects existing only as transformations of their causes, are to be obliterated, as though we could imagine broken glass without the glass.

4biii. THE ANALYSIS OF SPACE AND TIME

(c) Space and time are analyzable into regions. But then we also have the choice of saying that these regions are overlapping or merely contiguous. If the regions are contiguous, then they too are separable—i.e., any one of them continuing to exist in the absence of its neighbors. If the regions are made to shrink, we approach asymptotically to points. If we ignore the fact that the continuous shrinking of regions never does reduce any of them to a point, we may postulate that the smallest regions are points. How shall we reconstitute a continuous space and time from extensionless points, when an infinity of these points, like any one of them, has neither extension nor duration? This result should make us suspicious of every analysis, because it confirms that the products of analysis may idealize and distort the matters analyzed, however they may enhance our understanding of them. We prove that the products of analysis are inadequate to the matters analyzed by showing that these things, space and time, for example, cannot be reconstituted from the entities—e.g., points—which are created and introduced by the analysis. This realization should force us back to the given, starting again so that the elements and relations identified within it are sufficient for its reconstitution. Shouldn't we suppose, for example, that regions of space and time are overlapping, never merely contiguous?

4biv. THE ANALYSIS OF AWARENESS

(d) A unitary or unifying act of awareness may be divisible into momentary slices or spasms of awareness, where each of them is sufficient to join or span whatever phenomena are perceived. But here again, we have the problem of discrete moments, with no resources for joining them to one another. Is my apprehension of a sentence a succession of perceivings, each one having a different word or phrase as its content? How then do we explain the fact that every sentence seems to have a unitary sense, a unitary if complex meaning? Analysis is confounded by this question, if we assume, as intuitionism does, that awareness spans the array of things perceived, bridging and linking them. Words are read or heard in sequence, so that this unitary perceiving must endure for some span of time if it is to comprehend all the words of the smallest linguistic units which carry both meaning and truth, namely sentences. We may suppose that a unifying act of awareness is long enough to span a sentence, but still the problem is unresolved. For what shall we say about the relation of successive apprehensions, each one comprehending a sentence? How are they linked so that the meanings of discrete sentences may be integrated as paragraphs, chapters, books, or whatever? Analysis founders when we do not know how to individuate or bind these successive acts. Could there be a single, all comprehending act, one that endures through a lifetime, or merely a waking day? We are reminded of Kant's transcendental unity of apperception as it stands clear of every division while unifying all diversity within itself. This transcendental unity is, however, objectionable in itself because of being an inferred condition for experience, not an inspectable given.

It is worth remarking that we may avert this problem altogether. Understanding words or any other sequence, musical notes for example, is not like stringing beads, where each act of awareness adds to or completes a sequence of understandings. There are alternative, cognitivist views. They propose that we listen or look for patterns of meaning, where successive words or notes satisfy or revise these thought-directing hypotheses. This is not an idea that intuitionists could favor, because it grounds our understanding of sense or order in hypotheses about their likely future course. These hypotheses are usually uninspectable. Intuitionism must deplore them.

4bv. THE ANALYSIS OF CONCEPTUALIZATIONS

(e) Integrated conceptualizations, meaning theories or plans, invite two kinds of analysis: We want to differentiate the notions comprising the theory, while telling how they relate to one another. As ideas, these are Plato's Forms, or the objects of Husserl's eidetic reduction. The intricacies of their classification and dissection may be as complicated as Descartes implies when he argues that every idea not simple in itself is a complex of simples. Thought's objects are, however, not so clear as our visual metaphors encourage us to believe. Differentiating them from one another, then discerning their relations to one another is too much like finding the right-colored shirt in a dark closet. This is the motivation when some of Husserl's interpreters substitute words for the inspectable *eidos* which he emphasized. For then our survey of ideas avoids all the obscurities of trying to isolate and identify them. We have instead the easy availability and resources of a public language. The phenomenological and eidetic reductions are superseded as we read the Oxford English Dictionary.

4bvi. THE ANALYSIS OF LANGUAGE

(f) We may be eager that our theories and plans should also be extracted from the limbo of uninspectable thought in order that they may be expressed in words or other signs. That would enable us to identify particular terms, testing them for equivocation and redundancy. We might hope to eliminate some terms, while clarifying others. We could demand that relations among terms be perspicuous, even reformulating the theory until it exhibits a form that we call proper and "canonical." We could also abstract from the theory in order to examine just the language used for expressing it. What are the meanings of, or rules for using its many words? What are its grammatical forms? We may, as analysts, become philosophical grammarians. We may then care less for the fact that language is used for expression and communication, more for its logic and vocabulary.

4bvii. The analysis of values

(g) Integrated values are an invitation to distinguish, then justify, the constituent individual values. What does each of them require of us? Is the value applicable to the circumstances where we propose applying it? Does it cohere with the other values applied there? What is our motivation for endorsing it? Analysis might start from these or similar questions on the way to either of two contrary effects. Analysis may be deflating, as we compensate for too easy a deference to values which may not withstand this series of questions. But equally, reflection upon the values espoused may have a result like that of reflecting upon the words of ordinary language. Rather than a universe of discourse with its rules exhibited in the logical geography of their imagined uses, we may discover a universe of values, perhaps with criteria for measuring each value's compatibility with other ones. If the first outcome makes us sceptical, this second one may elevate values to a transcendental status, leaving us to make the world intelligible by thinking about it in the terms used for appraising it.

4bviii. The analysis of subjectivity

(h) If phenomena are unified because of being my affections, then we shall have to be more accurate in telling what I am and how I am affected by them. What, for example, is the source of unity in me for those sensory data which are aural as against those which are visual or tactile? How are these sensory domains integrated within me? If we answer that I am conscious of all of them, then we need tell about the conditions for the unity of my awareness. Is my self-consciousness punctate like a staccato beat, or continuous but changeable like an ululation? Are these many phenomena still unified when I sleep, and if so, how? Can we solve those problems without having to resort to an uninspectable transcendental unity of apperception?

Analysis, through all of these eight domains, is a search for those elements and relations required for the unity considered. It is short-sighted, therefore, if we suppose that intuitionism turns analytic only as it regards language. Each one of these alleged unities is a challenge to analytic intuitionists, as Descartes and Husserl are no less carefully analytic than any linguistic analyst could hope to be. None of this should obscure the complementary emphasis upon unity and synthesis. Unity is presupposed every time that an analytic intuitionist goes about dividing one or another of these eight bases for unity. There is always an essential reciprocity between these two, the one as a network of differentiations, the other as its totality.

4c. The three irreducible unities of intuitionist method

Analysts are always at risk of losing this necessary unity, either because of taking it for granted while devoting themselves to its analysis or because analysis seems to justify the claim that unity is only derivative, as the aggregate or configuration of the matters which analysis has identified. But unity cannot always be derivative if intuitionism is sound, because intuitionism presupposes three irreducible unities: first is the unity of the given; second is the unity of first-order awareness, as the given is perceived; third is the unity of second-order consciousness, as mind comprehends both its first-order acts and their given. The derivability of these unities from the matters identified by analysis is, therefore, no kind of reduction; but only a test for the adequacy of an analysis: can we re-create the unity in imagination from the elements and relations identified by the analysis?

Analysis may establish that some unities do reduce to their elements and relations; but this only implies that these unities are co-terminous with those elements properly arranged. Having the elements rightly configured, we have the unity. We have started from a more or less clearly perceived unity, resorting to analysis so that we may better understand its constitution. Analysis has then established what we already expect, that these unities do have constituent elements and relations. It is all-important, therefore, that analysis should not obliterate the basis for unity by denying the relations on which it depends, as happens when Hume applies his principle that everything distinguishable is separable. Hume supposes that the unities themselves have disintegrated, though it is only his analysis which is deficient. It is all the more significant now that there are the three unities for which analysts have no satisfactory analyses, namely the given, first and second order awareness. Even successful analyses would not entail their dissolution, for these three are necessary conditions for the very conduct of intuitionist analysis: something is given, it is perceived, then analyzed.

4d. Where unity, not analysis, is our aim

The analytic style current among intuitionists often obscures their respect for unity. There are familiar expressions of this respect in science, behavior, politics, morals and culture. Consider, for example, the dispute between these two accounts of science: One, as it waits for science to construct a perfected and comprehensive hypothetico-deductive system; the other, as it regards science historically, describing the successive but unpredictable changes of conceptual paradigms. bare intuitiEach of these views is stated in ways that emphasize their opposition, though onisms of form. Both stress the unifying force of ideas. Each one makes the world intelligible by using ideas to project differentiations and order onto the sensory given. What is the difference between these attitudes? Surely, there are several differences; but only one is significant here: Hypothetic-deductive systems, like Plato's Forms, are to apply atemporally without regard for a thinker's situation; conceptual paradigms, after Hegel's Ideas, change with the circumstances of the thinkers who formulate and apply them. Both of them have this one effect: Each of them unifies the sensory given, thereby creating a unitary thinkable world.

Notice that this prescriptivist application of ideas has its counterpart in the use of values. We see their unifying effect wherever intuitionists suppose that the differentiation and order of an imagined course of behaviors is dictated by one or a set of priorities. So, family, work, status, or sport might be the deciding value as I select among the things to be done. Add value to ideas, and we have both the components required for introducing unity into political life. Ideas alone might seem bloodless, but an idea espoused as a value is an ideology. Its application is not different in kind from the use of conceptual paradigms for directing scientific inquiry, where the rigorous application of the idea is impelled by a value, namely justice or truth. This joining of values and ideas is generalized where intuitionists consider the unity of cultures. For here, values and ideas are joined as rules. They prescribe the behaviors which distinguish a culture—e.g., as within its science or politics. Participants in the culture may have learned these rules unselfconsciously, therefore in a way that confounds the intuitionist understanding of that learning process. However, we may also consider a culture's adult members as they reflect upon their behavior, wanting to identify the rules which direct them, making them uniform and predictable. Each of us may be able to formulate one or a few of the rules which prescribe our behaviors. Some few of us may be able to discern the coordination of our many rules, hence the unity of our culture.

All of this, from its expression in science, through personal behavior to politics and culture, is intuitionism in the shadow of Hegel. His views about the prescriptive force of ideas and values are so consequential as to make us forget the other determinants of intuitionist unity. There are three to remember. First is the unity of a given whose parts are integrated by internal or external relations. Nature, theories, poems, paintings, and songs embody relations of both kinds, and each of them may be claimed as given. Second is the act of attention as it gathers and holds the diversity of things given. Kant speaks to this notion of unity as he argues that mind's unification of space and time is a condition for the unity of experience. Third, and more potent still, is mind's self-perceived unity. How to be in the world without losing oneself in its diversity? This is, for Descartes, Hegel, Heidegger, and Sartre, mind's task as it accepts the responsibility for being the pivot about which all the world turns. No matter then if it is easier and safer to dissipate one's identity among the several things claiming our attention. Mind cannot escape the demands of its own unity. A more careful specification of the bases for it are deferred to Chapter Four.

4e. *Not every unity is founded within the mind*

A different, more sceptical question is relevant here: Is there a basis within our inspecting minds for all the unities which intuitionism describes or presupposes? Are they only the products of inspecting mind, or its self-inspected foundations? Is the Sun unitary because of an idea in Descartes' mind? Are space and time unified because of the transcendental ego? Is culture unified because of our power for reflecting upon and articulating the rules which direct our behaviours? All of this is dubious when we can account for the unity of all these things in terms which are independent of anything that intuiting mind can do. There is only this one qualification: Mind does create some unities, as it makes coherent stories, businesses, and buildings. None of them, however, need be explained as the products of intuiting mind as it spans a content or creates a unitary given. Some other account of mind's unity-making would seem to be required. This alternative will say that mind invents and uses plans for manipulating words and things. It will be plausible now, as before, that mind should be decisive in creating some unities. But we shall have no motive whatever for saying that mind is the source or condition for the unity of every other thing. Intuitionism wants to say that it is because of insisting that all the reality of everything inspected, its unity included, should stand before our inspecting minds. It does not, as nature, culture, and even mind itself, are unified in ways that exceed inspection. Hypothesis, not intuition, is the only basis for knowing whatever unities these things may have.

5. The temporality of things given

One consideration is critical for both the given and our inspection of it. Is the given presented over time or at once; is it inspected through a span of time, or in a moment having no temporal spread? This might seem to be an issue that will be decided by inspection; but that is not so, because this is a place where the conflict of intuitionist views expresses dialectical disputes which are otherwise suppressed. An intuitionist decides his position in regard to these dialectical questions, and then uses his method in support of his choice. These opposed views about temporality illustrate this practice. They remind us of the contending inclinations of Plato and Parmenides on the one side, and Heraclitus and Kant on the other. Platonists suppose that the objects of intuition are eternal and that the inspection adequate to them must also be atemporal. Kant responds that every given and every inspection of it occurs in time. We excuse him the spontaneity of the transcendental ego as a pecularity of his argument in the First Critique.

Notice the inclination to coordinate claims about the given and our perceivings of it. If the given is temporalized, then our inspection of it is also alleged to occur through time. If the given is atemporal, then intuitonism aspires to having an atemporal view of it. There are also mixed cases. Husserl agrees with Kant that time is the internal form of intuition; but then he also supposes that the apprehending of essences is the highest order of intellectual activity. These essences are immutable, hence, timeless. Does Husserl declare that inspection also occurs in a timeless moment? He wavers; a mind apprehending essences thereby contemplates a world of eternal possibilities; time is transcended, by these objects and by mind as it perceives them, though mind's temporality is its signature. There is more than a hint of the same irresolution in the claims of ordinary language analysts. They start in time, reflecting on a succession of locutions. Then, when analysis has done its work, they step back to survey the "logical geography" of the word considered. The spatial metaphor is significant, because of implying that differences in the rules for using the word are contemporaneous, time being irrelevant to them. So should understanding be confirmed in an instant as we survey the network of this word's uses, and thereby its constraining rules. Both examples remind us of Plato. He supposed that dialectic, like Husserlian and ordinary language analysis, is a temporal process, one that prepares us for, then projects us into, the timeless contemplation of Form. There may also be intuitionists who start by reflecting aimlessly on timeless things, only to pass into time and the successive appearances of this originally timeless given. Leibnez and Hegel are close to describing this circumstance as they consider the possibility that God might have a previous, atemporal view of the history which He now creates and surveys. But all of this reverses the order of our experience in a way that falsifies it. Most intuitionists say, with Plato, that we start in the middle of time. They add, as he denied, that we never exceed it. Every content and our perspective upon it is, they say, temporalized. Even mathematical relations are held to this claim, as Kant's views about the status of mathematical truths, that they are synthetic, have this claim about temporality as their principal justification.

Temporalists disagree, however, among themselves. What is time's character? Is it continuous, as in Bergson and James, so that both the given and our reading of it are continuous? Or is time episodic and sequential, as in Russell and Hume? This dispute, like the one distinguishing temporalists from atemporalists, is not resolved by self-inspection. For this is one of the occasions when philosophers profess intuitionist scruples only so that they confirm "empirically" those conclusions which are already espoused. These are issues more dialectical than empirical, matters for which the evidence supplied by experience is equivocal. This is the reason for saying that intuitionist claims about them are the expression of decisions which are made independently of inspection. Intuition is invoked to endorse these *a priori* determinations.

6. Certainty

Intuitionism affirms, through all its variations, that mind is the measure; that is, that its judgements about the given and itself are unimpeachable. This point is so familiar, and so characteristic of intuitionism, that it deserves separate attention. For all intuitionists agree that judgements about the given are irrefutable—i.e., *certain.* Error is possible, but only if we claim more clarity or detail than is present within the given; or if we are careless in searching through it; or if we use inappropriate words to signify the differences and relations within it. This does not mean that our every assertion is a necessary truth, as "$7 + 5 = 12$" is necessary. It does mean that judgements are irrefutably true of the given, whatever its character, if they acknowledge or affirm those properties or relations which are present within it.

6a. What things are certain

Descartes invoked an evil demon to subvert this assurance though no phenomenalist is discouraged by it. Plato is not deterred either. He claims certainty about sense data and the Forms. Ordinary language analysts concede that we may infer too much from the locution considered at any moment, as C.I. Lewis argued when making the same point about the difference between "terminating" and "non-terminating" judgements. All of them agree that we cannot be mistaken when remarking and reporting the matters before us. Inference, too, is exempt from error, as Descartes said in the *Rules,* when each of the steps is inspected and certified by inspecting mind. Accordingly, this point is indifferent to the fact that the matters inspected are sensory or conceptual. Mind is certain of all these things, if only its claims to certainty are restricted to the matters before it. There are cognitivist and behaviorist doubts about certainty, as we may deny that the given is presented to an infallibly discerning mind. But these are not intuitionist doubts. Intuitionism is unreserved in its commitment to the immediacy of the given and to our infallibility as we perceive it.

All of this supposes that acquaintance, sometimes culminating in description, is our natural stance as we think the given. This theme is generalized. Certainty is also claimed when mind's attitude is the one of prescription or construction. On the one side, mind is certain in regard to what it does, including its use of innate ideas or words, or the making and using of conceptual systems. On the other side, mind is certain of what has been made: it has direct access to the world that is rendered intelligible or created as mind uses these thoughts or words. Remembering Descartes, we add that nothing is, or could be, better known to mind than mind itself as it projects ideas and creates experience. Whatever its character, all of the given stands before us, and all of it is seen as it is.

6b. The conditions for certainty

Can we also explain and justify this intuitionist certainty by identifying its conditions? We do that in two steps: first, by considering the principle sources or error; second, by telling how to eliminate them. One source is the making of predictions or inferences about matters not currently observed. These are speculations, and nothing which might count as knowledge can come of them, because inference and prediction are notoriously fallible. Knowledge, with its implication that we are not and cannot be mistaken, is more demanding. It requires the certainty which they can never guarantee. The other source for error is the gap that exists between the knower and known, be it spatial, temporal, or conceptual. So, things some distance from me are obscure, things remembered are uncertain, and a conceptual system anomalous with my own is unintelligible. The conditions for certainty are plainer as we reflect upon these sources for error: we need only bar speculation while closing the gap between knower and known.

Intuitionism accomplishes both results in the simplest way. First, it abjures speculation in all those subject matters which are fundamental, as mathematics is fundamental and meteorology is not. Second, it closes the gap between knower and known by supposing that all knowledge is self-knowledge. The details of this second point are left to Chapter Four, but we can see the outlines of this claim already: Mind is constituted of its receptivity and activity, where the given is received within the mind or created there. Turning upon the given to alter or regard it, we perceive ourselves. Freud and Kant, arguing that important aspects of mind are unavailable for inspection, are inimical to this intuitionist objective. Husserl and Sartre try to save this account by locating all of mind's activity within the circle of inspectable events. It seems to me that they fail when the greater part of cognitive activity and motivation escapes inspection. Nevertheless, their argument for mind's comprehensive availability to itself exhibits these three principles, each one a defense of certainty.

6c. Three principles in defense of certainty

6ci. THE SUSPICION OF ARGUMENT

A first principle is the intuitionist suspicion of argument. Intuitionists have little patience for a tortuous sequence of inferences, since no result is fully credible unless there is available, within the given, some datum having all the properties signified in the argument's conclusion. There is no point to wasting subtlety on the argument when its conclusion is only hypothetical until we confirm it within the given.

The impelling clarity of certainty, and the aversion for argument and inference, are expressed most succinctly in Plato's *Seventh Epistle*. Dialectic is superceded as the method for achieving truth when mind is already in sight of the Forms. Seeing them plainly, we have no use for argument. Descartes approves of inference, but he carefully restricts it in ways that satisfy intuitionist scruples. Mind is directly acquainted, he supposes, with simple ideas and their complexes. Demonstration proceeds as mind constructs complexes from these simples, or as it analyzes complexes into simples. Conviction, he says, results when we follow an argument step by step, never having all the steps within a single encompassing view, but seeing that the conclusion does follow necessarily from its antecedents. Self-evidence is superior to conviction. It requires that we regard the entire skein of an argument in a single, sweeping glance, seeing the conclusion as it is generated from its premises.

Every inference that is complete in this formal way is acceptable to intuitionists. Their impatience turns upon formal arguments which are meant to apply, though they may not, to something beyond themselves. For we cannot be certain that a valid argument is true of the world. There is also an aversion for those diverse opinions offered and defended in the course of unresolved disputes, each one laying down an interpretation and claim in regard to the matter at issue. This is to say that Descartes would have us use inference as it applies to geometry, not as we use it in law. Inference as it advances to necessary truths may justify our certainty. Inference as it defends a plausible but indemonstrable hypothesis never can do that, because no inference is reliable, however valid formally, if we are left to wonder about its material truth or authority.

This impatience for argument is not to be confused with the discussions to which intuitionists resort as they compare and coordinate their separate discoveries. The discussions among ordinary language analysts and phenomenologists are cases in point, where disagreement is controlled by everyone's submission to the given and by the understanding that it is more often the ambiguities of linguistic expression and not differences among the several givens which make comparison difficult. Accordingly, discussion, even discord, never implies that any one of the participants is less than certain about his or her reports. Their exchange of information serves the rather different objective of establishing the commonalities and dimensions of the given.

6cii. BELIEF AND THE EVIDENCE FOR BELIEF

A second principle in defense of certainty is the conflation of belief with confirmation. We are to believe only those claims which are supported, in the moment of belief, by evidence which precludes their error. Belief must always satisfy the conditions for knowledge. Descartes is emblematic; "I am, I exist," he affirms, with belief and confirmation coming in the same moment. That the datum persists, so that confirmation may be repeated, is incidental, because Descartes' assertion would not have been falsified had he been annihilated after that first moment of self-experience. This example is odd only because of being a claim that something *is,* not a claim about *what* it is. Descartes understood this qualm, and he tried to satisfy us by minimizing the difference between *is* and *what,* encouraging us to believe that all truths about our nature are discovered in the moment when we confirm our existence. This is very dubious when our character as thinkers is more problematic than the discovery that we exist. Nevertheless, our discovery of the *cogito* is a standard for intuitionist method, as Descartes asserts and confirms essential truths about a phenomenon on the basis of a single comprehending glance.

There are, of course, other examples. They include Plato's view that *nous* apprehends the *is* and *what* of the Forms in an instant, and also the intimation that we may see all the logical geography of a word, all of axiomitized science or Husserlian *eidos,* in one comprehending stare. This may be all that Hegel's Absolute requires for seeing the world in its totality—while also observing itself. These examples satisfy this one necessary condition; namely, that the subject matter given is self-sufficient, hence, complete. Belief is confirmed in the moment of belief, becoming knowledge, where thought requires no reference beyond the given for understanding *that* or *what* the given is. The *cogito* is our paradigm, if all its structures and activities are apparent to self-reflection. But so are the Forms, the grammar of ordinary language, a unified field theory, and every sense datum alleged to be complete and self-sufficient. Nature is complete as it is to known to its maker, the Absolute. Any mind regarding these things will have its beliefs about them confirmed in the moment of thinking them.

6ciii. CONSERVING ESTABLISHED BELIEFS

A third principle defending our certainty of the given is apposite here, where the desire for certainty makes us conservative, discouraging hypotheses for which no perfect confirmation is possible. Why risk error when knowledge of a self-sufficient given is already available or secured? The effects of this attitude are conspicuous when intuitionists write of scientific inquiry.

Science is problematic. Its hypothesis are often mistaken. At the best of times, its claims are underdetermined by the evidence. Intuitionism deplores these expressions of speculative thinking. It is forthright when expressing its antipathy to fallible, overextended scientific theory. Yet, intuitionists are all the while intimidated by the intellectual and social power of science. They are eager to capture science for themselves, restraining its intellectual thrust into matters imperfectly known while assuming its authority. Intuitionists hope to do this by declaring that their discoveries set the boundaries for intelligibility and truth. Science is to be conducted within the circle of these truths. So, Husserlian phenomenology and ordinary language analysis fix the limits within which any "merely empirical" science must proceed. Are we psychologists studying purposive behavior? Then we shall have to formulate our studies within the framework established by these intuitionist truths, agreeing, for example, that awareness and attention ("I am aware of. . . ," "I am attending to . . .") establish the context for studies of human purpose. All knowledge is to be founded in our acquaintance with these structures. The contingent and changeable expressions of these truths are left to science, as anthropologists can study the different things which occupy the thinking of people in different cultures. These scientific claims are fallible, so that scientists can only trade in beliefs. That leaves intuitionists to provide the matrix of founding truths.

Still more pernicious is the use of this intuitionist assurance in defense of tribalism. Scientists properly ignore the intuitionist dictum that ordinary language is or ought to be the arbiter for formulating our claims about every subject matter. Science is able to formulate and justify its own ways of representing the world. Culture and morals are more vulnerable to intuitionist claims about certainty, because those who speak most expertly about them are not disinterested in the way of scientists theorizing about matters of fact. These experts are more likely to be engaged in the affairs about which they report, as connoisseurs and priests are engaged. When they turn upon a culture, finding its apotheosis within themselves, we may suffer the presence of that culture's zealots. We are not surprised that they couple the fiercest assurance about their own ways with suspicion and distaste for anyone different from themselves. Intuitionism is not usually so dangerous.

7. Summary

These are the six factors that were promised at the beginning of this chapter. These six, i.e., the given, its mix of necessities and contingencies, our attitudes regarding it, with temporality, certainty and unity, are the defining aspects of the method which I am calling *intu-*

itionism. These factors together justify our saying that this method is emphatically psycho-centric. More than the measure of all that is and is not, intuiting mind gathers the things known into itself, becoming their condition. This is the intuitionist *telos.* It is the outcome already prefigured in the intuitionist ontology and psychology.

Chapter Four

The Intuitionist Ontology and Psychology

I f every method has ontological and psychological assumptions, then intuitionism must have them too. Identifying these assumptions is the problem for this chapter.

1. The intuitionist ontology

1a. Some particular intuitionist ontologies

A method's ontology is a more or less explicit claim about the least features of those things to which the method applies. If we suppose that our method applies directly to the world, then we shall have to suppose that method's ontology is also the world's ontology, for then the domain of the method's application is just the world. Intuitionism makes this conflation. It identifies reality with the given, thereby implying that reality satisfies the requirements for being given: Reality is exhaustively inspectable, it says, with nothing hidden from the mind perceiving it. Many things are said to be inspectable, including the material world, percepts, thoughts, words, sentences, theories, and all the dimensions and modalities of practice and experience. Intuitionists may emphasize one or another of these things, but always with the understanding that each of them can be claimed as real only to the extent that it is inspectable. No thing can exceed inspectability for the reason that everything uninspectable is not.

This concern for the ontology of intuitionist method should not be confused with the ontologies of particular intuitionist theories. It is the affinities among these theories, not their idiosyncracies which concern us. Compare for example some ontologies of our century—e.g., those of William James, the logical atomists, ordinary language analysts, and those conceptualists who use hypothetico-deductive theories or conceptual paradigms to differentiate reality.

The elements of James' ontology are the sensuous contents of the stream of consciousness. These include sensory data and ideas, as well as those relations which determine that the experience is subjective or objective. The ontological constituents common to Russell's and Wittgenstein's logical atomism are the atomic sentences which appear as arguments in truth-functions, and the truth-functions. The ordinary language ontology is comprised of words as they differentiate our universe of discourse, and of the sentences in which the words are used. The ontology of conceptual systems, including theories in hypothetico-deductive form and conceptual paradigms, is like the one of ordinary language analysis, though the emphasis is reversed. Ordinary language analysis devotes itself to the things that could be said about possible states of affairs. It anticipates that truth claims will be made about actual states of affairs, but it leaves them to science and practice. Conceptual systems have the opposite bias. We use them for making claims about actual states of affairs when truth, not only possibility and meaning, is the important thing to us.

These several ontologies are conspicuously different from one another. James is an intuitionist of content. Russell's logical atoms are sentences describing elementary sensory phenomena, so that he is as responsive to content as to form. The others are intuitionists of form. The given they describe is the set of differentiations with which mind is to think the world. At one extreme, as in Russell, the empirical data are important to the given, hence, to reality and ontology. At the opposing extreme, empirical data are so shadowy as to be incidental, as when ordinary language analysts consider the uses of words while supposing that it is these words, and not any empirical contents, which determine what is differentiable within the world. No one considering these various points of view would doubt that each one has a distinctive ontology.

1b. The ontology common to all intuitionist theories

These differences must not be suppressed, but neither should they obscure the affinities which result when all of these thinkers use the intuitionist method. So, logical atomism, ordinary language analysis, and the concern for theories are similar in their emphasis upon the conceptual structures which mind uses for differentiating reality. This is not language as studied by newspaper readers or telephone company engineers. These philosophers use language in the manner of Plato and Descartes when they supposed that innate Forms or ideas are required for making a thinkable world. The affinities among intuitionists are deep and essential, not casual and random. They constrain the many intuitionisms of form, but also the various intuitionisms of content. Every intuitionist supposes that there is something, be it sensory data, thought, words, or sentences, which fills the mind as we think or perceive the world. No matter that philosophers differ in the words they use to signify this act, whether they call it perceiving, reading, acquaintance, conceiving, or apprehending. Their point is the same: Some content is presented, inspected, and seen—hence, known. Some givens will have been created by the mind itself; others will have been set before it. Either way, they are contents that are present to and confirmed by mind as it inspects the given.

1c. Three questions

My account of the intuitionist ontology is formulated at this more abstract level. Rather then ask about the explicit ontological claims of individual intuitionists, we identify those ontological views which are presupposed by everyone who uses the intuitionist method. There are three questions to answer as we specify the elementary and pervasive features of this method's domain. First, what are the least features common to every intuitionist given? Second, what is mind's relation to the given? Third, what is the status of both the things which are not and cannot be given, and the things that are inspectable but not currently inspected? Do they exist? If not, have we justified the tacit but persistent intuitionist claim that *esse es percipi?*

1ci. What features are common to any given?

Let us start with the first question, asking what qualifications the given need have in order that it be thought or perceived. There are two considerations: The given is discernible because it is *differenti-*

ated and *manifest*. The given is differentiated within itself. It is manifest because of its relation to the mind which thinks or perceives.

We start by identifying three factors which make the given differentiated. First is articulation, meaning definition and contrast. The simplest given has some distinguishing quality. A complex given has qualities contrasted so that one may be seen as the prominent figure for which the others are ground. Second is the requirement that differentiations be ordered in space or time so that all the parts of a complex are perspicuous while being minimally connected. This is the case where spatial, or metaphorically spatial relations, the "logical geography" of a word for example, enable us to survey all of a set of things or properties differentiated. It is familiar too where the notes of a melody are differentiated through time. These spatial and temporal relations have the effect of spreading the differentiations before us for easier inspection. Connection in space and time is not, however, the same as integration; space and time do not, by themselves, create a comprehensible totality. For this, we require a third consideration, namely a system or logic such that every item differentiated is related, however indirectly, to all of the others. The effect of this third factor is plain in the case of tunes, where melodies having the same temporal values—e.g., the durations and intervals of the notes—are different from one another because of the distinguishing harmonic relations within each tune. Music, theories, and figures are conspicuous for being integrated in this other way.

This third consideration is, nevertheless, more problematic than the other two. Every intuitionist requires that the given have differentiated qualities or parts ordered in space or time; but many intuitionists ignore the third requirement. Plato is emblematic. He supposes that Forms are integrated by way of the relations, sameness and difference; but he is not convinced that our understanding of individual Forms requires that we apprehend all Forms as a coordinated totality. Nor is it plain that all of them can be perceived in that totalizing way. For Plato says that all Forms are expressions of the Good without telling how we might perceive all of them as its differentiated expressions. His account of the Forms seems incomplete, either because of the weakness of the system generated by the relations of sameness and difference; or because there is a deeper tension between the value-neutral logic based upon these relations and the order of Forms originating in the Good. Then too, Plato may have cared more for the individual Forms as they relate to the flux and less for the integrated totality of Forms. Either way, his irresolution carries over to the many intuitionists, including ordinary language analysts, Husserl and Hume, who are content to pass over the given without the benefit of an all-coordinating logic.

These three conditions for a differentiated given are to have these two effects. They are to assure that the given will be visible so that there is something differentiated and ordered to be thought or perceived. Equally important, they are meant to assure that nothing is hidden. Still, they do not establish by themselves that the matters differentiated and ordered are manifest, meaning present and luminous to inspecting minds. The things in a dark closet are differentiated, spatially connected, and possibly integrated by color, shape, purpose or age; yet, we do not see them.

1cii. WHAT IS MIND'S RELATION TO THE GIVEN?

We have an explanation for the manifest quality of the given only as we take up the second of the three questions above, the one of mind's relation to the given. This is at first sight a question that is properly left to the following section, where we consider intuitionism's psychological assumptions. That would be its proper place if intuitionism were like the hypothetical method in allowing for a clear distinction between the ontology of the domain to which it applies and the psychological faculties required for applying it. But that distinction is obscured in the case of this method to the point of disappearing. Why it disappears and the idealistic implications of that fact are two of the points to be emphasized below. Just now, we suspend this otherwise reasonable jurisdictional claim in order to consider the possibility that the given is manifest not for any reason intrinsic to itself, but only because of occurring within the phosphorescent, illuminating ether of consciousness.

This is a notion that was already familiar when Plato wrote of the Forms as eternal objects within world soul. The *Republic* speaks against this point because of suggesting that the lesser Forms are illumined by the Good and not by their presence to mind. But this may be an incidental and unintended consequence of Plato's claim that the Good is like the Sun in being the condition for both the existence and the visibility of the things seen. The more abiding emphasis within Plato affirms the reciprocity of knower and known. Each is adequate to the other, where the Forms are visible because of being differentiated and ordered, but where they are manifest only because of being present to *nous.* These two are the eternal dyad. Their reciprocity is the paradigm for intuitionist thought. Descartes exploits our instinctive assurance about this coupling while personalizing it. Other intuitionists position themselves between these two, with universal consciousness at one extreme and personal consciousness at the other. A personal consciousness may attend to a given that is either particular and ephemeral—e.g., sense data—or universal. It is harder to imagine a universal consciousness having a less then universal content. In between are the various orders of social consciousness, with commensurately social contents, as the arguments against the possibility of a private language are claims for the necessity that the given be social. This is the notion that all the members of a linguistic community know the same rules and behave in ways that are universally recognizable and predictable within the community. The rules are manifest as we know what to say and when to say it, what shall count as a solecism, and what to acknowledge as a correct formulation of the rules themselves. We are, says this view, beings who live in a world made articulate and perspicuous by the ways we talk about or act within it. The essential complementarity of mind and world is essential now as before. The given, whether we call it theory, sensation, experience, or the world, is manifest because of being thought or perceived. We illuminate by our thinking an already differentiated manifold; or we create that manifold, making it luminous in the moment of creating it.

Let us suppose, by way of recapitulation, that we have answered the first two of the three questions above: The given is a differentiated manifold, but one that is dark until illumined by our thinking. This ontology is perilously close to being psycho-centric. It only falls short of that extreme when the manifold is credited with having reality of some kind prior to the time when mind attends to it. But is this a possible exception? Can it happen that there is a given whose existence is independent of the mind inspecting it? Realists take for granted that this is so, but then intuitionists want confirmation: how do you know that anything does exist independently of its being given? We might infer from the regularity of something's appearance before us that it does exist when we are not perceiving it, but that is only speculation. The inference might be mistaken. Intuitionism abhors speculation, preferring that the only reality to which it lays claim is the one set before it. *Esse es percipi,* it says. Nothing can exist if it is not given to thought or perception. This is the idealist core within the intuitionist ontology. Its plainest expression is the prescriptivism and constructivism of so many intuitionist thinkers. They agree that mind creates the given, thereby avoiding any hint that the existence and character of the inspectable world might somehow, sometime, evade inspection.

1ciii. WHAT IS THE STATUS OF THINGS WHICH CANNOT BE GIVEN, OR WHICH ARE INSPECTABLE, BUT NOT CURRENTLY INSPECTED?

The third of our questions is pertinent now. Why does intuitionism affirm that things inconceivable but not contradictory cannot exist; and what status does it claim for those things which are knowable—i.e., thinkable or perceivable—but not currently or already known? Some thoughts about the first question lead us to an answer for the second one.

1ciiia. Things inconceivable but not contradictory

Common sense has said that things unknown and unknowable, though not contradictory, might exist. That is conceivable. Intuitionists respond that this is shallow. Conceive it, they say, then tell what you are thinking about as you do that. Their point is that we cannot conceive of these allegedly existing but unknowable things without imagining them in some way. Imagining them in any way, however abstractly, requires that we think of them as having certain properties, as nothing exists in the absence of the property or properties which give it identity, hence, existence. What properties might these be, intuitionists ask? We are to respond by citing one or a few of the properties which might be ascribed to unknown existents. Notice however that each of the properties mentioned is conceivable, as they must be imagined in order that we may ascribe them to these unknown existents. These "inconceivable" things exist, apparently, only because of having conceivable properties. They exist as inspected, so that it never was correct to identify them as things that exist while being inconceivable.

This is a bad argument, because we can speculate that unimaginable but internally consistent things exist without having to imagine their properties. How do we designate them? In the way proposed above; they are the things which are unimaginable but internally consistent. We can ignore the weakness of the intuitionist argument in preference to the information it reveals about intuitionist strategy: every claim is to be justified by requiring that its subject matter be exposed before the mind's eye.

1ciiib. *Esse es percipi*

This design is plainer when *esse es percipi* is defended as a doctrinal claim and not merely as the unexpected outcome of a dialectical argument. Intuitionism, we remember, eliminates everything which mediates between knower and known, as when Plato affirms that *nous* is directly acquainted with the Forms. These Forms are constitutive of Being, so that a mind knowing them knows everything that is; all of Being is perceived. The effect on Plato's intuitionist successors is a reluctance to acknowledge that there might be existents which exceed our power for inspecting them. This persuasion is difficult to sustain when we move beyond Plato to Descartes, Locke, and Berkeley. They identify the given, all or in part, with sensation. But then two implications, both of them intolerable, have to be considered: that the existence and character of things having sensible effects upon us may exceed our perceiving them, and that some other existents may not be presentable by way of sensation or thought. These modern intuitionists want to respond in the way sanctioned by Plato and their method: Everything existing is seen, so that anything not perceived does not exist.

This last sentence is, I know, mistaken as a claim about history. Locke does not say that real essences or things having them do not exist; merely, that we cannot know them. Descartes never denies that material things exist, though they are not directly inspected; to the contrary, God guarantees their existence. Even Berkeley agrees that one uninspectable thing, namely God, exists. Nevertheless, my categorical expression of their views is correct to the spirit of their intention. Consider as evidence this remark from the Second Meditation:

> I am, I exist: it is certain. For how long however? Well, for as long as I think, for perhaps it could even happen that were I to stop all thinking, I would with that completely cease to be.

Descartes is saying that my existence is conditional upon my perceiving myself to exist. His formulation is paradigmatic for every intuitionist claim about existence. Having some property, because of doubting for example, is not sufficient for existence, because existence must also be manifest and confirmed. Nothing exists if it is not given and seen to be given.

We might think that Descartes is foolish to be worrying about his existence during those times when he is too busy to be reflecting upon himself or merely asleep. We have to remember, however, the motive for his concern. Claims to existence are dubious. The things might not exist, if there is not sufficient evidence to confirm their existence. Our knowledge of mind's existence, as much as the existence of every other thing, requires this evidence.

Descartes allows that existences other than himself might be known mediately, by way of ideas and judgements whose clarity and distinctness testify to the fact that God guarantees the existence of the things they signify. Other intuitionists are sceptical about God's intervention in securing our knowledge of things. They suppose that Descartes' criterion for his own existence is the standard for every existing thing: each of them exists only as we know that it exists because of having it directly before our inspecting minds. It is not surprising, therefore, when Hume reduces the existence of things to the force and vivacity of our impressions, or when Kant identifies existence with the vivacity and coherence of those "objects" which are visible to the mind which has made them, or when Quine argues that existence is the value of a bound variable. Each of these solutions satisfies the demand that existence be ascribed to only those things which are constituted by the manner of their appearance before our minds. But then it also follows that nothing exists unless it is directly inspectable in this way, where mind's ability for confirming that it knows something is a condition for the very existence of the thing known. This is the cost for securing mind in its knowledge, the cost of assuring that nothing claimed for existence will escape our inspection of it.

1ciiic. Things inspectable but not currently inspected

This solution is not sufficiently comprehensive. For what shall we say of those things which are inspectable though not currently inspected? Do they exist? Let us distinguish between things existing necessarily and contingently. It is odd to say of necessities—the laws of logic, for example—that their force, hence, their existence, depends upon our perceiving them. Why? Because they apply within all possible worlds. We might try to bring these necessary truths under the claim that *esse es percipi* by saying that they obtain only because of constraining our thinking. We "see" the effect of these laws when there are no violations of the principles of contradiction and excluded middle within the given (though two thoughts or sentences may contradict one another). We see the law of identity satisfied, where things exist just because of those properties which establish their identities. Still, this is no answer. The fact that we see the force of these laws does not establish that they would not obtain if their consequences were not perceived. To the contrary, it seems that inspecting mind is not more than witness to a force which is altogether independent of it. That fact is already implicit in this characterization of our seeing them, for we see just the consequences of these laws, not the laws themselves.

1ciiid. God saves the things uninspected

This is one apparently irreparable deficiency in the intuitionist claim that nothing exists if it is not perceived. Is that claim more tenable when applied to contingencies? There are two accounts for them, each one affirming that *esse es percipi*. First is Hume's argument that things exist only as perceived, where existence is only the vivacity of our impressions. Second is Berkeley's view that things uninspected but inspectable persist in being because of being perceived by God. Which is better? Shall we say that inspectable but uninspected things pass out of existence, only to be revived as they are given to our finite inspecting minds; or that everything real is given forever to that eternally self-inspecting mind known to us as God. There is perhaps one reason for preferring Berkeley to Hume: We can defer to God when saying that necessities, like contingencies, fall to the requirement that *esse es percipi,* for these are, we speculate, the rules for God's own thinking, rules which God may have set for Himself. They obtain only as God thinks Himself, in all possible worlds.

1ciiie. The pairing of intuition and ideality

We discover that intuition and ideality are paired, the second as a necessary consequence of the first. All the antecedent developments of intuitionist method have pointed this way. Here, in Berkeley's dictum, these two are compressed into a phrase having maximum force and brevity. Idealism is well-known but imperfectly understood until we regard it as the consequence of intuitionist method. For intuitionism, with its ferocious impulse to confront things as they are or are made, does not allow a different result. Nothing can exist if it is not inspected, because it is only the things inspected which satisfy the demand that we have evidence to confirm our claims about them. The conditions for knowledge are to be the conditions for existence. The domain of existents shrinks and expands in synchrony with changes in the stock of those contingent truths which satisfy the conditions for knowledge. But always, the test of existence and its condition is the requirement that mind have confirming evidence for its claims about the things that exist. Knowing nothing of matters uninspected, we cannot make true claims about them. Where the only existents are the one prefigured by truths, it follows that anything not signified by a truth is not. Are there, might there be, truths unknown, hence, existents unknown? That could not be so, because truth has no ambit but the one of inspecting mind. It is only here in the light where mind registers or creates the given that truth is made and sustained.

1ciiif. Some idealists in spite of themselves

This result is unstable. We may be prepared, as intuitionists of form, for the claim that all the differentiations and relations of things credited to the world originate in our conceptual or linguistic systems. We may believe, as intuitionists of content, that reality merely subsists, just half-complete, until it is inspected. But only the boldest thinkers will dare to say that mind is responsible for the very existence of things. Berkeley, Hegel, and Hume were ready to say it; but what of the many intuitionists who are less attentive to the systematic character of their method? Many of them are oblivious to having to choose between the nonexistence of things uninspected, and God's eternal vigilance. Advised of the choice, they will avoid making it. Common sense and its commitment to things uninspected but inspectable will save them, they hope, from having to make it. Even the carefully systematic thinkers avoid this choice. Heidegger, for example, refuses to consider the reality of things whose existence is independent of our perceiving: there is only "man-in-the-world," where the hyphens speak for the mutual dependence of each part as it is conditioned by the other. What happens to the life-world during concussion or sleep? Heidegger never tells us. Nor does Carnap tell us how the world carries on during the times when no one is using a conceptual system for thinking it. Carnap has promised to "construct" the world, though without telling what happens to it when he has turned away to do other things.

Requiring that intuitionists should provide for the world's existence at times when they are not attending to it will seem ridiculous only as we suppose that philosophers should not be taken seriously in what they declare of their intentions. Are Carnap and Quine excused for the hyperbole of saying that the existence of things depends on the fact that we use a conceptual system for thinking them, so that we have conceptual relativism and internal realism?[1] No, they are not. There is no exemption from having to accept the implication of this view or from having to justify it.

1d. The three parts of intuitionist ontology

Intuitionists who believe that the world's existence does depend upon our thinking or perceiving it should be willing to say that common sense is mistaken; the world does not exist when it is not thought or perceived. Whitehead does say that. The world he proposes, has these three constituents: actual occasions—which become, then perish as moments of perceiving—eternal objects, and the God who sums and surveys the tide of actual occasions while thinking the eternal objects. This theory is an example for those ontologies which best represent the conceptual demands of intuitionist method. It accepts the implication that a world unperceived or unthought would not exist, and then it provides for the world's existence by saying that there is a God to think it. This provides, however dubious the explanation, for the enduring existence of whatever things are not currently thought or perceived by human minds.

Hume has no explanation whatever for the existence of inspectable things which are currently uninspected, so that theories of this Berkeleyian sort ought to be, I suppose, our reference as we schematize the intuitionist ontology. There are three parts. First is the differentiated given, a manifold having spatial or temporal spread, and perhaps some system of logic to unify it. Second is the mind to which this manifold is present. This is a manifest reality, one that is altogether articulated and perspicuous, a reality where nothing is hidden. Every method has presuppositions about the character of the mind using it, but intuitionism is peculiar because of supposing that mind is also a fixture within the method's ontology. That is so in these two respects: first, as intuitionists account for the manifest character of the given, saying that this content is luminous and evident just because of being given to, or created by, a conscious mind; second, as intuitionists affirm that all reality devolves upon our minds, where *esse es percipi*. Third, and more dubious, is that perpetually active and all-comprehending mind, that God which sustains all of reality when finite minds are distracted or tending to parts of it only. The first two considerations are primary, as finite minds and the given are joined in the reciprocity of activity and passivity, subject and object. The third factor compares badly to them, because it is a creature of inference, hence, alien to a method which acknowledges no reality which is not inspectable. This is a damning flaw within intuitionism, one revealing that the method's scruples are inconsistent with its ontology. But then, God, *nous,* or the Absolute is essential, however uninspectable, if intuitionism is to be saved from having to tell why it is that some parts of reality are not annihilated when they are not thought or perceived by our finite minds. This is the three-part ontology to which intuitionism recalls us. These are its seismic depths, even within the well-scrubbed and bowdlerized versions current among us.

1e. Using intuitionist method while ignoring its ontology

Philosophers who are unhappy with the intuitionist ontology may want to be more cautious about using the intuitionist method. We may be inclined to use it because of confusing the reasonable insistance that our claims about the world be verifiable with the peculiarly intuitionist expression of this demand. Intuitionism requires that everything acknowledged as real should be inspectable as given, whether presented to mind or created by it. It promises that nothing real will be hidden, and that all our claims about reality will be confirmed immediately as we inspect the matters given. But then intuitionists are obliged to endorse the intuitionist ontology while explaining away the many things for which it does not provide. These include the modalities—i.e., both possibility and necessity— things as distinct from their facades, wholes such as space-time,

inferred entities—including black holes and habits—some relations—
e.g., second cousin twice removed—numbers as distinct from their
signs, and a moral or creator God. It might also be true that mind is
not altogether visible to itself, so that many of the mental activities
which are essential to intuitionism's psycho-centric ontology might
be uninspectable.

Intuitionism is forever precarious so long as it identifies reality
with the mind-inspected given. Yet philosophers ignore the peril, because this constricted notion of reality helps to confirm one deeply
rooted view of our philosophic task. Philosophy, we sometimes suppose, is to be an exalted practice, one that surpasses opinion and
private interest on the way to seeing the world as it is. This is to be
more than judgement and sagacity, being instead the mind's clear
sight of those differentiations, relations, structures, and laws which
are constitutive of our world. There is to be nothing of controversy in
this, for we are to surpass dispute, seeing things as they are. Reality
has been identified with the given so that philosophy, as vision, will
be competent to know it.

1f. An alternative method, its ontology and psychology

A different ontology, one adequate to things not inspected or
even inspectable, would require that we relax the demand for verification. We need not see things directly in order to secure their existence or the truth of our claims about them. We may think about the
world, using hypotheses to represent the things alleged to exist there.
Our revised ontology will recognize two orders of being. Proximately, there are the signs which are terms within our hypotheses and
the rules for composing well-formed thoughts or sentences from
them. More remotely, there are possible states of affairs, and the subset of possibilities instantiated, meaning actual states of affairs. Everything that intuitionism might wish to describe, and all the things it
cannot describe are accommodated in this way, though always with
the proviso that we are separated from the things perceived, thought,
and described by percepts, thoughts and words, hence by a tissue of
natural and conventional signs. These more remote realities are never
inspectable. Our hypotheses about them are fallible, so that knowledge claims are probabilistic only. Intuitionists prefer the immediate
access which their method promises, because of fearing that we shall
lose touch with the world. But too much of reality is inaccessible to
them.

There is one deep affinity between intuitionism and this hypothetical method. Both acknowledge mind as the agent for applying the method: intuiting mind as it inspects the given, speculating mind as it uses signs to represent possible states of affairs. Intuitionist minds are incorporated into their method's ontology as the ground for all the world's intelligibility and existence. Speculating minds are, by comparison, the activities and powers of any creature or machine that is able to formulate and test its hypotheses. Snails do that, though we humans do it better. There is no impulse now for conflating method's ontology with its psychology, because hypothesis does not require that the ontology of its domain should be reduced to some derivative status within the mind which uses it. Hypothesis only requires that we should describe both the domain to which it applies—i.e., proximately to signs, more remotely to their objects—and the faculties and activities which are required for making and using signs.

There is every likelihood that this agent will prove to have the same ontological status as some of the things that are known by way of its hypotheses. Like them, it may be an exhaustively physical system. This is a point to be confirmed as we identify the hypothesizer's powers and activities. Could they have any realization other than a physical one when our knowledge of the physical world requires that we be causally related to it? One more general consequence is already in sight: this hypothetical method will likely place us within the world known. Intuitionism is exactly opposed: it locates all the bases for intelligibility and existence within us.

Every method presupposes an ontology and a psychology; but intuitionism is unique for making its psychology so fundamental to its ontology. We turn now to the intuitionist psychology, having confirmed already that mind is basic to this method's psycho-centric ontology.

2. The intuitionist psychology

2a. What does mind reveal of itself?

What do intuitionists discover about mind as they turn upon themselves? What are the psychological presuppositions for thinking or perceiving any given, our self-reflection included? This second question should be answered in the terms of the first one, because intuitionism can say nothing of mind until self-inspection has confirmed it. We are obliged, therefore, to press this first question another time: what is discovered about mind as we introspect? The intuitionist answer is that mind is an activity having two mutually dependant expressions. First is the act of registering or creating the intellectual or sensory manifold. Second is consciousness as it perceives both this given and itself. The considerations favoring this notion are considered in more detail below. Let us start, however, in this more querulous way, asking sceptically if there is any one list of characteristics which every inspecting mind cannot help but discern. This is the appropriate first question for a method which promises a consensus about the things inspectable. But then the answer is all the more confounding when intuitionists never do agree about mind's self-discoverable nature: there is no set of properties which every self-inspecting mind confirms in itself.

2b. Discord among self-inspecting intuitionists

James and Bergson say that experience is continuous, every datum connected to others by relations that are spatial, temporal, and dynamic. Hume was equally convinced that the data are discrete. Allowing only for conjunction and succession, he was convinced that there are no other kinds of relations to bind the data; and no thinking subject. James couldn't find one either. Kant sometimes agreed, saying that there is only the continuous experience of "me" accompanying my experience. Yet other writers, from Augustine and Descartes to Sartre, say that mind discovers itself while thinking and perceiving other things. These examples come, mostly, from intuitionists of content. Are their differences resolved by the intuitionists of form, as ordinary language analysis might show that some of these descriptions are badly formed. That is not so, as we prove by speaking coherently on either side of these several disputes. Descartes could exploit the personal and reflexive pronouns of ordinary Latin and French; while Hume and James described experiences that were, presumably, similar without relying upon their English equivalents.

The lesson of these examples is that every "discovery" credited to introspection has its contrary in the findings of other intuitionists. We might explain this variation by saying that experience differs amongs introspectors, but that inspection never errs. Intuitionists would not agree. They suppose that our self-description of essential mental structures should have universal application, where every inspecting mind finds these same structures within itself. This assumption violates the principle that every claim about mind should be founded and confirmed within the given, as a claim about the universality of mind's structures cannot be; but let this pass. For if minds are everywhere alike, we have the more urgent problem of having to explain and excuse the discord among self-inspecting intuitionists. What does explain it?

2c. *Disagreements founded in differing a priori* assumptions

The disputes would be settled if Hume or Husserl were to look more carefully or intently, one or the other admitting his error. But this does not happen. The opinions do not change; and not because of different techniques for self-inspection or because of idiosyncracies within the given of each reporter. These contrary opinions turn instead upon *a priori* assumptions which neither side will acknowledge. These assumptions are an embarrassment when intuitionists should not have tacit assumptions of any kind. Why? Because these assumptions about mind are hidden or disguised, though intuitionism requires that no claim be unavailable for certification by direct acquaintance. Every intuitionist is compelled to turn himself inside out, converting *a priori* assumptions into inspectable, empirical facts. He must look within the given for data which confirm those beliefs which be brings to it. This nearly guarantees that intuitionists will disagree about the given, because of having diverse and opposing views about the things to be discovered there.

There may be a residue of phenomena which every thinker would report after purging himself of a priorisms, though the perpetual disagreements among intuitionists suggest that this core is not easily identified. We might explain this by saying that the *a priori* is hard to locate and harder to discount. Still, finding and rejecting it would leave us some distance from a solution for the disagreements among intuitionists. That is so, because one issue is paramount: *Mind as inspected tells us very little about itself.* We cannot tell, from inspection alone, what mind is, a brain or spirit; or how mind produces whatever is manifest to us. We cannot distinguish very clearly among its several activities, especially the conceptual ones. These ambiguities and uncertainties invite a priorist characterization, as though mind were starved in self-perception of the order which these conceptualizations provide. There will be no adequate theory about mind deriving only from our self-experience, because a comprehensive theory, one telling what mind is and does, will postulate structures and activities which mind cannot inspect within itself. These ideas about mind are imported as unexamined a priorisms, or they are hypotheses subject to testing and revision. Either way, our claims about mind are theoretical and speculative. They cannot be disguised as the reports of a naive, self-inspecting agent.

The way ahead is obscured; we risk losing direction as we try to identify the psychological presuppositions of intuitionist method. There are two things confusing us. First is the consideration just cited: inspection by itself, hence, intuitionist method, is incapable of discovering and confirming mind's character. The evidence for saying this is: the discord among intuitionists as they describe mind; the admission by that most zealous of self-inspectors, Husserl, that some of mind must be "transcendental," therefore uninspectable; and the discoveries of cognitive psychologists as they suggest that many cognitive functions, including conceptual organization, learning and memory, are not inspectable. Second is the view shared by Hume, James, Carnap, and other intuitionists that intuitionism does not have psychological assumptions; there is, they say, no conscious or self-conscious thinker required for discerning or creating a thinkable given. Intuitionists on the other side—e.g., Descartes and Husserl— do believe that there is introspective evidence confirming their view; but it is pointless using the evidence of our self-experience to arbitrate this difference of opinion if, first, the evidence can be interpreted either way, and if, second, one's views about the existence of a thinking subject have theoretical origins which are independent of our self-experience.

2d. Using inference to identify the intuitionist psychology

Accordingly, we shift directions. Rather than list and evaluate intuitionist "discoveries" about mind, we consider that notion of mind which is presupposed by intuitionist practice. My procedure is Kantian, because I believe that the psychological presuppositions for intuitionist practice may be correctly inferred, without the need for confirming, introspectionist evidence. It would be good for intuitionist scruples if self-inspecting mind could discover the structure and activities presupposed by the method; but there seems to be no comprehensive account of mind for which self-awareness is, or could be, the final arbiter. Only inference supplies a relatively complete specification of the psychological conditions for intuitionist thought.

Is there one set of presuppositions shared by every intuitionist, or could it happen that different forms of intuitionism make different assumptions about the character of inspecting mind? The presuppositions I shall list are the ones appropriate to intuitionism as it is described in the preceding chapters. Anyone making those claims for intuition is committed because of using the method, to that view of mind which is described below.

It might be alleged that any one of various, alternative sets of conditions would be sufficient for explaining any particular activity claimed for intuiting mind. In the least favorable case, there would be several or many competing sets of conditions, each one sufficient for explaining that mind inspects, as it registers or creates, something given. Intuitionists would respond to this challenge by testing each one of the several alternatives against their self-experience, thereby eliminating every alternative but the correct one. I don't believe that the evidence of self-inspection is adequate for choosing among the different possible claims about mind's structure and activities. The variety of alternative lists of intuitionist presuppositions would, therefore, confound me. Happily, this forced choice is only speculative. There is, so far, no list of psychological conditions alternative to the one adduced below.

2e. Views that are explicit, implicit or presupposed

One set of distinctions helps to avert confusion as we identify these conditions. Particular intuitionists may have as many as three distinct view about mind. First are those claims which are formulated as self-descriptions. These are the *explicit* views. Second are the *a priori* assumptions about mind's character. These help to determine, they may even decide, what the explicit claims shall be. They are usually *implicit*. Third are the *presuppositions for intuitionist practice*. Explicit and implicit claims are likely to be similar because reinforcing; but they might differ radically from those views about mind which are presupposed as we use the intuitionist method. It might happen, for example, that explicit and even implicit *a priori* claims are spartan, though presuppositions for the intuitionist method are complex—as happens, for example, in Hume. I shall return to these differences later, when answering the charge that some philosophers are misrepresented by my list of intuitionist assumptions. Now to the question: What is presupposed about the character of mind when intuitionist method is applied. I shall begin simplistically, adding details as the scope and bias of intuitionist assumptions are clarified.

2f. Four inferred claims about intuiting mind

Intuitionism supposes that mind is divided between its passive and active parts. These two are complementary and mutually conditioning: nothing is registered by passive mind if active mind does not see it; there can be no act of inspection if nothing is given, passively, to be seen. This reciprocity is apparent when mind attends to a given which has been presented to or created by it, then again when self-conscious mind must be present to itself in order that it may be inspected. There are four topics anticipated here, each one requiring elaboration. They are: a) mind's receptivity, b) its intentionality, c) self-consciousness, and d) status as a substance.

2fi. MIND'S RECEPTIVITY

(a) Mind is passive to the given because it is a sensorium where the data to be thought or perceived are first registered and held, however momentarily, within it. The idea of a sensorium is inherited from the visual metaphor which dominates intuitionist thinking, as the eye receives sensory data, presenting them as an inspectable array. Mind as sensorium duplicates these two functions: this is the luminous medium where the given is possessed and shown. This visual metaphor is, of course, quickly generalized beyond sensory data to include every kind of intuitionist conceptualization, as clear and distinct ideas, Forms, words, and theories are also candidates for receptivity.

The one perplexity with these conceptual givens is their way of violating the assumption that receptivity is logically prior to mind's activity as it regards or makes the given. There are, for example, the theories used for differentiating and ordering the sensible world. Receptivity to both the theory and the experience it has created, and then reflection upon them, come after the time when the theory and experience have been made. Activity has preceded receptivity. Does this imply a prior order of receptivity? Are we conscious, as intuitionism requires that we should be, of this prior receptivity? Kant's discussion of synthesis is a reference point for these two questions.

Mind is receptive, Kant supposed, at two moments: later, when the sensory data have been synthesized, and earlier, when those data are first received. There is, however, this difference between the two moments: we are conscious of the finished experience but not of the unschematized sensory data. This last assumption is intolerable to intuitionists, because of implying that something might exist without being seen. Here is one of the places where Kant's transcendentalism is careless of intuitionist scruples. It may be the concern for these intuitionist rules which explains some of those intimations in the First Critique that sensory data are consciously received by the transcendental ego.

This pattern is duplicated in several other intuitionist theories. We are assumed to be conscious, for example, of the words and uses summoned by ordinary language analysis; but what of the occasions when these words were first learned? Mind will have been receptive at both times. Can intuitionists say that it was unconscious when the words were learned? There are also the conceptual systems we learn and apply, as we learn the rules and instincts of a political system. Consciousness in applying these rules compares to our inferred receptivity when the system was learned. But is it true that our earlier receptivity is only inferred? Intuitionism starts in the naive pursuasion that the matters used or reflected upon have been received by a mind that is conscious of them. That confirmation is impossible after the fact, as there is no way to confirm within a synthesized experience that Kantian mind was self-consciously receptive to unschematized sensory data. Inspection will have to occur, and be seen to occur, at the moment of receptivity. One thinks of Heidegger's intuitionist instincts as he argues that our prototypic perception is the "pre-Socratic" one of a world know holistically and without the mediation of those conceptualizations which divide and then reintegrate the given in ways that are appropriate to theory but false to the world. This is the purist reaction when inspection-as-acquaintance has been recast as synthesis, leaving us with nothing but inference as testimony to our original receptivity. It is that earlier receptivity that intuitionists must recover for self-conscious, inspecting mind. Every intuitionist who argues that mind uses a conceptual system to create a thinkable experience should agree that mind proceeds self-consciously, as much when assembling the materials from which it makes the conceptual system as when applying the system to create the experience. Too bad then if this intuitionist demand is not satisfied by the evidence: we are not aware of being receptive at these earlier moments in the history of making experience.

2fii. MIND'S INTENTIONALITY

(b) When intentionality is added to receptivity, we have the idea of mind as a theatre, with an audience of one. There is the stage, or sensorium, where data of every sort may be presented, and that witness to whom everything is plainly displayed. We perceive, think, talk about, remember, dream, or desire the matters set before us. These are intentional attitudes. They play upon the given.

Intentions are also distinguished in this other way: as naive, prescriptive or constructive. Where our notion of mind is still close to the metaphor of thought as vision, intention is seeing or acquaintance. That notion is extended as we allow that mind looks *at* and *for* its objects. These prepositions signify mind's transition as it passes beyond the mere registering of matters given. Where nothing specific is anticipated, mind can only contemplate the matters which appear adventitiously before it. A mind impelled by its anticipations is different. It fastens upon the data for which it has been searching. Success in finding them alters the feelings or ideas which have moved it, so that mind withdraws from looking because it is satisfied; or it formulates and acts upon some new objective.

A mind searching for, or within, an appropriate given is not yet a mind having the ability to determine the character of the given. That would be prescriptivism; and it requires that inspecting mind be empowered in special ways. It was sufficient before, when contemplation was the only task, that mind should intend the given by registering its presence. Judgement in this case is only the mental nod which signifies that, yes I see it. Judgement has a different ring when mind is looking for something within the given: yes, we say, I have found what I am looking for, or no, it isn't there. The prescriptivist attitude is different from either of these two, because it would have mind assume the responsibility for imposing some or all of the differentiations and orders that are to be present within the given. This implies that judgement will be a determination having two distinct moments, one preliminary and the other occurring when the given has been transformed by mind's activity. Initially, we are to determine what differentiations and orders can be imposed; on the other side, we are to satisfy ourselves that certain impositions have been made.

Kant's transcendental deductions are, in part, a justification for this two-step procedure, as the inspection of synthesized phenomena testifies to the efficacy of thought acting prescriptively. Two notions of judgement are implicit here, one for each step. Sensuous intuition, meaning unschematized sensory data, is judged in the respect that it is differentiated and organized. Judgements occurring after this schematization are like the ones ascribed to mind when we assume that experience is set before us, then perceived. Judgements of this second kind are an appraisal or finding, as we observe and affirm that some quality or relationship is present within the given.

Kant's prescriptivism is only part of the way to constructivism, because mind as he described it does not have responsibility for the character and existence of everything that is. Kant agreed with Plato and Descartes that sensory data are received not made. They argued that ideas are used as spectacles for projecting differentiation and order onto the sensory given. Kant transforms ideas into rules, making the transcendental ego responsible for organizing and unifying the data. But either way, prescription is not construction; mind has not created the data which are differentiated, then unified. Constructivism is more extreme in just this way: It insists that mind should create the given from materials of its own making. There is an anticipation of this more powerful intentional attitude in the making of plans. Plans direct behaviour as we alter our circumstances in ways that satisfy desire. We do this in circumstances that resist our determination to remake them, so that mind normally concedes an alien, thought-resistant given. There are some times, however, when mind refuses to submit; it withdraws from the material given into imagination and fantasy. Here is a place where the given has no character but the one we bestow.

Are there constructivists of this radical sort? Fichte was one. Carnap is another; "When I have constructed the world. . . ," he has remarked early in the *Logical Structure of the World.* Nor is that an idle boast if we take seriously the purport of his semantical frameworks, where every difference and relation that may be ascribed to the world is introduced as a predicate in the system. In these circumstances, the only things credited with existence and character are the ones that mind has created. Saying again that *esse es percipi,* we mean that nothing exists unless, first, the properties ascribed to it are founded within the conceptual framework, and, second, the sentences affirming its existence cohere with—e.g., are deducible from—

the other sentences already formulated and integrated into that formalized theory used for thinking the given. What worlds, what conceptual systems, is mind to create? That is decided by will as it acts in behalf of our values. Where do these values originate, in transcendental whim, practical interests, or culture? Carnap emphasizes our practical interests, though the answer is left obscure, because we may wonder if mind as he describes it is not necessarily transcendental.[2]

This transition from naive acquaintance to the prescriptivist ordering or constructivist making of the given marks a fundamental change in the orientation of our intentions. Before, we looked at the given or looked for certain things within it. Now, we are to determine, as an act of thought and will, that the given is to be organized in the ways determined by our interests and values. This difference transforms the metaphor of mind as a theatre. Before, mind's passivity was the condition for its activity, as receptivity was the prerequisite if active mind was to have an inspectable given. Now, mind's activity has precedence. We determine our purposes and values. We satisfy these objectives by inventing the plans or conceptual systems which will order the data given in ways appropriate to our aims. In the extremity, nothing is given so irrevocably that it might frustrate our determination to see it altered—e.g., as Nietzsche thought that Venice is the purist expression of human will. Constructivism is the intuitionist passion carried to its limit: Knowledge is guaranteed when the gap between knower and known is eliminated finally, because mind has created everything that might be known. How does mind secure its access to all the things which it has done? That is the next point.

2fiii. MIND AS SELF-CONSCIOUS

(c) We can imagine that a mind looking naively at the given might so enjoy the detail as to forget itself. But that will not happen when the balance within mind is revised, with active mind having responsibility and power for making the given. Self-consciousness will then be our normal condition, as we clarify our values and invent the plans which will see them realized. Also important to prescriptivism, though not to constructivism, is the requirement that mind take the measure of its own position relative to the data it will order, where these are phenomena which it does not altogether control. In all of this, intentionality becomes self-consciousness at the moment when power and responsibility, or weakness and need, turn mind upon itself.

Three assumptions are vital to these claims about self-consciousness: first, that mind must be self-conscious, or capable of being self-conscious, at every moment; second, that the self which is observed is cotemporal with, hence, fully available to and known by the self that observes it; third, that I discover in self-consciousness both that I am and what I am. These assumptions embellish the point that inspecting mind is self-enclosing, with immediate and faultless access to everything present within itself. These are cornerstones for a subjectivist, idealist metaphysics. Let us consider each of them in turn.

2fiiia. Mind must be self-conscious

Intuitionism is not content to assume that mind is often or always self-conscious. Mind, it supposes, must be perpetually self-conscious. This would not seem to be required where active mind is attracted and absorbed by a senuous given, yet our self-consciousness is a necessary condition for mind's inspection of the given. Why? The answer has three parts:

(i) The simplest is the view that passive mind vibrates as we are affected by the content received; we are as though shaken into self-perception, experiencing ourselves as we are affected by the given. The *must* in "must be self-conscious" is mechanical; we could not help but be affected and awakened by the impact of the given.

(ii) There is this ambiguity: Where lies the power for directing awareness? Where lodge the ideas which are used prescriptively? Where is it that plans are made and applied? Where is the critical power for evaluating the truth of judgements and the success of plans? Is volition a blind force or is it controlled? These are questions that cannot be answered so long as we suppose that the only division within mind is the one between passivity and activity, for all these powers require some further differentiation within active mind. Intuitionists must distinguish between first- and second-order awareness, that is, between consciousness as it attends to the given and consciousness as it evaluates, directs, and revises that first-order awareness.

These two levels are conspicuous already in Plato and Descartes as they distinguish mind's ideas from the percepts they clarify. Descartes also requires that judgements be made about the things perceived and that assent be given or withheld by a mind operating in its self-reflexive mode. Kant's transcendental psychology, in the First Critique, is only the elevation of these second-order responsibilities to a place where they are not inspectable, though Kant relents in the Second Critique, where some of them are, and have to be, inspectable. Which of Kant's texts is correct: Is mind self-inspectable, or not, as it makes or directs experience? We might answer that mind need not be self-aware as it corrects, clarifies, or redirects its own first-order perceivings, as a thermostat or automatic pilot is self-correcting without being self-aware.

These examples might be taken as proof that second-order activities may occur in the absence of that self-conscious, self-reflexive attitude which is so often the referent for our talk about reflexivity. But this is only half true, as a mind that recognizes and then alters some condition within itself is, to that extent, effectively self-aware. The only thing missing is the mind's second-order awareness of this, its second-order efficacy.

(iii) There is, however, a separate and compelling reason for the intuitionist coupling of second-order responsibility and power with self-awareness. For why is it that we *must* be self-aware, not merely in the respect that we evaluate and redirect first-order activities but also in the regard that we are aware of being self-directing and self-correcting? The preliminary answer is that *esse es percipi,* where nothing exists if it is not seen to exist. This is true of everything given, whether it is sensory data, words, or a conceptual system. But is that enough? Can the given exist if the act acknowledging it does not itself exist? Mustn't I confirm my own existence while, or even before, I take responsibility for the existence of those other things which are given to me? We are reminded another time of Descartes' uncertainty about the duration of his own existence and his resolution of that question: It is only my self-awareness which confirms both the continuity of my existence and the existence of anything else that I perceive.

2fiiib. Self-reflection is concurrent with the other things inspected

Intuitionism risks an infinite regress, where the existence of every mental activity of whatever order requires certification by a higher-order reflexive act. It averts this result by taking up the second of the three assumptions listed above as essential to our claims about self-consciousness. This is the notion that self-conscious reflection is simultaneous with the activities or phenomena on which we reflect. I see myself reflecting upon these other things in the very moment of perceiving them. That is so, because there is no gap between first- and second-order reflection, no distance for the mental light to cover as it passes from the one to the other. Both are perceived as they occur. But is this answer sufficient if we are to avert the regress? If second-order awareness is cotemporal with first-order awareness, why couldn't third-order awareness, or any one still higher, be cotemporal with this first-order activity? We might agree that these many acts are cotemporal, though cotemporality makes the regress unnecessary. Mind is to certify the existence of its first- and second-order awareness in the act where I see the reflected light of my second-order being in the lower-order activities perceived. I see, for example, my directing second-order awareness in the revisions made to the words I write. But then this reflection of what I am and do is not different from me, because the reflected light is cotemporal and co-terminal with its source. Second-order awareness illuminates, and sees, all of itself in the same moment.

Notice too that mind averts error because of knowing every part of itself in the same moment. A time-lag between first- and second-order awareness would require that we resort to memory for information about mind as it was. But memory is fallible, so that the certainty required of mind can be guaranteed only if the inspecting mind and that which it sees are co-terminous. There is no distance and no mechanical medium to separate them, no finite time required as mental light is refracted from the given into the mind's eye. More than close to myself, I am identical with myself.

2fiiic. Self consciousness *that* I am, and *what* I am

The third of the assumptions made by intuitionists when they think of self-consciousness is relevant here, as we consider this notion of identity. There is something problematic about it, because first- and second-order awareness cannot be identical with one another lest there be one act only, rather than two functionally different acts. There must be some other thing to which identity is being ascribed, where these acts are identical with one another in only the mediated respect that both of them are acts of this thing. It will be that mental substance which is composed of receptivity and these two orders of awareness. Self-knowledge is, accordingly, a project having these two distinct tasks: I must establish *that* I am, and *what* I am.

The responsibility for both tasks falls to self-consciousness. It has discovered that I am, while exposing all that structure which is constitutive of what I am. Much of what I am may not be perceived at any particular moment; but nothing is hidden. All the complexity of receptivity and the two orders of awareness, as much as the given, is there to be perceived.

This transparency is essential if I am to be responsible for all that I do. For I, as a self-conscious agent, must be free to choose, on every occasion, the content and manner of my intending. I cannot do that if knowledge of myself is incomplete, because this ignorance of myself would extenuate my responsibility for the choices I make. But nothing within me has, or could have, escaped me, for I must always have been self-conscious in the moment of intending every object, with no chance that I could evade my responsibility for deciding the mode of my intending—e.g., doubt or belief. Even when apparently unselfconscious, I must have been self-aware, for no other agency is empowered for making these choices in my place. There is no one else who could have done for me what I have myself done. It is I alone who have directed and revised a succession of first-order intentions. Only my preoccupation with the task at hand may have prevented me from stepping back from these circumstances to notice the power and responsibility which I bring to the given. But then I do already know all of this about myself, because I know what I am as surely as I know that I am.

2fiv. MIND AS SUBSTANCE

(d) This is the moment for telling what these claims imply about mind's character as a substance. Mind, as intuitionists have presupposed it, is that amphitheatre where experience fills the luminous, conscious ether. Self-consciousness establishes the arena's perimeter, and it directs those beams of intentional light which play upon the given. This is a mind always in touch with itself, nothing hidden, with powers for contemplating or making the given. This mind is self-enclosed, and possibly self-sufficient. Here I am, a self-encircling monad, with guaranteed access to the given and myself, and with unconditioned powers for attending to them as I will. It may be true that I have not created some large part of the given, including everything sensible and the laws of logic. But then it might also be true that every differentiation within the given and every rule for making it is my creation. What kind of substance is this, so free and powerful as to be self-sustaining, perhaps even self-creating? There are metaphysicians who agree that the psychology presupposed by intuitionist method identifies a substance so important that all of nature should be characterized in its terms. The monads of Leibniz, Whitehead's actual occasions, and Hegel's Substance-for-Subject are examples. They would have us tell what the world is merely by generalizing to all of being from the psychological presuppositions of intuitionist method.

2g. *Five questions*

All four of the issues significant for intuitionist psychology—i.e., mind's receptivity, its intentionality, self-consciousness, and status as a substance—have now been considered. This is a place for taking our bearings. There are several things to consider. First is the intuitionist requirement that each of these claims about its psychology should be testable by way of direct inspection. Are they confirmed in that way? Second is the need for integrating the results of this psychological investigation with the preceding ontological one. Third is the possibility that there might be altogether different explications of the intuitionist psychology. Are there plausible alternatives to the one considered here; or arguments telling why no alternative is possible? Fourth, we need remember that the psychology ascribed to intuitionist method will seem an impertinence to the many philosophers who might be charged with intuitionism. Many of them have renounced it. How can we plausibly ascribe it to them? Fifth is the validity of this psycho-centric ontology. Is it credible and complete, or even plausible?

2gi. Is THE INTUITIONIST PSYCHOLOGY INSPECTABLE?

(a) Can we use the intuitionist method for confirming this method's psychological presuppositions? We remember that intuitionists do not agree about mind's inspectable character. Their disputes were my justification for preferring inference to inspection as the means for identifying the character of inspecting mind. But now with mind's receptivity and two orders of awareness described above, we need ask if any part of this alleged structure exceeds our powers for direct inspection.

The answer from principle is that nothing within the structure of self-encircling mind should be hidden to self-inspection. Mind should be altogether visible to itself. If some intuitionists continue to deny that they discover this structure within themselves, there are others, Descartes and Sartre for example, who say that this description is not so much an inference as a report of the various orders and reciprocal relations within our minds, all of them apparent to everyone who turns upon himself. This cannot be true of every activity claimed in behalf of inspecting mind as the following argument proves.

Kant supposed that mind's capacity for unifying the forms of intuition is inferred, not perceived. That unifying act could not be perceived, because the perceiving would have occurred within time while the unifying act that was to be the object of our perceiving would have occurred outside of time, as its condition. The one should have been inaccessible to the other.

We might hope to evade this difficulty by saying that mind's self-perception of the act which unifies time is "transcendental," like the act itself. But where is the support for this? Kant does suppose, in the Second Critique, that transcendental mind has direct access to itself as we direct will in accord with reason. But Kant has never agreed, in the First Critique, that transcendental ego has direct access to itself as it imposes the conditions for a unitary experience. It could not have that access if Kant is right in saying that self-experience is always temporalized, for then the self-perceiving act will occur within time, while its object, the time-unifying act, will occur, inacessibly, outside it. Intuitionists cannot deny that mind unifies our experience of time, because that would deprive mind of responsibility for the unity of its sensorium. Mind would then be less then self-sufficient, though intuitionists have no other entity to which they might appeal when explaining the unification of mind's receptivity. With only self-consciousness available to create that unity, they are forced to choose between a limited autonomy and the paradox that this most fundamental condition for conscious experience is not inspectable.

The desire for total inspectability is consistent with the demand for certainty and the requirement that *esse es percipi*. But Descartes and Sartre do not perceive the entire structure which they ascribe to inspecting mind for the reason that they could not. That is so for these two reasons: first, because the argument of the last paragraph shows that one of the claims made in behalf of mind and its autonomy precludes an act of confirming self-perception; second, because mind reveals very little of its character to direct inspection. It is likely that Descartes and Sartre have formulated the greater part of the intuitionist psychology as an inference from the claims of intuitionist method, before using it to determine their "self-perceptions." They have discovered the structure which they assume.

2gii. Does the intuitionist psychology cohere with its ontology?

(b) How do these psychological presuppositions cohere with the ontological ones? This second question reminds us that intuitionist psychology has cannibalized its ontology. A method's ontology is constitued by the elementary features of that domain to which the method applies. Ontology is, therefore, normally distinguishable from those claims about mind which are presupposed by the method's applications. This distinction is subverted where intuition applies as much to knowing oneself as to thinking some perceptual or intellectual given. Add to this the verificationist dictum of intuitionist method that *esse es percipi,* and we have the claim that a mind visible to itself and responsible for seeing or making the given is the necessary ground for whatever exists, itself included. Intuitionist metaphysicians may disagree about the character and status of this mind, some calling it the one God who thinks all of reality, others allowing that there may be one or many finite monads. There is, however, this one essential point common to all of them: Descartes' *cogito,* properly explicated, is the foundation for all that is or may be.

2giii. Is the subjectivist psychology the only one appropriate to intuitionist method?

(c) Could there be some different psychology for explaining the applications of intuitionist method, one that is stripped of this subjectivist, idealist bias?

2giiia. Three of the justifications for intuitionist method do not require the subjectivist psychology

This psychology supposes that mind is autonomous but isolated, though nothing like this view of mind is encouraged by three of the four justifications through which intuitionism moves as it validates itself. We remember these four as naive realism, representationalism, prescriptivism-constructivism, and common sense. Only the prescriptivist justification at its constructivist extreme coheres perfectly with the notion of mind as self-encircling and self-sufficient. The common sense justification is vague about mind's autonomy and isolation, while naive realism and representationalism insist that mind is placed among those other things which are perceived and known. Mind's isolation and self-sufficiency are by no means essential to these other justifications.

This is the appearance but not the deeper impulse. Intuitionist method is impatient of these other, mind-independent realities. It knows nothing of them, however frequently we postulate their existence in order to pacify our superstitions about things existing apart from us. *Esse es percipi:* we know nothing of any existent additional to the ones we inspect. Naive realism and representationalism defy that principle by making ontological assumptions which exceed anything which might be established by the intuitionist method. They do this because of being motivated by an unsupportable, because unverifiable, theory that we live and move among things which are independent of us.

This idea is based on a mistake. Those who believe it have confused, as Kant would say, the transcendental object with noumenal reality. The transcendental object has no reality apart from mind's expectation that organized phenomena will exceed their current appearances, completing themselves in a possibly infinite series of future appearances. Noumena are those things which cannot be known or even considered. They fall just short of nonbeing. Intuitionist method is false to itself and guilty of bad faith when it defers to these allegedly mind-independent realities in order to commend itself. The citation of these three less rigorous justifications is, therefore, irrelevant to the autonomy and isolation presupposed by intuitionist method.

2giiib. Plato's intuitionist psychology

The issue is however still undecided, for there is one other quite prominent alternative to this Cartesian psychology. That is the one of

Plato. He might have agreed that *esse es percipi,* meaning that the Forms are seen eternally by *nous.* But then *nous* is characterized by its transparency to and love for the Forms, not by self-consciousness. What is more, *nous* has no personality, no individuality. Though self-sustaining in its relation to the Forms, it is not self-encircling—because of being self-conscious—or free within that enclosure to choose by its own lights. Why prefer the Cartesian psychology to this Platonic one, when many intuitionists, including ordinary language analysts, those who use conceptual systems for differentiating reality, and Husserl sometimes, are closer to the spirit of Plato then to Descartes?

The short, Cartesian answer is that Plato's view are mistaken; applications of the intuitionist method, even the applications he considered, require a psychology richer than the one he described. Intuitionists who say this might argue for it in either or both of two ways: one, a diagnosis of Plato's claim, the other, a statement about the conditions for our knowledge of anything, Forms included.

The diagnostic argument is an explanation for Plato's assertion that *nous* is universal, without individuality or perspective. Two things explain this claim. First is Plato's belief that individuality and perspective are obstacles to the knowledge of Being. For Being is intelligible in itself, and not in any way dependent for its existence or character on our ways of thinking it. We know Being only as we discount or overcome personal identity and perspective, as we do in representing it mathematically. Second is the complex argument which says that personal identity is founded in self-consciousness and that self-consciousness cannot be the basis for our knowledge of the Forms because it is corruptible. This conclusion assumes that the Forms are unchangeable and that like knows like, so that any mind knowing the Forms must also be uncorruptible. But what is left for knowing them if we have discounted that part of mind which is responsible for personal identity, perpective, and judgement? Only receptivity and that first-order consciousness which merely attends to the given. Awareness of the sort demanded for knowing the Forms is not judgemental, as the eye need make no judgements as it is filled by the Sun or the things on which it shines. So is judgement irrelevant when we cannot help but see the intelligible order of things.

The second of these two claims has begun as a reflection on this first one. For Plato has not denied the reality of self-consciousness, but only its relevance for our knowledge of the Forms. Yet Plato errs:

Self-consciousness is not merely the individuating and personalizing contingency to which splintered *nous* is temporarily bound. Consider that receptivity which is filled and differentiated by the Forms. That medium, so vaguely discerned by Plato, is the sensorium which Kant described as the condition for receptivity, and more specifically as the forms of intuition. These forms are unified, meaning that every place or moment in space or time is connected to every other one. This unity is a condition for perceiving any complexity having spatial or temporal span, then for comparing its elements. So, we require the unity of time for hearing a melody and even a chord, however brief its duration. Time is all the more obviously required as we consider the chord in more detail, listening for the individual notes, then for their harmony. Plato's Forms are more like the chord than the melody: we would, perhaps, apprehend all of them at once, not one at a time. We might also see in that instant that the Good is the principal Form, and that the Forms differ from one another. But then we would also make comparisons, remarking that individual Forms are like or unlike a succession of others. There are an infinity of Forms. Even Plato might have allowed that *nous* would require time for making the comparisons. But then we could not make them if receptivity were not run through and grasped as a unity by self-binding self-consciousness.

Intuiting mind is more than a self-perceiver or faculty of judgement, and more than a will. Intuition requires that self-consciousness should supply the conditions for our having access to the matters we perceive, judge, and desire. It requires that we be literal about mind's self-sufficiency. Mind is cause of itself. It is, says this psycho-centric ontology, the guarantor of all the conditions for what it is and does. Plato has ignored these conditions without proving that they are dispensable. His psychology is, therefore, naive and incomplete. Intuitionist psychology requires that we acknowledge the existence of that self-conscious agent who supplies all the conditions for observing, or even making, the given.

2giv. Those who reject the intuitionist psychology while using the method

(d) The fourth question is timely now, for what shall we say of those intuitionists who reject that psychology which is, I say, presupposed by their method? We can respect the vigor of their opposition to it, for this is a psychology which fails the intuitionist rule that nothing is real if it is not inspectable. Hume's objections are familiar; but intuitionists of our time are equally insistent. Here, for example, is Carnap:

> Egocentricity is not an original property of the basic elements of the given.[3]

> The existence of the self is not an originally given fact. The sum does not follow from the *cogito;* it does not follow from "I experience" that "I am," but only that an experience is. The self does not belong to the expression of the basic experience at all, but is constructed only later, essentially for the purpose of delineation against "others."[4]

I interpret this as meaning that we do not discover a self among elementary experience, for the reason that there is no one to bear these elementary data.

> The "self" is the class of elementary experiences. It is frequently and justly emphasized that the self is not a bundle of representations, or experiences, but a unity. This is not in opposition to our thesis . . . a class is not a collection, or the sum, or a bundle of its elements, but a unified expression for that which the elements have in common.[5]

Carnap is repudiating the subject which I have described as a first presupposition for intuitionist thinking. That would be final, as the statement of his beliefs, but for the distinction made previously between a philosopher's views, whether explicit or implicit, and those notions which are presupposed by his method. There is often a conflict between a writer's views and his presuppositions; and that is nowhere balder than the examples of Carnap and Hume.

A first-time reader may notice than quash the instinct that Hume's impressions and Carnap's elementary experiences are noticed, compared, and connected. Something sensible and live, something that is more than a construct from these elementary data, has written a book about them. But then we dismiss these reservations as a failing in us, as an inability to set aside our own persuasions while reading the philosopher with an open mind. The original question does, nevertheless, persist: Who is it that attends to these elementary experiences? What is the character of that agent who wrote the book? Carnap anticipates, then tries to divert our curiosity.

[T]he question whether, at the bottom of all autopsychological objects, there lies the "self" as a final unresolvable unity, is not a question of order, but a question of essence: thus, to pose and answer the question is not the task of the constructional system, but of metaphysics.[6]

Metaphysics, however, is the "pseudo-science" whose every assertion is meaningless. There is, therefore, no way of specifying the psychological conditions for using intuitionist method. The agent who is passive to elementary experiences, and active in making and using a semantical framework for differentiating and ordering them, is itself just the class of elementary experiences or an exile in the purgatory of metaphysics. We are reminded of Hume: Impressions are received, ideas are regarded and compared, inferences are made and habits are acquired but there is no subject who perceives, thinks, and learns.

We avert this result by distinguishing these two things: first is the inability for locating a self within experience; second is the claim that there is no self which is passive and active through the course of experience. Carnap, like Hume and James, is the purist who says that the self cannot exist if it is not discerned within experience: *esse es percipi*. We may respond in either of two ways, saying first, in the style of Descartes and Sartre, that he has not looked carefully enough or in the right way; or second, that the existence and character of this thinker is inferred as a condition for those activities which Carnap so firmly avers.

These and related distinctions are also pertinent to William James. He is more insistent than anyone in rejecting Kant's transcendental ego. The unity of experience is, he says, founded in the relations which are already intrinsic to it. This is not compelling when we recall that Kant's transcendental ego has three roles. In the first, it unifies experience by providing least relations for otherwise atomic data; in the second, ego turns upon itself so that reason may direct the will; in the third, ego contemplates the experience it has created. James reformulated the first two notions in order that he might dispense with the transcendental ego. He assumes, without explaining the third one. The products of this subject's activities are observed; they are, says Kant, "presentations." So has James described the stream of consciousness, all its continuities standing before us, in ways which presuppose this receptive, inspecting subject. For this reason, James as much as Carnap and Hume is inconsistent.

No thing is real if not given, they suppose, though our receptivity to experience, and all the ways for describing, differentiating, and organizing it testify to the existence and character of that uninspectable agent whose existence they deny.

There are many intuitionists who are, like these three, divided against themselves. All of them suppose that a given of content or form is set before our inspecting minds, whether presented to or made by us. There is Husserl's phenomenological reduction, Russell's emphasis on acquaintance, Heideggerian talk about "presencing," Wittengenstein's claim that the logical form of sentences is displayed and seen, the claim of ordinary language analysts that mind surveys the logical geography of a word, and the view common to many philosophers of science that we use a conceptual system, whether a formalized theory or paradigm, to create a thinkable world. Only Husserl, among these intuitionists, is careful to provide for inspecting mind. The others ignore or deny it. To them, preeminentely, we need apply the three rubrics mentioned before. Their explicit views about mind—and even their implicit, *a priori* assumptions about it—may deny the reality of receptive, inspecting mind. But all of that is betrayed by their reliance upon the intuitionist method. For intuitionism is committed irrevocably to mind as it thinks the given, with no remission for those who use the method selectively or uncritically. One cannot squint, as though to see only a little bit, without using the eye. Nor can we be intuitionists without invoking the intuitionist psychology. These philosophers of science and language, each one as spartan as Carnap, must choose between their desire for confirming, direct inspection, and their distaste for the *cogito*.

Plato has seemed to provide a discreet middle way, as he supposes that a detached, intellectual vision of things has no implications about a mind having more complexity, individuality, and perspective than *nous*. But that was mistaken when Plato thought it, as it is mistaken now. The character of intuiting mind is ever more plainly articulated as we move from Descartes though Leibniz, Kant, and Hegel to Husserl and Sartre. Their explicit claims about mind have come to approximate those notions which have always been presupposed when the intuitionist method is used, as the mind that Sartre describes is uncompromisingly responsible, free, self-conscious, and self-sufficient. We should insist that every intuitionist make his explicit views cohere with the ones presupposed by his method. Let intuitionists be answerable for their psycho-centric ontology. Let them explain the paradox that a method which makes inspectability a condition for existence has psychological presuppositions which inspection cannot altogether confirm.

2gv. Is the psycho-centric ontology complete?

(e) We also require an intuitionist response to the last of these five questions about their ontology and psychology; namely, is this psycho-centric ontology complete? Substance implies individuation, self-sufficiency, and agency. Mind, as created and sustained by self-consciousness, would have all three powers; but then it would also have some other properties. Here are three which defy the requirements of inspectability.

There is, first, no activity without agency, as it is a wheel that turns. Every agent has properties which are specifiable independently of the properties of its activity. How shall we characterize that agent who is receptive to the given, aware of it and perhaps responsible for making it, then aware of itself? Intuitionism perpetuates the Cartesian idea that mind is identical with its activity, though Descartes ignores mind's structural properties and implies thereby that mental activity is groundless, like the spinning of a nonexistent wheel. Mind will have some structural properties if it is to act in any way. Its structure is probably the one of body and brain, with the implication that very little of it is known to inspecting mind.

Second are the dispositions which intuitionism ascribes to mind, as when it supposes that we may recall ideas not currently inspected. Dispositions are the properties of structures, as the capacity for memory devolves on structures having definite paths of access to the data they store. Free-floating dispositions, dispositions without a ground in structure, are inconceivable, as there is no capacity for running apart from the legs which might run. We cannot tell, very often, what dispositions a structure has, so that intuitionism is doubly embarrassed; it cannot use intuition to identify all of mind's abilities or that structure where these powers reside.

Third, an all-encircling and all-sustaining self-consciousness implies mind's perfect self-sufficiency. Mind would be the power which isolates us from other things. But this is a fiction when the structure on which mind depends is a body having to sustain itself within the world. This is a body acting under intelligent direction while accommodating to its circumstances, a body which derives information and nourishment from them. Mind, far from being the activity which secures our isolation, is the set of activities which extend body's useful relations to the things about it. Some of these relations are representational, as we use words to signify things which are important to us. These representations are the maps we use for finding our way into the world. Finally and always, we are bound to those other things by the dynamic and reciprocal relations which sustain us and them.

3. The alternative again

All three of these considerations bear upon the substantial, probably material character of the agents endowed with mind. But this third point has an additional and separate implication, one that is even more deadly to intuitionist prospects. Intuitionism declares that the only things we might know are the ones confirmed directly by inspection. This explains the intuitionist impatience with those inferences and representations which are unconfirmed by our direct inspection of their objects. Intuitionism fears and despises everything that is speculative in either way. Suppose, however, that mind is only a power of body, and that all of body's relations, within and without, are mediated by more or less complex chains of causal relations. Everything known will be mediated by the effects that other things have upon us, that is, by natural signs, or by way of those conventional signs, meaning thoughts and words, which we use for representing the things known. Knowledge claims will be formulated as hypotheses representing possible states of affairs, with a premium upon confirming evidence and the coherence of accepted hypotheses. We never shall have the certainty which intuitionists have prized. Our every claim about the existence and character of things existing independently of us will be speculative. Knowledge will be warranted assertibility. Intuitionism will be defunct.

What of our persuasion that we do inspect and know some things set before our inspecting minds, feeling and sensations being the most obvious examples? This must be a mistaken impression if our minds are only the activities of body, because every bodily process is causal and mediated. The activity misconstrued as inspection is a succesion of interpretations, where each interpretation classifies some affect in the way prescribed by a rule. Experience is real; but this activity displaces inspection as an explanation for it. Seeing an apple, we see it as red and expect that it will continue to look as it does. As the color changes and the shape sags, we modify the expectation by changing the interpretive rule. We prepare to observe the apple as it changes in a more or less predictable way.

How is the experience of color created? We do not yet have a complete answer, though we do know how to compose images, as in television screens; and we can imagine the combination of image generators with internal, self-monitoring systems. We understand better how the successive interpretations of sensory inputs are organized mechanically, for we build machines which scan sound, heat or light in order to register and organize a pattern of sensory differences. Most of these machines do not monitor themselves, though there are some that do that. There are even machines that represent some part of the world symbolically before acting upon it, and beyond that, machines which program themselves. Machines too can make and test hypotheses. Mind's use of its signs, whether natural or conventional, and its facility for making and changing the rules which direct its interpretations are more complicated than the behaviors of these machines; but mind may not be more mysterious. For nothing is inspected. There is, as Peirce was first to say, neither a given nor a power for inspecting it. We don't need either one. The world is accessible to us by way of the signs we use for representing it.

Chapter Five

Topical Metaphysics:
Cause and Effect

1. Systematic and topical metaphysics

I ntuitionism is pervasive in all of philosophy, and dominant too in metaphysics. This is true whether metaphysical thinking is systematic, wanting to comprehend all of being within a set of mutually conditioning relations, or topical, preferring to divide reality into discrete subject matters.

Intuitionist metaphysics of the systematic kind starts in either of two ways. On the one side are those intuitionists who suppose that some difference discovered within the given expresses the fundamental structure of all Being. Plato seems to have proceeded in this way when he inferred from the difference between stable names and ephemeral sensations to the one of Forms and the flux. On the other side are the metaphysicians who are drawn to their method's psychocentric ontology. Having discovered and characterized their own subjectivity, they generalize about all of nature or being, saying that reality is constituted only of myriad finite minds—e.g., Leibniz's monads and Whitehead's actual occasions—or one cosmic mind—e.g., Parmenides' One and Hegel's Absolute.

Topical metaphysics takes its inspiration from Hume's principle that everything distinguishable is separable. Sensory data may satisfy this principle, but so do words and whole theories. Topical metaphysicians claim the right to consider any one of these allegedly separable matters without more than passing regard for every other one, as a theory of space and time might ignore the fact of motion, while a theory of time is indifferent to the character of space. Intuitionism has nearly boundless resources for this topical way of thinking. There are, for example, Husserl's Ideas, and more available still, the many distinctions within ordinary language. We can isolate talk of space from that of time, and both of them from talk of matter, cause, morals, and divinity. We are to believe that each of these topics is autonomous, so that we might provide a comprehensive theory about it, without regard for the words or evidence that are appropriate to those other, equally self-sufficient topics. Reality is understood, for the purposes of these topical analyses, on the model of a picture gallery, where adjacent paintings are considered separately; we may choose to be richly informed about one, while caring nothing for the others. Topical metaphysics, is, therefore, one kind of essentialism; it implies that every separable topic has an isolable nature, without mutually implicative relations to other topics.

Suppose that we extrapolate beyond the array of various, more or less comprehensive analyses to the time when all of the issues which are important to systematic metaphysics have been considered, individually, by topical metaphysicians. For we may expect that these individual results will be expressed as an encyclopedia of being-in-the-aggregate. The one remaining problem for topical metaphysics will be the one of justifying the principle for ordering its separate analyses. Is the principle external to the matters aggregated, as alphabetizing them would be; or is it integral to them? Is it also true that an internal, integrating principle is itself just one more, separable topic? Topical analysis never asks this question because there is, so far, no complete or almost complete set of topics to be integrated. Still, the parallel between systematic and topical metaphysics requires that we anticipate the completion of both kinds of metaphysical inquiry. The standing of its integrative principle becomes, at that moment, a vital question for topical metaphysics.

With Chapter Six reserved to systematic metaphysics, this present chapter is devoted to the affects of intuitionist method within topical metaphysics. I doubt that topical analysis is more than provisional: first, because no topic is isolable from every other one; second, because the status of a final integrative principle leads in either of two ways: to the claim that the principle is conventional so that the many topics have no integration in Being, or to the claim that they are intrinsically related so that the contrary presumption of topical analysis, that they are isolable, is mistaken. Nevertheless, topical metaphysics is the standard for contemporary metaphysical inquiry. Most metaphysical analyses are topical, and most metaphysicians deride the possibility that metaphysics could be systematic. It is important that we consider things as they are, identifying the intuitionist biases within topical analyses.

2. Two kinds of topical analysis

Analyses are provoked in either of two ways.

Some of them begin as we reflect on something that is perceived within the given, though imperfectly understood. What is intentionality, as revealed in self-experience or prefigured in ordinary language? What do we discover of law, cause, time, or morality in our experience of or talk about them? We sometimes imagine that these two resources, sensible experience and ordinary language, guarantee a fresh, unbiased view of the matters at issue, as we might go about a garden, or swamp, focusing only on birds or bullfrogs, ignoring all the rest. This is intuitionist philosophy as it turns its back on the formulations and problems inherited from our dialectical past. We are called to the things themselves, or at worst to the concepts or words used by ordinary people as they think about or describe these things.

The alternative starting point for topical analysis is the history of philosophy, that tangle of good and bad starts, of vigorous defences and poisonous assaults. This is the refuge to which intuitionists go when the other, more naive, beginning has failed them, when they discover themselves in the midst of an old dispute while hoping for a new start. Topical analyses of this second kind are often parasitic upon the systematic theories they wish to discredit, as analysis tests the hypotheses of systematic but nonintuitionist theories by measuring their claims against something which is "incontrovertible" within the given. Hume does this when he invokes sensible experience against Aristotle's views about cause and effect. Aristotle, says Hume, is guilty of speculative excess: look at the sensory given to see if you perceive the necessary connections or causal powers which Aristotle ascribes to nature. Gilbert Ryle argues in a similar way: first, by opposing arcane philosophic views to the counterintuitive ones of science; then, by saving us from these equally bizarre results by affirming, in his *Dilemmas,* the ordinary language solutions. Ryle and

Hume have wanted to quash those speculations which exceed a reliable given. Analysis, as they use it, is a defense of intuitionist purity. Each one turns his rhetorical skills upon the speculative enemy, faulting his logic, damning his theory at every place where speculation threatens to ignore, deride, or reinterpret the unimpeachable given. No wonder that these analyses are counted successful if they merely destroy the offending speculation, leaving the given intact. No intuitionist thinks it odd that these analyses fail to answer, or even respond to the questions that are raised and possibly answered by the other, more speculative theory. For why bother to formulate a solution if these questions drive us beyond ordinary language or the sensible given to hypotheses which may not be confirmed within either of them?

3. Cause and effect as an example for topical analysis

Cause and effect is a topic which has received both kinds of analysis. Hume is the dialectician committed to defending the sensory given from Aristotle's too speculative claims about it. Whitehead is an intuitionist of that other, naively programmatic, sort. Isn't it peculiar, however, that these two examples of topical analysis should come from the books of philosophers whose own work is ardently systematic, never merely topical? Hume and Whitehead never write of causality without considering what they regard as its significant conditions and implications. Why cite them as examples of topical analysis?

I do that for several reasons. Hume is our modern source for the principle that everything distinguishable is separable. His analysis of causality is paradigmatic for the applications of this principle. He uses it to "establish" that causality does not require essential reference to matter and motion; they are, he says, irrelevant to cause and effect. Whitehead is equally adroit at separating causality from every reference to them. Also conspicuous are the analyses formulated in Humean and Whiteheadian style, analyses that are neatly scissored from Hume's and Whitehead's theories, then left to stand alone as self-sufficient topics for analysis. Causality is, therefore, a plausible example of the topics chosen for analysis. My objective has two parts: first, to expose the intuitionist bias in the Humean and Whiteheadian analyses of cause and effect; second, to argue that no metaphysical notion is adequately formulated when it is separated from every other one. Topical analyses are never more than provisional. We are always impelled beyond them as we analyze some particular issue from the standpoint of that theory, however provisional, which coordinates our notion of the whole.

4. Hume's theory of cause and effect

4a. The singularity of causal relationships

We start with Hume. He has denied that interaction, matter, power, and necessity are pertinent to the relation of cause and effect. But then Hume makes no sense of the occasion when red paint splatters over my floor from the bucket right now falling, bottom up, from a ladder. Is it constant conjunction which justifies me in calling them cause and effect? What if it is Jackson Pollock using similar means to produce a unique effect? Are we barred from saying that Pollock is the painter, and cause of the pictures bearing his name? There are of course circumstances where the title "author and cause" is not so freely given, and others where the identity of the cause is not so plain. Suppose that Pollock had kicked a ladder so that a bucket had fallen as above. Should he have been credited with painting the floor? If several artists are in a competition to hit a canvass from twenty feet with squirt guns filled with paint, we may be uncertain about the identity of the winner if each gun is loaded with paint of the same color. But we can settle these difficulties by putting a different chemical marker in each of the guns, or by agreeing that we lack the information required for settling them. What we cannot do, or should not want to do, is deny that there is cause and effect in singular complex events, whether or not constant conjunction is observed or alleged. We need to identify those factors intrinsic to individual events which justify our saying that every particular effect is created by its antecedents.

4b. Hume's reductive analysis

It is not apparent that Hume started with a prejudice against the idea that cause and effect might be intrinsic to singular events. It is only his arguments against the Aristotelian notions of cause which oblige him to say that causal relations are only the ones of constant conjunction. The argument having this result has several mutually enforcing parts. First are the claim that sensory data are distinguishable—hence, separable—and the claim that these sensory atoms are connected to one another by spatial and temporal relations. There is no provision in these two claims for the interaction of causes, or the dependence of effects upon their causes. We are barred from introducting these considerations when Hume remarks that we have no impressions of them and no power for inventing ideas of them or inferring to what they might be. That is so, he argues, because ideas are only the copies of impressions, and because the only permissable inferences are the ones going from an impression or idea to the idea of its familiar associate. We are left with only these impressions and the ideas of impressions remembered or imagined. They have no relations but those spatial and temporal ones which are perceived or imagined. These are circumstances where the existence and character of every atom are independent of the existence and character of every other one, and where no sensory atom is the generative condition for any other. We do speak of causes and effects, but only to signify constant conjunctions, as hitting one's thumb with a hammer does usually correlate with pain. What is the difference between these causal conjunctions and those others which are merely accidental, as it is accidental that every other human breathes when I do? Hume cannot tell us, so that his explication of causal relations has these two costs: On the one side, he has obliterated the cause and effect relation within singular events; on the other side, Hume has no way of distinguishing the true causal conjunctions from constant but accidental conjunctions.

4c. Hume's intuitionist motives

Hume's argument has both of the features which are typical of views defending the given. First is the choice of given, and the avowal that every thinkable difference and relation is founded within it. Second are the arguments which defend the given from adulteration and misdescription. Where impressions and ideas are the given, it is uninspectable relations, aspects and conditions, meaning interaction, necessity and causal powers, which are purged. We are left with only the sensible given. Nothing, Hume says, is real if it is not perceived. But little or nothing of final, formal, material, or efficient cause is inspectable, so that these are merely the over-descriptions, hence the misdescriptions, of things given.

Motives are important. What could be Hume's motives as he takes this analytic sledgehammer to the Aristotelian world, breaking it up so that there may be no place to resist the demand that all of it be exposed to inspecting mind? It may be true, though the evidence for saying it is exaggerated, that Hume was the canny modernist, using indisputable "empirical" ways of eliminating the constricting Aristotelian metaphysics. We have no impressions of the causes which Aristotle describes, so they cannot exist. Anything conceivable can exist, so that there is no reason in metaphysics or nature for denying that any impression we imagine might exist unconditionally by itself. All the claims that form our naturalistic view of things turn out to be prejudices, with nothing that Hume's principles would count as evidence for them. Why should Hume argue in a way that denies a fair hearing to these naturalistic assumptions? Only because Hume is determined to shatter every basis for the persuasion that there might be a world that stands apart from us while exceeding mind's power for inspecting it. This is an important step on the way to defending us from the demands made upon us by nature and the political order. It is a way of clearing the decks so that mind may have perfect autonomy in the way that it constructs and interprets its experience. We are saved from having to bend to a world that will not be reduced to the ambit of inspecting mind.

4d. Evaluating Hume's theory of cause

Theories are good or bad, accordingly as they explain or fail to explain the phenomena at issue. A good theory identifies those factors which are constitutive of, or the conditions for, a certain result. Having the theory enables us to understand what has happened and, sometimes, to predict what may happen. Hume's intuitionist theory of cause and effect is bad in each of these ways. It does not explain or even allow that cause and effect might be the factors within a singular relationship—e.g., as our universe may be the effect of a single explosion. It disables us for making people responsible for things they do, since no one, on Hume's telling, has any effect on anything else. Hume identifies causality with constant conjunction, though he cannot specify the conditions for recurring events or tell what the difference is between causal connections and accidental ones. There are other failures too, as Hume's theory entails that the world should be chaotic, because anything can follow anything else, and static because nothing should happen when antecedent events are not sufficient to produce changes.[1] The world is, however, neither chaotic nor static, so that Hume's theory is refuted by the empirical error of its entailments.

5. Unsatisfactory alternatives

Saying this risks a certain paralysis, because of seeming to imply that there are only the two choices: revert to Aristotle's views about cause and effect, or affirm Hume's intuitionist objections to them. The benefits of these alternatives may seem to be equally balanced: Aristotle's analysis is comprehensive and usually plausible, while Hume has excited philosophers to the point where we gladly ignore the phenomena to be explained out of respect for a theory which declares that we cannot explain them. Hume is faultless in his respect for intuitionist scruples, though he has nothing to say of that transformation which occurs in one or more of a set of causes as they interact. These failures cancel one another, so that we are left forever with these two, apparently exhaustive alternatives, the one a good approximation to the conditions for change, the other a minimalist account of change coupled to an annihilating critique of whatever speculations exceed the sensible given.

This result should be intolerable. We are deprived of a satisfactory metaphysics of nature because of fearing that any reformulated account will be as vulnerable as the one of Aristotle. That fear is reasonable only if we accept the intuitionist critique on its own terms, never bothering to question the assumption that every theory must satisfy the demand that its every claim be validated by inspection of the matters alleged. The way is clear to a revised metaphysics of nature if we discount these intuitionist scruples, for we can theorize responsibly without requiring that inspecting mind should certify our every claim.

6. Some reasons for providing a different theory of cause

I suggest the following sketch for a theory of cause and effect. My proposal is broadly Aristotelian, but different because of insisting that we need understand the efficacy of causes within the context of a revised theory of substances and their relations. Formulating this alternative has two effects: It reminds us that topical analysis falsifies its subject matters by dividing them from one another, and it recalls us to the many uninspectable aspects of a relation which is essential to nature. Hume is tidy but shallow. It is intuitionism which makes him so. Comparing all that needs to be said of cause and effect against the most that Hume can say of it is a test of his intuitionist method.

7. Two kinds of theory about causation

There is a fundamental difference among theories of causation. Some regard effects merely as successors to or substitutions for their causes. Others regard effects as transformations of causes, saying that causes endure through the course of their transformation.

7a. Substitution

Hume's notion of cause and effect is an instance of the substitutional theory, where these three features justify this classification: (a) Hume argues that change is a succession of discrete elements, where the existence and character of every element are independent of its antecedents and succesors. Every element is static. None is transformed in the course of its history within the serial order. (b) Substitution is determinable in regard to temporality, meaning that some instances of it are temporalized, while some others are not. We speak, for example, of sentences which are comtemporal, or atemporal, where one is created from the other by applying some rule of inference. This altered sentence is the substitute for, or successor to the first one, with no implication that one precedes or follows the other in time. Cause and effect is a temporalized substitution relation, where the effect succeeds, and may displace, the cause. (c) The order of succession is explained by a rule or law, as the order of sentences is determined by an inference rule. A causal law "explains" a sequence of events in the respect that the events are ordered as the law prescribes. This is, however, only a partial explanation, for it applies only to the character of the ordering relation, not to the existence or character of the events. What is it that produces them, thereby deciding their character? We know the answer in the case of inference, where successor sentences are created by the person or machine using the inference rule. We have to forget these generating conditions when we consider Hume's substitutional account of causality, because it affirms that nothing is created by its antecedents or by any other thing.

The issue will not go away. What is it that creates the events which satisfy, by their order, the causal laws or rules used to explain them? Is there some God who creates every next item in the sequence of causes and effects? Hume wouldn't like this solution, but then he leaves the matter unexplained. There is, he says, no reason why any event should have any antecedent. But this doubles the mystery by implying that the laws or rules covering the succession of causes and effects are weaker than the rules of inference; we cannot use a causal law for creating effects from causes, as we can use rules of inference for making successor sentences from their antecedents. What are the efficient and formal causes creating each of the individuals within a causal sequence? Hume can only reply that there are no causes of either sort.

7b. Transformation

The transformational notion of cause and effect is different in all three respects: (a) Change is continuous rather than sequential, so that no change is merely the temporalized complex of discrete and static individuals. Things are perpetually transformed, not usually to the extent that whole identities are lost from moment to moment, but rather because one or more of a thing's properties or relations are changing. That some properties and relations are relatively stable does not preclude the slow, or catastrophic, transformation of others. (b) The mere differences among things ordered do not presuppose temporality, as the numbers of a sequence are different from one another but timeless. Time is essential to transformations because the differences generated within them are changes. Yet temporality is still too vague a notion, for this is not the time of intuitionism, meaning time as a medium for the presentation and relating of differences, as when musical notes are heard in succession. Here, in the relation of cause and effect, time is assumed in a way that is essential to the dynamics of transformation. That is so because change embodies motion, thereby presupposing space and time. (c) Transformation provides conditions for both the character of the changes occurring and for their existence. The character of individual changes is determined by constraints immanent within the process. These include properties of the causes, and the properties of the medium where changes occur, as a particular geometry is an immanent constraint within the space where motion occurs. The existence of the changes is explained by the efficacy and persistance of the things transformed, as notes are sounded when a musician plays and his instrument vibrates.

8. A theory of cause alternative to Hume's

My notion of cause and effect is an alternative to Hume's intuitionist theory. It is transformational, not substitutional. Where the existence and character of every sensory atom are independent of every other one, and where before and after are the only relations important to temporalized succession, Hume could ignore both the internal character of the things sequenced and every other relation they might have to their antecedents and successors. None of this could be significant for cause and effect relations. Transformationalists say that Hume is mistaken; the internal character of things, together with relations additional to spatial and temporal contiguity, are vital to a thing's transformation. But then too, our notion of transformation is not adequate until we have a characterization of the things transformed. There is, accordingly, no satisfactory theory of cause and effect without a complementary set of notions adequate to substance, space, time, and motion. Each of them might be considered in some minimal way without regard for the others, but no one of them is adequately represented until we have specified the mutually conditioning features of all the others. My sketch of a theory about causation is a fragment in that more ample transformationalist account. It emphasizes the role of substance as the agency and subject of change, for we cannot talk in a more than provisional way about cause and effect until we have specified the character of the entities which are transformed, or mutually transforming. We start with a more detailed account of transformation.

8a. Whitehead's notion of process

Remember Whitehead's actual occasions. They are transformed internally, when each of them creates its own identity by integrating the prehensions of its antecedents in ways that are prescribed by its ideas and values. Notice, however, that Whitehead has not extended his notion of process and continuity from the becomings within actual occasions to the generative relations which knit past to present and future. This has the effect of confirming Whitehead's claim that actual occasions are discrete, with no dynamic relations among them. Aristotle distinguished points from lines, saying that the points are abstractions. They are ideal entities to which we approximate by the operations performed on lines—e.g., they cross at a point. Whitehead's actual occasions are too much like these points, for he does not argue or believe that every succeeding occasion is a moment or phase in a material evolution where identity is sustained through time and change.

8b. Generational continuity

We repair Whitehead's omission by saying that transformations are continuous in two ways. First, each one is a space-time worm, extending a trajectory in which there are no jumps. Second, each worm is qualitatively continuous, in the respect that there are no points within the process where the entities being transformed terminate for an interval, having neither qualitative properties nor a place in space-time, only to reappear after the interval with altered qualities in the same or a different place. (I am supposing that the "quantum jumps" ascribed to electrons which disappear, then reappear, is a provisional description, one that is mistaken when construed as a claim about their existence. These particles are, I infer, hidden or disguised, not randomly annihilated, then recreated.)

The idea that entities retain their identity through the course of their transformations is problematic because of seeming to imply the essentialist view that an entity preserves the core of its properties through the history of its interactions and changes. We soften this claim by introducing the weaker notion of *generational continuity*. This signifies that every subsequent phase of a transformation has evolved from previous phases, though few of a structure's current properties were there in its earlier history. Butterflies generated from caterpillars, and frogs from tadpoles, are examples, but so is this writing paper generationally continuous with a tree, and before that with the soil and seed from which the tree grew. These transformations are not aimless or unconstrained. There are two limits upon them: material circumstances and the laws of nature. We have an example of constraining material circumstances where the bucket of paint pushed from a ladder has a bottom but no lid. The changes occurring surge through the network of these decided facts. But now we add that process is the transformation of material circumstances under the regulation of laws, as when the paint falls and splatters. Every generational continuity is the extension of changes through the filter of material circumstances and constraining laws.

8c. Causal laws are immanent not imposed

It is most important to the ontology of these continuities that the laws directing them are not separable from the entities which are engaged and transformed. For change is not like a chess game where pieces on the board are separable from the rules of the game. These rules are made to apply only as we move the pieces, for they exist in the heads of chess players, not on the board. Compare this to nature where the constraints operating within it are intrinsic to the changes themselves—e.g., as the laws of motion are intrinsic to the geometry of that space-time where changes occur. We have an example of these intrinsic constraints in the growth of crystals. Each of them embodies some characteristic mode of geometrical design, where the changes within a growing crystal are constrained by the symmetries which regulate its growth. A more familiar example is the complementarity of lock and key, where the turning of the key is limited by the complementarity of their two forms. It is by no means plain that every law has exclusively geometrical origins, as economic and sociological laws apparently do not. Still, we have a basis in these geometrical examples for the claim that the constraining force of natural laws is founded, intrinsically, in the properties of the things transformed.

8d. Stabilities

These things, the material agents for change, are *plastic structures* or *stabilities*. They are structures because their parts are arrayed in space and time. They are stabilities, because the form of their organization is sustained, however briefly. These structures are deformable (transformable) through a range of alterations—i.e., they are plastic. The lines of possible change are present within structures and their environments, as they are at least partly decided by the relevant gravitational or electro-magnetic forces operating within a region. Organizations which are more loosely assembled, and the ones constituted by rules or laws which are not reducible to the geometry of space-time, will have additional, sometimes conventional, constraints upon change, as civil law and custom are limits upon social change.

These constraints, whatever their origin, establish a "space" of material possibilities, for they determine the set of possible transformations for this system. These are the possible changes for this array of material agents. This "space" is not, however, the "logical space" of Wittgenstein's *Tractatus*.[2] That is a space of all logical possibilities. Material possibilities are, by comparison, those which are not foreclosed by the material constitution of this system, with its internal, constraining laws. The possibilities of this space are, therefore, only a subset of the totality of logical possibilities ascribed to logical space. It was only a logical, never a material, possibility that there be a witch so malign that she could have made toads of princes, though each of those young men could have varied in remarkable ways from their historical selves. There were other material possibilities for each of them, given their material character and circumstances, and the laws operating within them.

8e. Stabilities compared to Aristotle's primary substances

This description of stable systems is very close to the Aristotelian one of primary substance. Aristotelian substances are, however, usually inert. The structures described here are dynamical systems. Each one is sustained by the equilibriating effect of actions occurring within and outside it, as the flower pot on a window sill will crack or vaporize if the conditions inside or external to it are radically altered. There are equivalent effects for economies, weather systems, families, human bodies, and governments. Each one of them is an expression of the fact that motion is not stopped but only directed through a network of relations. A system is self-sustaining and stable so long as there is a source of energy, no breakdown of its parts, and no intrusion overwhelming the balance of mutually adjusting, internal processes. There are, of course, differences among systems, as the elements may be bound more or less tightly—e.g., the cells of our bodies as against people within social orders. But overall, every stable structure is like every other one in being an organized system of reciprocally related parts. These are the only self-sustaining entities, where even their autonomy is compromised by the fact that each one depends for its continued existence and character upon its relations to other systems. Accordingly, Aristotle's primary substances are replaced, for the purposes of this theory about causation, by entities which are to be described indifferently as *systems, structures,* or *stabilities.* These are the entities which are created and sustained as material circumstances are transformed under the constraining force of immanent laws.

8f. Stabilities are conditioned internally and externally

We begin seeing the utility of this notion for a theory of cause as we remark the two kinds of changes occurring to these structures.

8fi. INTERNAL CONDITIONS

Some are internal, occurring as changes in the composition or reciprocal relations of the parts. These changes may be so disruptive that the system comes apart. But equally, these internal changes may be accommodated as the system achieves or sustains equilibrium. Stable systems are more or less firmly defended against the intrusiveness of external relations by the mutually sustaining force of their internal relations, though no stability is proof against every intrusion, as the integrity of any apple is no barrier to a worm.

8fii. EXTERNAL CONDITIONS: SYSTEMS ORGANIZED HIERARCHICALLY

The system's external relations are equally significant for its character. Every structure is located in an environment of other more or less stable structures. Some of them are independent of one another, meaning that the existence and character of one are independent of the existence and character of the other or others. There are many examples of this independence, as the riders on a subway car are independent of one another in both respects. But it is very difficult establishing this independence when we consider the many subtle effects that things do have upon one another, whether physical or psychological. Independence is apparently a merely ideal and limiting case within any structure's environment. The only systems truly independent of some specified system are the ones occurring within that "absolute elsewhere" familiar to relativity theory. Those are the only things so remote from a structure as to have no possible effect upon it.

Every other system—i.e., all the ones within a structure's environment—have some degree of effect, however slight, upon its character. They are, to that extent, conditions for its existence. Each of these proximate structures has, therefore, one of two relations to the system at issue: they overlap it, or they are nested within or without it. Home and school are overlapping stabilities within a child's life, as the gravitational fields of Sun and Earth overlap one another. Nested stabilities are equally familiar, as every stable system falls within a hierarchy of larger systems, each one having an integrity and stability of its own; the borough of Manhattan in the City of New York in the State of New York, being an example. Each order within the hierarchy imposes its own constraints, so that a lowest or lower-order system has certain of its options foreclosed by one or another higher-order system.

Many of these overlapping or nested systems are ephemeral, as people defer to one another when passing on a sidewalk. But then it does happen sometimes that structures engage one another in ways that are reciprocally sustaining. A marriage or city is created as reciprocal relations are established among their constituent stable systems. These constituent systems are the material content of the higher-order ones; though high-order systems are nevertheless a limiting force upon them, as a city's laws apply to people living within it. The regulative force of these higher-order systems is all the plainer when lower-order systems are created within them to the standards they prescribe, as businesses are started within capitalist economies and lisping speech is taught within the communities that prize it.

8g. The cosmological system as an example of internally conditioned, hierarchically organized systems

The inclusiveness of higher-order systems is also confirmed in another way. There is one system, the cosmological one, which establishes a comprehensive limit upon the independence of constituent systems, as there never was a time when Earth could have existed alone, without mutually affecting relations to other bodies. The parts of our cosmological system are located within a network of mutually conditioning relations where the existence and character of each one is forever a function of both its internal order and its relations to some or all of the other constituent systems.

Is our world constituted of one higher-order system in which all the other stabilities are nested; or is it instead a system of overlapping stabilities, many of them organized hierarchically but with no single one containing all the rest? We may live in a world where both alternatives obtain. One order—i.e., space-time—may be a highest-order constraint upon every stability occurring within it. This pervasive and constraining order may, nevertheless, be tolerant of the many different hierarchies which are generated within it, somewhat as Earth is equally hospitable to diverse cultures while constraining all of them in some common ways. We may distinguish, therefore, between universal constraints and local organizations.

This cosmological system, whatever its constituents and their relations, will be the one stability whose existence is not conditional upon anything existing apart from itself. That will have been true even at the moment of its inception, so that the primal explosion creating our universe originated, if it occurred at all, in a system, however small and dense, where equilibrium was disrupted by something in it. This closed system is, we infer, self-differentiating and self-sustaining, though neither of these properties entails that it is also a necessary existent. For the fact that our world is actual, and not merely possible, is a contingent fact when other possible worlds remain, so far as we can tell, possibilities only. Some necessities are rightly credited to our universe, as the geometry of space-time supplies the context where differentiation and order are prescribed to the systems generated there; but these are necessities pertinent to the internal order of our world. They are incidental to every claim about the necessary existence of the whole.

8h. Are there least elements within stabilities?

Is there also a least order, one whose terms are material particles—i.e., "simples" rather than systems? Probably there are, though we are likely to be mistaken if we think of them as material particulars of fixed character. Each of these particles is likely to be a chameleon, meaning that it assumes any range of properties, with every current one depending on its present relations to other things. There might be several kinds of elements, each one distinguished by the range of its possible variations. We shall have to distinguish, if this is right, between a particle's current, manifest properties, and that determinable essence which qualifies it for that range of other properties which are exhibited as its circumstances change.

8i. Aggregation and configuration as the bases for composition

How is it that first-order stabilities—e.g., protons—are generated from these material elements? How does it happen that successively higher-order stabilities are constructed from these simpler ones? There may be several conditions for the compounding of particles and then of structures, but two are conspicuous: aggregation and configuration. Aggregation alone may account for human mental abilities, as our brains may differ from snail brains principally because of having vastly more nerve cells, with all the additional synapses this implies. A brain of aggregated cells is one instance of a higher-order system which imposes regulative principles upon its constituents and their activities even as they are its only constituents. Configuration also creates higher-order systems having properties peculiar to itself, as three parallel lines acquire novel properties when reorganized as a triangle. It may be true that every stable system is founded in one or both of those relations.

8j. Summary description of stabilities

Summarily now, I suggest that aggregation and configuration explain the fact that many or all stable systems incorporate material particulars or lower-order stabilities, while establishing distinctive capacities and behaviors of their own. All of nature might be the assembly of these overlapping, nested and reciprocally related stabilities, all of them composed of protean material elements embedded in space-time. Its inherent geometry, together with motion, the qualitative diversity among the kinds of material particles, and the principles of composition—e.g., aggregation and configuration—might be sufficient to explain all of the qualitative differences within our world.

8k. The relevance of causality in a world of stable systems

This ontology of self-transforming and mutually conditioning stable systems compares to Hume's claim that sensory atoms are static in themselves and unaffected by their spatial and temporal relations to atoms like themselves. The notions of causality associated with these ontologies differ in corresponding ways. Where Hume has reduced causality to constant conjunction, this proposal of mine requires all of Aristotle's four causes. Let us start with the three that are less problematic: formal, material, and efficient causes. A reformulated notion of final cause is introduced some paragraphs below.

8ki. FORMAL CAUSE

A stability's formal cause is its organization. This is a constraint upon its operation, as the flow of work through a business is constrained by the organization of its parts. Molecules and genes, motion of every sort, traffic patterns, recipes, and games: each of them embodies a form. Some of these forms are inert, as in a statue where the form carved into stone is incidental to whatever changes occur within it. Statues are therefore bad examples of formal cause, not the emblematic ones. The forms more important to us, and to nature, are those which constrain the changes occurring within stable systems; for example the weight-bearing frame of a building or the drive-train of a car. These are limits on change and the sustaining forms of stability.

8kii. MATERIAL AND EFFICIENT CAUSE

Material cause is the stuff organized by form, as both matters and their behaviors are ordered. Matter is a cause in two respects. First, it has capacities and tolerances peculiar to itself, as copper but not cement is an electrical conductor. This first point is critical; for it is not sufficient that matters are well organized if they cannot behave in the ways required. Second, matter is the carrier of motion, as there are bodies having trajectories, but also the undulations of waves. It is these bodies in motion which are efficient causes. Their motion is the agency both of change and stability: of change as things impinge upon one another with no off-setting resistance; of stability when successive changes create a network of mutually accommodating and sustaining effects. Striking a match is an unsustainable change, as the match is lit and destroyed. Two stars drawn together until each circles the other are a stable system.

8kiii. EFFECTS

Supposing now that we have formal, material, and efficient causes, we need ask about their effects. What are they? Effects are the states of a particle or system. They express its constitution, as the truth of the Pythagorean theorem expresses the ordering of parts within a right triangle, and as honesty is the effect of having one sort of character. These states may also be the result of a thing's engagements with other things, and in the case of systems, the result of interactions occurring within them. The effect may be a change from a previous state, or the sustaining of an established condition, as baldness is a change, while health is a sustained effect. Baldness may seem to be like health because of enduring; but the two are very different. Health requires that its conditions should persist. Baldness, like death of every sort, endures without being sustained. The effect endures as the causes dissipate. We must not agree however to the next likely inference, for the absence of sustaining conditions in examples like baldness does not entail that there are, or might be, occasions when all the causes are dissipated as the effect occurs. No effect can exist for any time without the persistence of one or more of its causes. That is so because the effect is either a change in one or more of the causes or the sustaining of a condition in or among them. The effect exists only as they do. This is the existential necessity of causal relations, as baldness presupposes a tire or scalp.

8kiv. NECESSITY AND CONTINGENCY IN CAUSAL RELATIONSHIPS

It is plainer now that the relation of cause and effect is a mixture of contingency and necessity. It is, for example, contingent that circumstances are as they stand; other arrangements were possible. It is also contingent that the things assembled are qualified to act as they can or do; there are possible worlds where things having these structural properties behave differently. But now, as these causes assemble, there are necessities of existence and form to limit the result.

Existential necessity is that conditional relation just described. Effects presuppose their causes because of being changes occurring within them or because of being sustained by the relationship of their causes, e.g., baldness and health.

Necessities of form are the constraints exercised by formal causes as they restrict the behaviors of material causes. We know from experience that locks do not always open to the correct key, though it is necessary that they open in every particular case, other things being equal. This necessity is founded in the complementary shapes of lock and key, where locks and keys reduced to just these geometrical properties would open, necessarily and unproblematically, in every single case. The "other things being equal" clause is, therefore, a reference to those additional, material, and contingent circumstances which may interfere with these otherwise necessary relations.

Not every necessity of form is geometrical. We can better understand the force of these other necessities if we consider a game whose rules are binding for every move within it. There are different games with other rules, but this game is defined by its material conditions—i.e., its board and pieces—and by the rules which determine what shall count as a correct move. Nature may be like this game, as changes within it are a function of material circumstances and the laws which restrict the changes occurring or sustained within them. All the regularities in nature are evidence for the application of these internal directives and constraints. This inherentist, determinist story is not confuted by the probabilistic claims of quantum theory, for even there we find that natural laws restrict the possible outcomes of a process to a very few, some of them having only the slightest chance of occurring. We may have to agree that some necessities of form do tolerate these variations, but this diminishes their constraining force in only the smallest way. It does not begin to justify Hume's claim that anything can happen when causes are assembled and engaged.

8kv. FINAL CAUSE

We have provided so far for the notions of formal, material, and efficient cause, all within the context of a nonintuitionist alternative to Hume's views about cause and effect. How shall we extend this reformulation of Aristotelian notions to cover the idea of final cause? Can we do that without having to invoke the idea of conscious intention, or that of a teleology inherent in every thing, living or not? The notion we require is already implicit in our characterization of stabilities. These are, we speculate, complex systems which have achieved a sustainable equilibrium within themselves, while accommodating in a more or less sustainable way to those other systems from which they derive energy and information. What is it that explains the establishing and sustaining of stable systems? It is, I suggest, a principle that is realized through the agency of formal, material, and efficient causes, though it applies to each stable system, and then to all of nature as a whole. That principle, our final cause, is the principle of least energy.

Imagine a relationship of mutual dependence, one that binds two friends. Each one is dissatisfied by the accommodation between them, so that both would like to withdraw from it. Neither one does withdraw because the cost of doing so is greater than the price of leaving things as they are. For "cost" and "price" read *energy*, where the relationship continues because the energy required for sustaining it is less than the amount required for dissolving it. This bond was formed when each of these two agents were willing and able to use quantities of "free" energy to alter the other one's patterns of behavior. But even then the quantity of energy available for securing a bond was limited, so that diminished effort was the one sure outcome: the turbulence between them would come to nothing, and they would part; or they would secure a less costly but sustainable relation to one another. Starting again was unlikely if they failed: separating is costly when the accommodation between them is already established.

Where is the source for the energy required to make or undo a stable system? Quantities of free energy are often generated within systems already established, and in the relationships of these systems. This energy is "free" in the respect that it may be diverted to other activities without harm to the stability of the system or systems where it is generated. There are three possible outcomes as the energy is used for altering a system or systems already established, or for creating new ones. First, it is possible, though unlikely, that energy might be generated and diverted, indefinitely, in behalf of some effect or accommodation which is never realized. Second, a new or altered stability is achieved, third, the energy is diminished or redirected.

Final cause is just this principle of economy: The result achieved and sustained is a consequence of the least amount of energy required for achieving it. Excessive energy is sometimes used, as we humans often use too much of it because of being ignorant of the amount required; but natural processes operating without human intervention do not typically overshoot the mark in a similar way. In them, the energy required for a new stability is more often proportionate to the energy expended. That new or altered stability sustains itself until its sources of energy are depleted or until the energy turned against it is superior to the energy available for sustaining it. The principle of least energy is, therefore, two things: On the one side, it is a mechanical principle operating by way of formal, material, and efficient causes; on the other side, it is a regulative principle operating on, within, and throughout nature. It is a final cause only in respect to having this regulative effect.

We are saved from having to regard natural processes as moving "toward" equilibrium for the sake of this principle. That teleological view of things is inappropriate and unnecessary when this least energy principle already operates within material processes as a mechanical principle. Notice too that no moral virtue goes with it, as fascist states are stable because of restricting the expression of energy, while democratic ones seem profligate in wasting it. Least energy is morally interesting only to stoics as they remark this character of things in order that they may accommodate more soberly to them. Final cause does not tell even these stoics which stabilities to prefer.

8kvi. RECIPROCAL CAUSATION

We come by the way of these considerations to a notion of causality that is appropriate to stable systems while integrating all four of Aristotle's four causes as interpreted above. This is the idea of *reciprocal* causation. Consider the molecules comprising any stable physical system. Each of them is reciprocally related to all those contiguous with it, and through them to all the other molecules constituting this thing. Each of them has a character of its own. Nevertheless, the character and existence of each molecule are partly conditional upon the character and existence of those others which engage it. This is the reciprocity between them. Every stable system is, in this way, reciprocally related to its neighbors, and beyond them to all the other stabilities that may affect it. Their reciprocity integrates all four of the causes mentioned above, for it is matters configured and constrained by form while in motion which establish these more or less sustainable, mutually conditioning relations.

The systems so created have a certain inertia, as the internal, reciprocal relations of their parts make them resistant to the intrusions of things external to them. But these systems must also be related to those other ones which supply their energy, and perhaps their information. Their reciprocity is a measure of their need for these two kinds of nourishment, as rocks are more autonomous than cities. There is of course no special virtue to reciprocity, as there is no virtue to a solar system or to bandits stealing from one another. Reciprocal causation, like the stabilities themselves, is a morally neutral but pervasive feature of that self-transforming nature where stabilities are regularly created, then breached, dissolved, or incorporated.

9. Hume on stable systems and their causes

This completes my sketch of a world rather different from the one that Hume describes. He says nothing whatever of stable systems, and his remarks about cause and effect are useless for understanding these systems as each one is established and sustained by the transactions occurring within and without it. We might try to justify Hume's neglect of stable systems by saying that the idea of them is merely a theory different from his own. But this is a feeble reply, because we have both the theory and the many things which confirm its applicability—e.g., human bodies, economies, galaxies and atoms. Each of them is established and sustained by the transactions occurring within and about it. It is not only a theory Hume ignores; he also neglects the entities and events comprising our world. Hume's ontology with his theory of cause and effect is oblivious to these realities. That makes his theory useless as any sort of precedent for an adequate metaphysics of nature.

10. Why we defer to Hume

Why is it that we take Hume so very seriously while knowing that his views are irrelevant to the transformations and stabilities occurring within nature? The answer seems to be that Hume is an intuitionist, speaking to philosophers who are themselves, mostly, intuitionists. If he can make the given safe for inspecting mind, eliminating every trace of speculation from our claims about it, then he has satisfied intuitionist scruples whether or not he has anything useful to say of nature. One says this while agreeing that the sensory data which Hume has emphasized are important to all our inquiries, whether practical, scientific, or metaphysical. These percepts are good evidence of nature and being, but they are not all of either one.

11. Some twentieth century Humean views about cause

No one who is mindful of nature's independence of mind and theory can forever agree that Hume's given is our one proper subject matter or that his views about cause and effect are adequate to the realities perceived. We turn, therefore, from Hume himself to Humeans writing about cause and effect in our century. Many of them are philosophers of science. Does this guarantee that their analyses of causality are more sensitive than Hume's own theory to its role within nature?

Consider the one formulation which dominates Humean thinking in our century. It suppose that we need not ascribe causal necessity or even causal efficacy to the relations among phenomena, because we have good scientific theories with which to describe, predict, and explain them. We are to assume that these theories are expressed in hypothetico-deductive form. The theories are ordered hierarchically so that most general hypothetical claims are the postulates from which lower-order theories, and then test sentences, are deducible. We formulate a theory so that we may understand the flux of sensory data; and now we apply the theory to circumstances that are or may be observed, deducing the theoretical or test sentences which explain or predict these phenomena.

11a. Hempel and Braithwaite on the use of hypothetico-deductive systems

Here are some passages from Carl Hempel and R.B. Braithwaite to illustrate this notion of cause. Both of them endorse Hume's view of it.

> [W]e are concerned with the nature of the difference, if any, between "nomic laws" and "mere generalization" . . . David Hume maintained that objectively there is no difference, but that a psychological fact about the way in which minds work causes us to ascribe necessity to scientific laws, the "idea of necessary connexion" being derived from our experience of the constant conjunction of properties and not from anything in nature over and above constant conjunction . . . I agree with the principle part of Hume's theses.[3]

> [T]he general maxim "Same cause, same effect," when applied to . . . explanatory statements, yields the implied claim that whenever an event of kind F occurs, it is accompanied by an event of kind G.[4]

Hempel and Braithwaite also agree about our reasons for formulating law sentences, as indicated by this quote from Hempel:

> Consider . . . the physical explanation of a rainbow. It shows that the phenomenon comes about as a result of the reflection and refraction of the white light of the sun in spherical droplets of water such as

those that occur in a cloud. By reference to the relevant optical laws, this account shows that the appearance of a rainbow is to be expected whenever a spray or mist of water droplets is illuminated by a strong white light behind the observer. Thus, even if we happened never to have seen a rainbow, the explanatory information provided by the physical account would constitute good grounds for expecting or believing that a rainbow will appear under the specified circumstances. We will refer to this characteristic by saying that the physical explanation meets the *requirement of explanatory relevance:* the explanatory information adduced affords good grounds for believing that the phenomenon to be explained did, or does, indeed occur. This condition must be met if we are to be entitled to say: "That explains it—the phenomenon in question was indeed to be expected under the circumstances!"[5]

Let us suppose that we apply Hempel's criterion of explanatory relevance as we explain that a key has opened a lock. We are to construct the system of hypotheses from which we deduce this result. Only as we have this system of laws do we justify our expectation that the lock will open as the key is turned. Still, the character of explanation is unresolved, for what is the object of our understanding? Is it only the system of laws from which correct predictions are derived; or is it some factor intrinsic to the relationships they signify? We might expect that these philosophers of science will acknowledge that the predictable relationship of lock and key has its foundations in the complementarity of their shapes, where geometry alone would make it necessary that this lock should open to a key of complementary shape.

This proposal is unacceptable to everyone who believes with Hume that the only basis for cause and effect relations is their constant conjunction. Everyone of that persuasion refuses to concede that explanations are founded in the relation of a law sentence or theory to the phenomena it represents. They prefer saying that explanation devolves only upon the relations of sentences within hypothetico-deductive systems. Braithwaite says it in the following way.

It is not necessary for . . . higher-level hypotheses to be established independently of the law which they explain; all that is required for them to provide an explanation is that they should be regarded as established and that the law should logically follow from them. It is scarcely too much to say that this is the whole truth about the explanation of scientific laws.[6]

There is, I infer, no ground or reason within the phenomena for the relationships signified by the law sentences deduced from a formalized system of laws—i.e., no factor additional to their constant conjunction. Everything that is significant for explanation is founded exclusively in the relations of these sentences.

This is odd, because it converts those necessary relations which are intrinsic to the geometry of space into the formal necessities of a syntactic structure. Necessities are purged from nature in order that they may be captured and exhibited within the systems which thought creates then uses for projecting form onto sensory data. The "ultimate explanation for a scientific theory," says Braithwaite, is "that of organizing our empirical knowledge in a way which will enable us to make reliable predictions."[7] This means, I suggest, that we are to use our formalized scientific theories for thinking of the world as if there were causes within it, though Hume has established that there is neither causal efficacy nor necessity within the things perceived. Hempel supplies an example. Semmelweis discovered that

> childbed fever was caused by decomposed animal matter introduced into the bloodstream through open surfaces. Thus formulated, the explanation makes no mention of general laws; but it presupposes that such contamination of the bloodstream generally leads to blood poisoning attended by the characteristic symptoms of childbed fever, for this is implied by the assertation that the contamination *causes* puerperal fever. The generalization was no doubt taken for granted by Semmelweis, to whom the cause of Kolletschka's fatal illness presented no etiological problem: given that infectious matter was introduced into the bloodstream, blood poisoning would result.[8]

This says plainly that we think causality into the world by way of the more or less explicit theories used for thinking about sensory data, though Hume has established that these data are, at most, constantly conjoined.

Is it true that causal laws are only the law sentences of our theories and not the regulative principles intrinsic to nature. Braithwaite answers in the following way:

> The nature of scientific laws cannot be treated independently of their function within a deductive system. The world is not made up of empirical facts with the addition of the laws of nature; what we call the laws of nature are conceptual devices by which we organize our empirical knowledge and predict the future.[9]

Why should we believe that laws of nature do not have regulative force *within* nature? There are two reasons: first, because the inference to uninspectable laws of nature violates the intuitionist stricture that everything real must be inspectable; second, because the inference to regulative forms existing independently of mind is unnecessary when we have an inspectable system of scientific law sentences, a system which makes correct predictions. No matter then if the world has no laws or causes within it. Intuitionism is satisfied that mind has its own forms for thinking the sensory given.

11b. Causality displaced from nature to the theories which make phenomena thinkable

This is a view which displaces causality from nature in order to provide for it by way of the semantical and syntactic features common to formalized theories. The motion of a cause is represented by its trajectory, as we plot the sequence of values for a four-place variable—i.e., three for space and one for time. Causal interaction is represented by plotting these trajectories as they cross or run together. The relation of cause and effect, hence, the efficacy of the causes, is expressed by the conditional—i.e., "if-then"—form of law sentences and by the universality of their quantifiers. The quantifiers imply that instances of the variables coupled within law sentences are constantly conjoined, as the universally quantified version of "If smoke then fire" implies that every instance of smoke will be coupled to one of fire. Causal necessity is just the deducibility of sentences predicting a certain correlation of events from the higher-order sentences of the theory. Causal powers, the dispositions qualifying things for change, are also to be represented by the conditional form of our law sentences, as 'can burn' means 'will burn if lit.' Accordingly, there is no aspect to our notion of cause which cannot be reformulated as a claim about the semantical or syntactic features of law sentences in their relations to a well-confirmed and formalized theory.

Why do these Humean philosophers of science require that this formalized theory be well-confirmed? Why couldn't we illustrate all the aspects of cause and effect by appealing to the semantical and syntactic features of a theory that is false? Why does truth or falsity matter when cause and effect are reduced to that formal and representational apparatus which is common to every formalized theory?

The reason for demanding a well-confirmed theory bears on its use. We are to think about the world by using a well-confirmed theory as we would use a pair of eyeglasses. Using the theory projectively, as a false theory could not be used, we think of the world as though there were causes and effects within it. We turn the theory upon the small details of our lives, thereby confirming the popular superstition that these things are suffused with cause and effect relations. We need only be careful that we do not overinterpret this projective use of the theory, for our Humean notion of cause and effect requires that we distinguish the flow of sensory data from those causal ideas which have no reference beyond the semantical and syntactic features of the formalized theory. Hume argued that our habits of expectation enable us to think about the world as though cause and effect were intrinsic to it. These logical empiricists substitute well-confirmed and formalized scientific theories for Hume's habits. But now as before, we are to have it both ways: we may think of nature as though causes and effects are present in it, though nothing occurring there is either cause or effect.

11c. Some advantages of these theories

This modern formulation does have two considerable advantages. On the one side, it dispenses with habit, a notion which is like causal necessity and causal power in having no inspectable referent. On the other side, it distinguishes between accidental conjunctions and nomic ones. It is an accident that every other creature breathes when I do. Anyone noticing this constant conjunction might have formed a habit of association, hence, an expectation about cause and effect. We establish that this conjunction is not lawful by showing that it cannot be deduced as a law statement from our sciences, though we can use them to explain it. In all of this, our hypothetico-deductive theories differentiate, organize, and unify the sensory data. Mind moves back and forth, looking first within the data or previous theories for clues useful for constructing a better theory, then using its revised theory for making the data more coherent than before. Mind is first the tailor who makes the suit, then the customer who wears it. Having established and projected the conditions for a thinkable order, we now see and enjoy the "world" as ordered within the system.

11d. Scientific theories as appropriated by intuitionists of form

The "logical empiricism" of this view is plainly an evocation of traditional intuitionisms of form. First is Plato's claim that order is discoverable in sensory experience because inspecting mind is equipped with a set of ideas used projectively. This implies that order in nature is, more fundamentally, order among the ideas with which we think it. Everyone wanting to learn of natural order and its conditions is encouraged to examine the ideas or sentences used for thinking about the world, rather than nature itself. Second is Descartes' belief that ideas are more economical and perspicuous if they are arranged deductively. At best, mind will survey the entire skein of ideas or sentences at once, seeing both the axioms and the theorems derived from them. At worst, we shall have to advance in steps, satisfying ourselves that every next line follows necessarily from the ones before it. Descartes supposed, as logical empiricists do not, that axioms should be self-evident. Still, their idea was his: Scientific truths are to be formalized so that they may stand before the mind's eye as a comprehensible expression of all the differences and relations properly credited to the world.

This interpretation of mind's role may seem a caricature to those who read Ernest Nagel's *Structure of Science,* R.B. Braithwaite's *Scientific Explanation,* or Carl Hempel's *Aspects of Scientific Explanation.* These are writers so well-versed in scientific theory and procedure as to make the rest of us tremble. It is, however, their conflation of philosophic motive with scientific learning which promotes the intuitionist bias, leaving it unexamined. Nature, as they describe it, is an aggregate of distinguishable and separate events, where these events reduce to sensory data. The only relations credited to these data are of two sorts.

First are their spatial and temporal relations. Kant has inferred from Hume's phenomenalism that space and time are merely the forms of intuition. This implies that the spatiality and temporality of sensory data reach no farther into the world than the sensorium of inspecting mind. There seems to be no place where Nagel, Braithwaite, or Hempel repudiates this Kantian view, saying that the spatial and temporal relations of the phenomena covered by scientific theories are independent of our minds.

The other relations credited to sensory data are the ones specified by our theories as we use them for thinking about the data. These are the relations used for sorting and organizing our percepts. They include the causal relations which are imputed to phenomena as we say, for example, that aspirin stops headaches. We are to realize, even as we say this, that these causal relations have no place within the world itself, that they devolve entirely upon the semantical and syntactic features of the theories used for thinking or talking about the world. Never mind that nature all but disappears, only surviving to the extent that it is visible through the projective machinery of our theories. Perhaps we should not regret its demise, for nature in itself is unintelligible if theories are the source for all that is intelligible within the sensory manifold. This reduces nature to the status of a thing-in-itself, to something that is dispensible because it is unthinkable.

11e. All of form displaced from nature to mind by way of theory

This is the last step in a remarkable evolution. Descartes, following Galileo, isolated human experience from the subject matters of physics. Mind would be the authority regarding logic, values, and itself when science had established its responsibility for our claims about nature. The distinction between primary properties, as science discovers them, and the secondary properties which dominate our human experience of nature had marked this division. Now, contemporary intuitionists writing as philosophers of science have restored the unity of thought and experience. They do that on the side of intuiting mind and Kant's First Critique. All of form, meaning every difference and relation, is to originate within the mind. The schematized given, now described as the "world," is said to be intelligible just because mind thinks about it in the ways prescribed by our theories. All the bases for intelligibility within nature are reformulated then relocated within them. These scientific theories do, of course, tell us about the details and correlations of events within the world; but that is merely secondary to the uses for which the theories are appropriated by intuitionist philosophers. For we need remember that philosophers of science write as philosophers, not as scientists. They do have prodigious information about science, but they are not investigators of nature. Nagel, Hempel, and Braithwaite are careful observers of scientific practice; but more fundamentally, they are in-tuitionists of form, classifying and clarifying the structures with which inspecting mind thinks the given.

11f. Nagel's formulation of the causal principle

These eminent philosophers would no doubt reject my charac-terization of them as intuitionists of form, greatly indebted to Hume's intuitionism of content. Ernest Nagel, especially, has deplored the a priorism of those who claim a privileged, transcendental point of view. Still, this philosophic appropriation of scientific theory for pre-scriptivist, intuitionist purposes operates in him too. Several things confirm this. First is Nagel's assumption that causality is a principle of uniformity operating upon or within thought or theory, rather than a productive relation among things. Nagel's bias is emphatic when he summarizes a discussion of some alternatives:

> What is the upshot of this discussion of the logical status of the princi-ple of causality? Is the principle an empirical generalization, an *a priori* truth, a concealed definition, a convention that may be ac-cepted or not as one pleases?[10]

These are options within thought. None of them acknowledges that cause and effect might be a transforming relation among particulars, because Nagel supposes that causality is only a principle for organiz-ing our thought about the world. This is plainest where he remarks that the notion of cause is essential to the task of scientific inquiry.

> [T]he actual pursuit of theoretical science in modern times is directed toward certain goals, one of which is formulated by the principle of causality. Indeed, the phrase 'theoretical science' appears to be so gen-erally used that an enterprise not controlled by those objectives would presumably not be subsumed under this label. It is at least plausible to claim, therefore, that the acceptance of the principle of causality as a maxim of inquiry (whether the acceptance is explicit or only illus-trated in the overt actions of scientists, and whether the principle is formulated with some precision or only vaguely) is an *analytic conse-quence* of what is commonly meant by 'theoretical science'.[11]

I take this to mean that causality is essential to the world as thought, where scientific theories are the instruments of thought. The world is intelligible, says Nagel, only as causality is one of the principles for organizing our thoughts about it.

There is one ambiguity in Nagel's account of these views: might he be reporting rather than endorsing them? This might be the more likely interpretation if Nagel had not endorsed Humean views about causality, thereby denying that cause and effect might be the terms of a productive relation within nature. Still, Nagel, no more than Braithwaite or Hempel, is an orthodox Kantian transcendentalist. All of them suppose that the categories and rules of thought are maxims that we may change if our purposes or circumstances require it. We could, for example, do our scientific theorizing without the principle of causation, though our science would be less effective because of making the world less comprehensible. Should we nevertheless dispense with cause and effect as a principle of explanation when so many physicists hardly mention them? That is unnecessary when the idea of cause and effect has been reduced already to the metaphysically innocuous one of uniformity—i.e., to constant conjunction— and when the derivability of true predictions from our well-confirmed theories is our only way of distinguishing accidental conjunctions from the lawful, "causal" ones. Cause and effect remains, therefore, an essential notion for thinking the world.

11g. Summary

Intuitionists of form have appropriated scientific theories, using them to differentiate and integrate the sensory given while adding such metaphysical nuances as this hypothetico-deductive reformulation of Hume's views about cause and effect. All of this serves the purposes of thought as it schematizes the sensory given. None of it counts towards a philosophy of nature, because nature's own character is never allowed to disrupt our preoccupations with the making of a theory adequate for thinking the given.

This charge may seem to be very farfetched when the theories used for thinking the world are the ones of science. For surely, nothing surpasses them as representations of whatever is deep and determining within nature. The appearance of irony or paradox is superficial. Intuitionists are drawn to scientific theories because of their power for differentiating and integrating the sensory given, not because these theories may be construed realistically as a correct specification of the decisive variables within nature. Scientists typically regard their theories as important in this latter sense. Intuitionists do not. A theory's penetration into the generative conditions within nature is irrelevant to them, except derivatively as it leads to the formation of additional laws for thinking the sensory given.

We confirm this bias by seeing it expressed in a familiar example. Consider the idea mooted before: that nature is comprised of more or less stable systems, each one independent of some others, but all of them nested within or without, and overlapping, many more. Causality is the generating and sustaining relation within and among these systems. It is the productive and sustaining relation within a self-transforming and self-stabilizing nature. There are three ways to understand this claim: as a characterization of nature in itself; as speculative overdescription of the sensory given; as a set of ideas for thinking the given.

Philosophers of science like the ones mentioned here would refuse to consider these notions in the first way, because they devote themselves to clarifying and justifying the forms and procedures of scientific thinking. They make no claims about the character of that reality which is independent of our thinking it. The second alternative would have been congenial to Hume, and perhaps to these philosophers of science, because no one who inspects the sensory given will discover self-equilibriating systems within it. This is an idea that is introduced by the hypotheses used for thinking the sensory given, not one that might be confirmed by inspecting it. "Speculative overdescription" is, therefore, one likely intuitionist response to this proposal. The third alternative is the one most likely to be preferred by intuitionist philosophers of science, because this hypothesis about stable systems is the gloss of one physical theory: We can use thermodynamics as a system of laws for thinking about the world as though it were constituted of stable systems. What we cannot do, if we are intuitionists, is imagine that our ways of thinking the given signify deep structures within a reality that is independent of mind for its character and existence. Intuitionists reply that no world of that description is thinkable. The only world that they would have us know is the sensory world differentiated and integrated by the ideas, rules, or theories used for thinking it.

This is the intuitionism of form. Hume's notion of cause and every scientific claim is made to satisfy its prescriptivist aims.

12. Whitehead's notion of cause

There are two plausible starting places for intuitionist metaphysics. One is the given as its is perceived or thought. Hume and his twentieth-century successors start here: Hume as he deflates Aristotle's claims by demanding that we confirm them within the sensory given; the Humeans of our time as they reformulate the idea of cause in terms that are appropriate to the formal systems used for thinking the given. The other intuitionist starting point is the psychology assumed by intuitionist method: we may generalize about the world, or some feature of it, from our notion of mind as self-enclosing and self-sustaining, hence, autonomous. This alternative starting point is significantly different from the first one, as attention to Whitehead's views will show. There is, however, a remarkable convergence when the intuitionist passion for form overrides this difference, appropriating Whitehead's notion of cause as easily as it subsumes the Humean one. Where twentieth-century Humeans use scientific theories for reading cause and effect into nature, we shall see that historians and literary critics could as easily (though typically they do not) found their claims about interpretation on Whitehead's notion of cause. All that is prospective. We start with the particulars of Whitehead's views.

12a. Actual occasions

Fundamental to him is the idea of a subject which integrates its sensory affects by way of its ideas and values, thereby creating an experience focused by this subject's aims. Whitehead characterizes these subjects as "actual occasions." Each of them exists for a moment. It comes into being and perishes, while having no dynamic relations to any other moment like itself. Reality is composed of only these actual occasions and the eternal objects—i.e., the Forms—which are ingredient within their internal differentiations and orders. Every actual occasion "prehends" its antecedents by way of the effects they have upon it. These affects are sensory data, similar at least to the ones described by Locke. They are the given.

Actual occasions represent and know the world by way of these affects, though occasions differ in their powers for articulating and integrating them. At the lowest order of awareness, prehendings are merely felt; at higher orders, they are also distinctly perceived and represented symbolically. Every occasion, whatever its powers for representing the world, is a perspective on its antecedents. For Whitehead insists that his views are pre-Kantian: we know the things which have affected us by way of their effects upon us. Those objects for knowledge are the occasions antecedent to the knowing occasion. They are not, as Kant supposed, objects created by mind as it organizes its sensory data. It is this regard for objects known, not made, which justifies Whitehead's claim that his theory is a reversion to pre-Kantian themes.

12b. The problem of knowing an effect's cause

Whitehead's notion of cause and effect is all but explicit. We are acquainted with the effects and thereby with the causes, for the effects on us are the termination of their influence. We who look backwards, wanting to reconstruct the sequence of causal processes, are helpless to do that, because we can go no farther than the effects within us. Our predicament is the one that Locke described: We know things only as they affect us. Their real properties, including their ways of acting upon us, are unknowable.

12c. Causation eliminated

Whitehead solves this problem of knowledge in a most economical way. He reduces the relationship of causes generating an effect to the response of the subject affected. It differentiates and integrates its affections in the ways prescribed by its ideas and subjective aim. Each occasion is then prehended by its successors, though the transmission of this influence is altogether mysterious when nothing ever passes between them: "[A]n actual entity never moves."[12] There is, therefore, no mechanism whatever for explaining the fact that a successor occasion might prehend its antecedents. Imagine a streak of drops on a windshield. Whitehead's actual occasions are related in a corresponding way; each one is discrete, no one can depend in any way upon the others. There is only the sequence of actual occasions. Every one interprets its antecedents, then perishes. We have effects but no causes.

12d. Prehension

Whitehead almost disguises this implication by his use of the word "prehension." It suggests that we know the things affecting us, as we see the sun and not merely its effects upon us. This use of the word is misleading when compared to the more detailed claims of Whitehead's theory. Consider the prehendings of an actual occasion, one of those having the higher-order capacities for thought and symbolic representation. These prehendings are received and "felt," then clarified by the ingression, that is, the thought, of eternal objects. Using the ideas of heat and light, this occasion categorizes its prehendings, making them intelligible. What is more, it characterizes these affects as prehendings of the sun. Notice, however, that the whole identity of the thing seen is contituted within the prehending occasion: this occasion has interpreted its prehendings by assigning them to a putative object outside itself while having no way to confirm that there is any thing of that kind.

The thing "prehended" is reminiscent of the "transcendental object" in Kant's First Critique. We cannot help thinking of the world as if there were things existing apart from us while affecting us; but this is an idea of reason, not a fact. It is an idea having no confirmable, or even conceivable application to things existing independently of us. The attitude encouraging this realism is only the delusion of our human nature if, as Whitehead argues, nothing is prehended by way of its effects because no actual occasion acts upon or is acted upon by any other one.

12e. Actual occasions are self-caused

There is just one exception to the rule that Whitehead's views about cause and effect eliminate the causes. He does say that actual occasions are self-caused.

> An actual entity feels as it does feel in order to be the actual entity which it is. In this way an actual entity satisfies Spinoza's notion of substance: it is *causa sui*. The creativity is not an external agency with its own ulterior purposes. All actual entities share with God this characteristic of self-causation.[13]

There are two aspects to this notion of self-causation. First, actual occasions come into being *ex nihilo*. This is a conclusion entailed by the claim that actual occasions are discrete with no motion between them. No occasion will have "material" conditions beyond itself, so that each one is responsible altogether for everything within itself, including the fact of its existence. This coming to be, from nothing, is a mystery that we shall consider below. Second is the process of self-transformation. Prehendings are differentiated, then integrated in ways determined by an occasion's subjective form and aims. Subjective form includes moods and emotions. Subjective aims are a set of ranked values. These two, as much as the ingression of eternal objects, i.e., ideas, determine the final integration of every occasion's prehendings. The result of this process is a culminating unification. The occasion becomes what Whitehead describes as a "subject-superject." This is a unity reaching beyond itself to the fulfillment of its aims.

12f. New causal powers

Whitehead supposes that an actual occasion acquires new causal powers as its own prehendings are differentiated and integrated; other things will be affected differently because of this transformation within it. We might reject this claim, saying that nothing can be affected by this new occasion because it will perish without having touched or changed its successors. This is correct if we interpret Whitehead in the literal way required by his own words, for then the lack of dynamic relations among successive occasions precludes the influence of any one upon the others. Suppose, however, that we are more tolerant in allowing examples that might illustrate his more expansive views about cause because of preferring some of his more allusive language.

Consider the effects integrated within an actual occasion, as colors and shapes are unified within a painting. The power in this actual occasion is the analogue to the difference that a picture can make when it is seen and enjoyed. The antecedent does not act but is instead the cause of its successor because of the way that it is perceived. The antecedent makes a difference, not because of anything it has done, but rather because of what it is prehended as being. Its role as cause does not surpass the creating of a causal power within itself.

Anyone who is changed by the paintings he sees or the newspapers he reads is an argument for this complex notion. It combines Whitehead's two ideas of cause: One actual occasion prehends its antecedent when that earlier occasion has transformed itself. Both partners in this relationship are active, though in different ways. The antecedent is active as it completes itself. The successor is active as it prehends the antecedent, sometimes altering its own values in order to integrate this prehending within itself. Whitehead speaks to us as thinkers who position ourselves within the world by evaluating the things which affect us. This is the point that is generalized when Whitehead says that everything takes a position on the things it prehends, applying, however dimly, its own ideas and values.

12g. The experiential basis for this notion of cause

We see that Whitehead's notion of causality is alternately retrospective and prospective: the one, as an occasion prehends its antecedents; the other, as it completes itself in order that it may be prehended by a successor. This is the attitude that we should expect of an ontology which is founded within, then generalized from, human experience. For we do gather our perceivings and memories of things past on the way to projecting ourselves into the future. Nothing could be more plausible or familiar to a writer who is steeped in Descartes, Leibniz, and Kant, then Nietzsche and James. These are thinkers who founded or perfected the romantic conviction that all of the world is summed and then advanced within the pulses of human experience.

Whitehead's notion of cause and effect, like all of his ontology, expresses his reverence for this anthropomorphic idea. Still, Whitehead's causes are ineffectual. That is so, because his theory of cause is genetic, never generative. Each moment of experience has a succession of antecedents and successors, but there is no provision within Whitehead's theory for the generation of successors from their antecedents. No actual occasion is produced from or by any other one. Each one is like the impressions that Hume describes: It comes to exist unconditionally, then perishes. This confirms that Whitehead's notion of cause is one more instance of the serial, substitutional account favored by Hume. This is not process, but only succession.

12h. Whitehead's intuitionist assumptions

We can explain this result by identifying the intuitionist assumptions which entail it. Whitehead's intuitionism is explicit.

The philosophy of organism in its account of prehension takes its stand upon the Cartesian terms *"realitas objectiva," "inspectio"* and *"intuitio."* The two latter terms are transformed into the notion of a "positive prehension," and into operations described in the various categories of physical and conceptual organization.[14]

12hi. THE INTUITIONIST BASIS FOR PREHENSION

There are two assumptions, fundamental to intuitionist method, which help to make it plausible that actual occasions prehend their causes. This intuitionist support is not incidental when the dynamics of "prehension" are so very dubious because Whitehead has said these two things: that there is no motion between actual occasions, and that the antecedent has already ceased to exist at the moment when its successor comes to be.

One assumption is the conflation of thought's content with the object thought. Intuitionism has reduced the objects of thought to the inspectable given. We are to identify those objects with ideas and sensory data, or with schematized data, rather than use the contents as signs for thinking about matters which are not immediately present to our minds. We may suppose that we are thinking about objects standing beyond these inspectable contents, but that is, as mentioned above, a delusion. Whitehead does want to use these contents as signs of antecedent, now annihilated, actual occasions. How does this intuitionist argument help him? By supplying him with the content for thinking prehended antecedents, and with the justification for supposing that these inspectable contents are the living presence of the objects thought.

The other assumption is helpful now, for intuitionism affirms that *esse es percipi.* These data before the mind are not the remote consequences of things past, but rather the very presence of the thing prehended. They lie within it by virtue of their efficacy upon it. This confirms Whitehead in saying that a monad locked within itself does nevertheless have access to the things preceding it. Though now as before, nothing has been said to justify the claim that there is any relation between a current occasion and its antecedents.

Joining these two assumptions, we affirm that mind cannot know anything of the things prehended except their effects upon it. Equally, mind cannot know its efficacy upon other things. Hypotheses which might extend thought and knowledge beyond these immediacies are banned, because there is no way that we might confirm them—i.e., no way that we might have unmediated access to the things identified by the hypotheses. We are reduced, as Whiteheadian intuitionists, to the knowledge of mind's own inspectable becomings.

12hii. THE INTUITIONISM OF SELF-CAUSATION

The other notion of causality, that actual occasions are self-creating, carries still farther into the essentials of intuitionist thought. For how could Whitehead justify his claim that the world is composed only of self-creating moments of subjectivity? The answer has its inception in that oracular passage quoted several times above.

> I am, I exist: it is certain. For how long however? Well for as long as I think, for perhaps it could even happen that were I to stop all thinking, I would with that completely cease to be.[15]

Whitehead's actual occasions, like Descartes' *cogito*, exist only as they think. They cease to exist when prehendings are integrated in accord with a subjective aim; that is when the task of thinking one particular set of data is finished. Descartes requires that thinking should not be a sufficient condition for the *cogito*'s existence; it must also think itself in order that there may be evidence of its existence. Whitehead is not so demanding.

> The principle that I am adopting is that consciousness presupposes experience, and not experience consciousness. It is a special element in the subject forms of some feelings. Thus an actual entity may, or may not be conscious of some part of its experience.[16]

> Consciousness is a subjective form arising in the higher phases of concrescence. . . . It follows that the order of dawning, clearly and distinctly, in consciousness is not the order of metaphysical priority.[17]

Nothing, I suppose, has experience, unless it is conscious, so that Whitehead's objection to the universal applicability and priority of consciousness is intended as an observation about self-consciousness. If we read "consciousness" where Whitehead writes "experience" and "self-consciousness" where he writes "consciousness," then we may interpret him as saying that subjectivity exists whenever there is consciousness—i.e., thinking or experience. Consciousness, not self-consciousness, is metaphysically prior. This would not satisfy Descartes, because he wants inspectable evidence of something's existence before affirming that it exists. Even mind must provide evidence of itself to itself in order that we may be certain of its existence. Whitehead cannot agree, because he wants to generalize the notion of subjectivity beyond human experience to every existent. Where lower forms of existence might be conscious but not self-conscious—i.e., capable in Leibniz's terms of perception but not apperception—Whitehead softens Descartes' more rigorous standard. Still, he does agree that the existence of actual occasions is conditional on their thinking. They exist only as there are prehendings to unify. When that is done, they perish.

Let us consider these drops of experience. What are the steps as Whitehead argues that each of them is a momentary thinking? Three remarks help to focus the argument.

> [Descartes] laid down the principle, that those substances which are the subjects enjoying conscious experiences, provide the primary data for philosophy, namely, themselves as in the enjoyment of such experience. This is the famous subjectivist bias which entered into modern philosophy through Descartes. In this doctrine Descartes undoubtedly made the greatest philosophic discovery since the age of Plato and Aristotle.[18]

> This doctrine fully accepts Descartes' discovery that subjective experiencing is the primary metaphysical situation which is presented to metaphysics for analysis. This doctrine is the "reformulated subjectivist principle."[19]

> The actual things (Descartes said) "required nothing but themselves in order to exist."[20]

What is the argument for saying that actual occasions exist only so long as they think? There is no argument. Whitehead merely repeats, with some embellishments, Descartes' own views. How could one justify proceeding in this way? Only by supposing with Descartes that nothing is better known to mind than mind itself. Thought thinking itself is the stable center to which intuitionism forever returns us, with no obligation to provide the justifying arguments.

We are closer now to having an intuitionist explanation for the claim that actual occasions are self-centering. This idea has two aspects: First, the actual entity is the sole cause of its own development, after, second, being created *ex nihilo*. Autonomous self-development is not too surprising an idea if we consider the self-made man or the unhatched chicken taking all its nourishment from inside the egg. Creation *ex nihilo* is more problematic, for how could it be that something is created from nothing?

We normally think about this issue by using examples that are physical. We then befuddle ourselves by trying to imagine that matter might be created from nothing. This is easily done by following Hume's example: we imagine the thing by itself, without regard for its antecedents. But this "thought experiment" seems trivial when respect for the principle of sufficient reason and the principle that matter and energy are conserved combines with reverence for the Greek arguments that nothing can come to be from nonbeing. Could it be true that Whitehead is saved from having to consider these principles and arguments merely because his actual occasions are moments of experience rather than physical objects? A moment of experience might seem to be exempt from the principle that matter and energy are conserved; it might not seem to require antecedents that are sufficient to produce it. If we also suppose that Greek arguments against the possibility of existence *ex nihilo* are directed only to the existence of material things, then we might feel safe, if precarious, in saying that actual occasions are self-caused in this radical way. Still, that claim is unconvincing if there is no explanation telling how these occasions might come to exist in the absence of conditions.

Whitehead may have supposed that we justify the idea of existence *ex nihilo* by citing the paradigmatic case where the thing creating itself is a mind thinking itself. There are two considerations. First is the Cartesian claim that thinking has no material conditions; this is important if material things cannot be created from nothing. Consider now the things having no material conditions—and what is more, no conditions beyond themselves—for this invites the second point: that all the conditions for thinking are intrinsic to the thinking. Thinking, this says, is self-conditioned. Rather than emphasize the phrase, *ex nihilo,* we say that thinking occurs "spontaneously," meaning not that it occurs "from nothing" but rather that its occurrence is unconditioned or "free," Mind's lack of conditions is, therefore, just the freedom to create itself by thinking of other things while thinking itself.

12i. Self-causation and freedom

This is, I concede, only the inferred explanation for Whitehead's claim: he implies, without quite saying it. This is, however, the explanation which best coheres with the psycho-centric ontology of his intuitionist method. Intuitionism wants to say that self-inspecting mind is self-conditioning and self-sustaining. Mind is responsible for its own existence and development. It is not surprising, therefore, that mind should want to locate the inception of its existence in mind's freedom for thinking other things and itself.

Whitehead stresses the idea of "creativity," using it to signify the novel integrations produced within the many actual occasions. But it may also be true that the more fundamental expression of creativity is our self-creation. Self-creating self-consciousness is vital to intuitionists. They require that mind's freedom to think should be exhibited and confirmed as mind thinks itself. This assumes with Descartes that nothing exists, including the freedom to create ourselves, if it is not witnessed.

This will be a complex freedom. It will include the freedom to think oneself while thinking some other thing; and the freedom for thinking oneself while deciding what other things to think and how to think about them. Whitehead would not be alone in believing that this is so. Aren't there many intuitionists who testify to mind's freedom, all of them inviting us to inspect ourselves, discovering there our unconditioned freedom for thought. The "freedom" they claim for thought is our modern euphemism for the dubious claim that something might come to exist *ex nihilo*.

12j. Whitehead as the intuitionist metaphysician of form

This is a reconstruction of assumptions which Whitehead never articulates. It is, however, consistent with the things he does say; and it saves him the embarrassment of having nothing to say when asked to justify the claim that every condition for the existence of actual occasions is located within them. This also has the effect of making Whitehead the largely unacknowledged metaphysician for this century's many intuitionists of form. These are philosophers who suppose that everything intelligible within reality is founded in the systems that mind creates as it thinks the given. These may be scientific theories or the interpretations of literature, history, or morals. They may seem to be value-neutral or emphatically evaluative. Either way, these are mind's expressions as it affirms and exhibits itself in the act of making the world thinkable.

All of this is explicit as we join Whitehead's two notions of causality: the one as mind creates itself in its freedom to think, the other as thinking differentiates, then integrates a content. Interpretation, he might have said, is mind's freely chosen self-constitution. This is the way that mind comes to think the world and itself. This is all that is or could be intended when we say that mind is self-creating.

Interpretation engages all three of the aspects implied by Descartes when he writes of the *cogito:* Something is given then inspected by first-order awareness, while second-order awareness regards the complex data perceived, sometimes intruding upon them to provide ideas and values, or to withhold assent. Consider now an actual occasion, one having "experience" and "consciousness"— i.e., consciousness and self-consciousness. This occasion differentiates then integrates its prehendings by way of its ideas, moods, and values. All of its short lifespan is devoted to interpreting these affects. Turning upon itself in the act of self-constitution, this occasion takes the measure of itself as a thinker having a point of view. This is an agent which secures its existence in two ways: first, by interpreting the world in a way peculiar to itself; second, by regarding and affirming itself.

Did Sartre read Whitehead? Did Carnap realize that the semantical frameworks used for making the world thinkable are the devices of a monad affirming its own ideas and values, and thereby itself? It is likely that neither of them knew much of Whitehead. But that is a shame, when their intuitionism is so much in debt to the foundations which he refined. "Causation," Whitehead has argued, is "nothing else than one outcome of the principle that every actual entity has to house *its* actual world."[21] I read this passage in the following way: Mind creates a differentiated but unified world by using words, thoughts, values, or moods for making it thinkable. But then it also follows that mind creates itself in the act of thinking its world.

12k. Reciprocal causality and the nexus

We have to temper this reading of Whitehead lest it drive him to solipsism. That intimation is countered only as we remember that Whitehead has insisted that every actual occasion prehends its antecedents, while relating to their contempories within "nexus." No actual occasion is alone in the world, because each one is related within "societies" to myriad others, where only God prehends their totality.[22] This is one last place where Whitehead's theory of cause should be vital to him, for we expect that there will be some dynamic relation to bind the socialized occasions. The issues relevant now are familiar to us, because nexus should be similar, at least, to the complex, stable systems described above. I suggested earlier in this chapter that reciprocal causation is fundamental to the stabilizing of these systems, where each part of a system depends for its existence and character upon its reciprocal relations to the other parts. Could Whitehead agree?

Whitehead defines "nexus" by saying that "any . . . togetherness among actual entities is called a 'nexus.' "[23] Their togetherness is a kind of order. Whitehead describes some of the bases for order in the section entitled "The Order of Nature" in *Process and Reality*.[24] He acknowledges the several kinds of natural order, including the geometrical character of space-time, and the organizing effects of gravity and electromagnetism. He also writes carefully of the hierarchical relations of ordered systems, where larger-scale systems provide the stabilizing conditions for orders of smaller scale. Whitehead is sensitive in every significant way to the differences among systems that are independent, overlapping, or nested. Only one thing is awry: Whitehead's ontology of actual occasions and his notion of cause subverts this accurate and subtle rendering of stable systems.

The problem is that Whitehead has atomized what he calls the "extensive continuum." Its only constituents are actual occasions. Each of them is distinguished from the others by the antecedents it prehends and by the integration of its prehendings. These differences among actual occasions serve the double purpose of individuating and ordering them. Every occasion is unique because of being a novel interpretation of its antecedents; the many occasions are ordered, if only in the minimal respect that they are differentiable in their qualitative diversity. There is no intrinsic order of a more systematic and objective kind. Why is that so? For the reason that order among the many actual occasions has shattered into as many pieces as there are occasions: "The notion of 'order' is primarily applicable to the objectified data for individual entities."[25] This is a way of saying that order is only the relationship produced within every actual occasion by the integration of its prehendings.

Where is the reciprocity that would organize these occasions by limiting each one's freedom while sustaining it in some way? There is no reciprocity among them. Each one can only look backward to its antecedents and forward to its subjective aim. Relations to its contempories are only those of qualitative similarity and difference. This is the place where Whitehead looks past nature for a solution to the problem of order. He invokes the notion of God, saying that God is the actual occasion prehending all the finite occasions in their togetherness. But this is feeble when God's prehension of those occasions is different from the occasions themselves, so that the order in which He thinks them is only the order that God has imposed when thinking them as a totality.

13. Whitehead and Hume

Whitehead requires that his God should establish the relatedness of contemporaneous occasions by thinking them together. Hume also provides for the causality of things by thinking them together; that is, by thinking one when perceiving the other. Each of them is impelled to this result because of assuming that nothing can be ascribed to reality if it cannot be set before our inspecting minds. Too little of the dynamics within causal relationships is perceivable, so that Whitehead and Hume are obliged to reduce that relationship to something that can be inspected.

They are not bothered when their notions of cause and effect are useless for explaining the particular effects occurring at every moment throughout nature, where individual causes are altered or their properties and relations are sustained because of dynamic relations within the sets of causes. No matter that all of this is as commonplace as lighting a match or kissing a child; Whitehead and Hume cannot identify the factors which justify our saying that every single event in nature is a paradigm of causal efficacy.

The clumsiness of applying their notions to the particularities of ordinary practice and nature in general is not so intimidating to them, because neither measures himself against the demand that we make our theories adequate to matters of fact. Whitehead and Hume answer principally or only to this other demand, namely, that we formulate our theories in ways that satisfy intuitionist scruples. If theory is mute about the particularities and reciprocities known to practical life and science, then too bad for them. The principle virtue is fidelity to the intuitionist demand that we say nothing of the world unless inspecting mind can verify it. Whitehead and Hume are true to that principle, each in his own way. We are forced to choose: Cripple ourselves in knowing the world; or reject, then replace, their intuitionist method.

Chapter Six

Systematic Metaphysics: Mind's Appropriation of Being

1. Systematic metaphysics

M etaphysics is systematic when it formulates theories so that they may be applicable and adequate to all of Being. Topical metaphysics has said that its principle, separable if distinguishable, speaks to deep fissures in Being. Systematic metaphysics replies that every notion separated from those others to which it relates essentially is distorted and incomplete.

2. Two meanings of *systematic*

There are two familiar senses to the word *systematic,* one of them relevant here. Thought is systematic in an incidental way if it provides one or a set of rubrics for organizing data of some kind. A telephone director is systematic in this first way. Subscribers are listed on the basis of a double contingency: first on the accident of their names; second on the fact that first letters of their names come early or late in the alphabet. Organizing principles of this sort are extrinsic to the matters organized. They facilitate the addition of new entries and the locating of old ones, but they say nothing of the people listed. Systematic theories of the other kind organize their subject matters on the basis of properties which are inherent, as a table of the elements differentiates and organizes them by reference to properties intrinsic to them. Every systematic metaphysician claims to be systematic in this second way. Each one addresses himself to the categorial features which are intrinsic to Being.

3. The result to be explained

The questions for this chapter devolve upon the character of these inherent categorial features. Should we understand difference and relation, unity, existence, substance, change, and law in the terms of a mind thinking the given? Should we agree that mind as it thinks the given and knows itself is the example for every other claim about reality? These alternatives summarize the two derivative choices for metaphysics within the intuitionist tradition. Each of them assumes that Being is rightly appropriated by mind, either because mind creates a thinkable given, or because mind is the model for everything that does or can exist. All the world's inherent categorial features are to be acknowledged in the one way or the other: within the given, or within mind's own structure. These alternatives are derivative, because there is an ancient though abiding tradition which accommodates both of them, Mind, it says, incorporates Being. Every part of reality, this implies, is either a feature within the given that mind has thought, or some aspect of the mind which has created the world by thinking it.

My aim in this chapter is a reconstruction, part historical, part dialectical, of the motives and claims which promote this view. When that history has been reformulated, I shall say that twentieth century linguistic philosophy is heir to the holism and idealism of this tradition.

4. A prescriptivist creation story

The history to be reconstructed has one of its first expressions in Plato. He supposed that the perceptual world is a chaos, where nothing is fixed and everything evades identity because of changing before we can identify it. Only the mind's ideas are stable, each one distinguished from the others, all of them encouraging that analysis and explication which turns whatever is merely implicit into a comprehensive *logos* standing plainly before the mind. Plato sometimes describes the *telos* of *nous* as it rises to incorporate the Forms within itself. Yet, the myth of *nous* escaping the body in order to merge itself in the Forms should be set against the claim that the Forms are innate. Mind uses them projectively, making the data seem stable and intelligible by reading the order and form of our thoughts into the sensible world. This is Plato's adaptation of the Protagorean claim that man is the measure of all that is and is not. For as Plato urges, ideas stand visibly before the mind. Percepts and the sensible world they represent are thinkable only as the more or less obscure expression of these ideas. Mind determines *that* something is, but also *what* it is.

Consider now that the flux of sensations uninformed by ideas verges on nonbeing because of simultaneously being and not being any and every property. The perceptual world secures its claim to being, or even to becoming, only as it acquires the stability-in-identity which thought projects onto it. This has a startling implication: it implies that the sensible world is made orderly and intelligible, *that it is created,* by mind as it makes the flux thinkable. This is not creation in the sense that efficient causes generate their effects, as parents make children; but it is creation, nevertheless. Ideas are the formal causes prescribing whatever stable differences and order are present within the thinkable world.

Mind's creation of the sensible world is a notion guaranteed to embarrass us. Our minds are fallible and finite, much too feeble to claim responsibility for everything intelligible within the cosmos. How extraordinary that intuitionism evolves from Plato's formulation of the Protagorean view until we have, in Kant and Hegel, the apotheosis of Plato's creation story. Spinoza was wrong, says Hegel: The world is not merely Substance, but rather Substance-for-Subject. It is a differentiated and unitary object just because of being made unitary and intelligible by the Absolute. Some passages from the *Phenomenology of Mind,* one from the Preface and another at the book's end, suggest the dimensions of Hegel's project.

> Everything depends on grasping and expressing the ultimate truth not as Substance but as Subject as well. At the same time we must note that concrete substantiality implicates and involves the universal of the immediacy of knowledge itself, as well as that immediacy which is being or immediacy qua object for knowledge.[1]

The goal, which is Absolute Knowledge or Spirit knowing itself as Spirit, find its pathway in the recollection of spiritual forms as they are in themselves and as they accomplish the organization of their spiritual kingdom. Their conservation, looked at from the side of their free existence appearing in the form of contingency, is History; looked at from the side of their intellectually comprehended organization, it is the Science of the ways in which knowledge appears. Both together, or History (intellectually) comprehended, form at once the recollection and the Golgotha of Absolute Spirit, the reality, the truth, the certainty of its throne, without which it were lifeless, solitary and alone. Only

The Chalice of this realm of spirits,
Foams forth to God his own Infinitude.[2]

This last quotation, from Schiller, is Hegel's celebration of the Absolute's self-consciousness. It has emptied itself in an act of free creation, and now it reflects without mediation upon the differentiated but unified experience it has made. This is the Cartesian *cogito* and Kant's transcendental ego elevated to Godhood, where "I am, I exist" is *Genesis* reformulated as the story of epistemic creation.

[S]pirit then brings to light the thought that lies in its inmost depths, and expresses essential Reality in the Form Ego = Ego.[3]

We may wonder at the presumption of supposing that the sensible world is created in the act which makes it thinkable. But we concede that God can make anything He chooses. That He makes the world by thinking it, using formal rather than efficient cause, is no more surprising than his creating it as an act of will. Does it follow that finite minds can do as much, merely by using the ideas or theories available to us? Most of us are sceptical that mind, even a mind writ very large, creates the world by thinking it. What are the arguments which have convinced intuitionists that this might be true? How much of this is a metaphor gone berserk?

5. Three features for which to provide when making a world

Notice as we recapitulate the development of this intuitionist persuasion that anyone holding it must be ready to provide for the three following considerations. First are the differentiations which are present in, and constitutive of a world. Second is the three-fold unification of these events: spatially and temporally, dynamically by way of causal relations; and nomologically under the laws which prevail within a world. Third is the requirement that the world created be more than a plausible fiction; it must be actual, not merely possible because thinkable. All of this chapter turns upon the fact that intuitionist mind hopes to incorporate all three of these factors within itself.

5a. Differentiation

Plato supplied an intuitionist solution for the first of these claims as he argued that the sensory world is differentiated when mind thinks sensory data as the instances of its ideas. Kant substitutes rules for ideas, saying that mind's schemas organize sensory data in ways that are sufficient to distinguish dogs from cats. Other intuitionists of form substitute words or whole theories, but these are only the alternative formulations of a program whose outlines are unchanged from Plato's time to our own. Sensory phenomena are known, these intuitionists say, only as we use ideas, rules, words, or theories to mark out the properties and relations which distinguish them. This is the prescriptivism which legislates the world's character, saying or supposing that the world is intelligible to us only as it displays the differences which are established already within thought. There is, of course, the alternative view that we represent differences within the world by way of hypotheses about them. This supposes that the existence and character of differences and relations within the world are independent of the ways we think about them. It allows for error and makes a virtue of the requirement that we find ways of testing, then revising, our claims. But then all of this is anathema to epistemic creation, because intuitionism fears that a world whose differences are independent of thought may elude our knowing it. That is its motive for requiring that all the world's content and all its differentiating rules or ideas be set before or within our inspecting minds. The only world to which we have assured access is the one created and sustained within mind.

5b. Existence

This way of providing for the intelligibility of things is one-third of all that needs to be done if Being is to be incorporated within the intuiting mind. Existence and the three kinds of unity are still to be considered; there are many philosophers who have anticipated their reduction to mind. Yet, mind's incorporation of the world is never so assured before Descartes describes mind as it turns upon itself. He has solutions for both of the remaining issues, though his remarks about unity are only implied, leaving Kant to make them explicit.

5bi. Descartes' discovery that I am, I exist

Descartes' views about the intuitionist conditions for existence are plainly stated: *"I am, I exist,"* he says, "every time it is pronounced by me or mentally conceived necessarily is true."

This sentence is the conclusion to an enthymeme, where existence is presupposed at three places. First is the tacit claim that doubting exists, as when previously accepted beliefs are doubted. Second, we are to understand that doubting presupposes a doubter, on the assumption that activity implies the agent whose behavior this is. More generally, awareness in any modality—e.g., doubting, perceiving, affirming, or denying—presupposes the thinker who is aware in these several ways. If the thinking exists, then the thinker also exists. But, third, we have not yet established that this is *my* thinking, so that I am the thinker whose existence is confirmed. How is each of us to prove that it is he or she, and not some other agent, who is thinking? That is confirmed only as I turn upon myself, discovering in the presence of my own thinking the fact that mine is the thinking, and I am the thinker.

> Now, what shall we say of this very mind, that is, of me myself? . . . What, I ask, am I who seem to perceive this wax so distinctly. Do I not know myself not only much more truly, much more certainly, but also much more distinctly and evidently? . . . I manifestly know that I can perceive nothing more easily or evidently than my mind.[4]

Thinking exists, the thinker exists, and I, the thinker thinking, exist. All three of these truths, but especially the last one, are confirmed by my self-inspection.

There are, moreover, two aspects to me: *that* I am and *what* I am. Descartes distinguishes between these two and suggests that the fact of my existence is established before the ascertaining of my character.

> I have come to acknowledge that I exist, I seek to learn what I am— this "I" that I have acknowledged. It is most certain that thus pre-

cisely taken, the notion of this "I" does not depend on any of these things I portray in the imagination.⁵

What I am is more problematic than the fact that I am, thereby forcing this question: What is there about my existence, or about the manner of my knowing it, which makes my existence distinguishable from my nature?

Descartes' assurance about his existence seems to be founded in these two things. First is the argument that was emphasized in Chapter Three. If we affirm that doubting exists because there is sufficient evidence for it, then we need also affirm the existence of that second-order consciousness which is witness to the evidence. What is the evidence which obliges second-order awareness to recognize the existence of mind's first-order activities? Only, and here is the second point, the force and vivacity of active mind as it is set before itself. I exist, and know that I do, because of the intensity of my self-experience. Self-inspecting mind is witness to its own activity and presence.

5bii. HUME ON FORCE AND VIVACITY

All of our claims about existence may be reformulated so that they satisfy the requirements of this paradigm. So, with force and vivacity as his criterions, Hume defines existence in the following way:

> The idea of existence, then, is the very same with the idea of what we conceive to be existent. To reflect on anything simply, and to reflect on it as an existent, are nothing different from each other. That idea (existence), when conjoined with the idea of any object, makes no addition to it.⁶

Hume has also said that "whatever the mind clearly conceives includes the idea of possible existence."⁷ This obliges us to distinguish possible from actual existence, but there is no way to do that within Hume except by distinguishing ideas conceived or imagined from the impressions perceived. The ones merely conceived are faint when compared to the force and vivacity of the ones perceived. That intensity of experience is the only basis on which to distinguish the actual existents perceived from the possible ones imagined.

How could Hume plausibly conflate the evidence for something's existence, i.e., its forcible impression on the mind, with that thing's existence? He has two reasons. One is negative and sceptical; the other is a solution to the sceptical problem.

On the negative side is the bias of Hume's intuitionism: ". . . external objects become known to us only by those perceptions they occasion".[8] Hume denies, however, that things of this mind-independent sort do exist. What follows about existence? Should we say that nothing exists, just because nothing exists apart from our minds? Why do we reserve the notion of existence for those things which are not inspectable? Why not locate existence within our perceivings? Descartes has shown the way. He has freed us from having to distinguish the existence of things from that presence-before-our-minds which is the evidence for them. He does this by confirming his own existence within the evidence for it, as I discover that I am in the immediacy of my self-experience. We might protest the generalizing of this idea by saying that mind's experience of itself is unique, there being no other case where knower and known are identical. There is a gap, we might insist, in the case of every other existent known. But that claim is just a restatement of the realist superstition. Whatever is true of mind and our self-knowledge is rightly generalized to our knowledge of every other thing. Each of them is known, and each one exists, only as it is perceived. Things having that status are known to exist with all the assurance that mind has of its own existence. Notice, however, that the existence of these contingent things is derivative. They exist only as we do, because they are sensory affections in us. What is more, they incite our self-discovery, as mind need reflect on something given in order to perceive itself. Perhaps these contingent things exist merely as a goad to our self-discovery.

These last remarks are apparently false to Hume. He argues that mind reduces to the sequence of its impressions and ideas. We have, he says, no single impression or idea of ourselves, but only a bundle of associated impressions and ideas. This reminds us that Hume's explicit views about mind are contrary to the presuppositions of his intuitionist method, for Hume's reliance upon these assumptions is plain: impressions are seen, complex ideas are constructed from impressions by way of simpler ideas, simple inferences are made, and uninspectable habits are acquired. None of this is consistent with the bundle theory, because all of it implies the more ample assumptions of the intuitionist psychology. Even Hume, therefore, founds the existence of things perceived in the logically prior fact that mind perceives their existence as qualifications of itself. Nothing shall exist if it is not perceived. This applies as much to second-order awareness as to first-order awareness and its objects. Rather than confirm its own existence by inferring to itself from its perception of them, second-order awareness turns upon itself. How does it do that? Not by turning away from first-order awareness and its objects in order to focus upon itself. Perhaps by glimpsing itself in the act of attending to them. Either way, this is the self-reflexive act in which mind confirms its autonomy. Why is that so? Because mind is, so to speak, backed against the wall. Looking about for every other thing that might condition the existence of its impressions and acts, thereby attentuating its own responsibility for them, mind discovers only itself. For nothing exists if it is not perceived, and everything perceived falls altogether within the mind itself. Consequently, second-order awareness turned upon itself discovers both its autonomy and the fact that every other existing thing is conditional upon and embodied within it. Mind perceives itself as the self-encircling and self-sustaining condition for all of them.

Why should intuitionism be impelled to this result? Remember Descartes' objective: we are to verify our knowledge claims about every putative existent. We have an example of this more complex demand in the case of first-order awareness and its objects. Their existence is not secured until second-order awareness has recorded their mutually conditioning relationship within its more synoptic view. Nothing is certain, nothing is known, nothing can be said to exist unless mind perceives it. *Esse es percipi* This is the keel and condition for all the Being that intuitionism will acknowledge. Mind is the measure of all that is that it is, because mind embodies all of existence within itself. Yet, mind too exists because of being seen. This is the luminous center of the intuitionist ontology. This is mind as the ark of Being.

5biii. DESCARTES' FOUNDATIONAL ARGUMENT

We have discovered the basis for all existence in Descartes' remark that mind need be self-inspecting in order to exist. That is the passage first cited in Chapter Three.

> "I am, I exist" it is certain. For how long however? Well, for as long as I think, for perhaps it could even happen that were I to stop all thinking, I would with that completely cease to be.

A mind that is active or affected in any mode of awareness verifies the existence of these acts or affections by inspecting them. Seeing them as qualifications of itself, it confirms its own existence.

There is, however, a certain obscurity that remains as we consider the complex character of self-inspecting mind, for there seem to be three places where existence is established within it. The data which Hume describes exist because we see them as forceful, and more fundamentally because we see them as qualifications of a thinker which has discovered its own existence. This last point anticipates the second place where existence lodges, namely in mind's first-order acts of awareness. It is those acts which are qualified by having these data as their objects. These first-order acts exist for a two-fold reason. On the one side, they are seen to exist. On the other side, they too are the qualifications of that thinking subject which discovers itself, first as a necessary condition for them, second as a forceful presence in its own right.

This thinking subject is the third site for existence, and the ultimate foundation for everything perceived, hence for everything that exists. Yet, this perspective is our remote objective. Descartes never reduces the existence of everything to the evidence of it; nor does he suppose that the *cogito* is the one existing thing. God, essences, the extended world: all of them are said to exist without depending on the fact that we think them. We do know the *cogito* by way of self-experience; but all these other existents are known inferentially, as we reflect upon the evidence for them. Still, our scepticism is easily provoked, for what do we know of these things apart from the ways they affect us? Could we provide for everything that is significant in them by attending only to their ways of appearing before us? Phenomenalism regarding physical things, conceptualism regarding essences, and the idea of a personal God, all start here. Descartes encourages these views without endorsing them when he declares that I am, I exist; for now the existence of these things can be grounded in the one existent which cannot be doubted. We acknowledge all the while that physical things and essences do not easily reduce to our perceivings. Nor is God easily reduced to something contrived by imagination. For my existence is derivative. I do exist necessarily each time that I conceive or pronounce it; but I am finite and contingent. My existence is conditional upon that God whose existence is necessary because of expressing its perfection. Any reduction of God's existence to my own, is therefore, more than heresy or vanity; it is contradictory and perverse.

These reflections express some of the traditional realist wisdom in whose shadow Descartes lingers. He is not altogether prepared for the revolution he promotes. Still, he is just short of agreeing that intuitionism has displaced every ontological priority in the name of an epistemological one. For mind is first; first in being and first in knowledge. Nothing is better known to mind than the mind itself, where mind's existence and character are known immediately whenever mind is active in any way. Not at all a derivative and dependent thing, mind experiences itself as self-creating each time that it thinks itself or any other thing. It is just the matters thought and perceived that are derivative, for they exist as qualifications of our thinking. This is the principle from which other intuitionists will generalize as they populate the world with disparate minds or reduce all of Being to the ambit of a single mind.

We now have two of the three factors that are required if all of Being is to be incorporated within a mind or minds thinking intuitively. Differentiations within the world have been explained by way of the ideas, rules, words, or theories which differentiate the sensory given. Existence is the mind's own; or derivatively, its qualifications exist. This leaves only unity to consider.

5c. Unity

Three kinds of unity are ascribed to the world. First are its spatial and temporal relations. Second, individuals are related dynamically as causes having effects. Third, events are related nomologically, meaning that there are laws which coordinate their relations. Can any or all of these relations be reduced, without remainder, to relations which are credible to intuitionists? That is done, or tried in ways that follow from the assumption that all of the world's differentiations, and its existence are founded within one or many minds. The problem of the world's unities is, therefore, only the one of telling how mind provides for the relatedness of the phenomena perceived.

5ci. Nomological unity

We start with nomological unity, because this is already implicit in the claim that mind uses ideas, rules, or theories for projecting such differences as are discovered within the sensory given. We add that these differences are related systematically, where relations among the ideas, rules, or theories are the basis for whatever relations are ascribed to the phenomena. We say, for example, that three things are differentiated as lieutenant, sergeant, and private, with obligations to one another determined by this characterization. Nothing is a sergeant in any more essential way, so that the prescriptivist assignment of differentiating properties and relations does not arouse any lingering realist prejudices within us. Nor is there anyone who can dispute the character and relations prescribed, for this is a stipulation requiring nothing more than our acquiesence to make it valid.

The projection of nomological relations only becomes problematic as we take up those laws which have seemed to express some deeper, intrinsic set of norms—physical laws being an example. So, force, mass, and acceleration are to be understood as differences articulated within thought or language and then projected with their relations onto sensory data. These data become, thereby, the events which exhibit Newton's laws. Alternatively, we do not project these differences and their relationship onto the data but merely regard the law as a device for interpreting the data. Either way, the phenomena are unified by a law in two respects: first, as the distinguishable features of a single complex event are seen in their relatedness; second, as phenomena occurring at different times and places are seen as instances of what is generically the same complex relationship.

Laws, with the differences they coordinate, are the principal topic of confusion as intuitionists move facilely between the "material" and "formal" modes of speech. Where do properties and laws originate, in the world itself or within thought or language? Intuitionism has all but eliminated this difference, when every claim about the world is a shorthand reference to that product which is differentiated, ordered, and objectified by the mind's own activity. This geneological consideration is the important one as we distinguish the two modes. The formal mode specifies those ideas and relationships which mind has used prescriptively in the course of this history. The material mode is naive. It specifies only the content that is made intelligible by our thinking it. The formal mode articulates what the material mode can only express, namely, that differences among properties—together with the unity of properties under law—are features of the world originating in thought.

5cii. CAUSE AND EFFECT

There is only a short way to go as we extend this claim to the dynamical relation of cause and effect. This last phrase, "dynamical relation. . . ," seems to pick out one kind of relationship within the mobile, protean world. That insinuation is, however, only the artifice of the material mode. It implies that we are talking of a relationship which is independent of our thinking and speaking, though "cause and effect" is only the signature for some of the laws used for thinking the given. There are, we remember, physical laws of several kinds. Some, like the laws of motion, determine the invariant relations of certain variables—e.g., force, mass, and acceleration. Other laws are more explicitly causal (in the respect that they invoke efficient rather then formal cause), as we say that matches light when struck. Notice, however, that these causal laws have the same role as laws of the other sort: They differentiate and unify sensory data so that we might think of them as the stable constituents of an objective world.

There might be this quibble. My example is a low-level causal generalization, though laws used for thinking the given should be deducible from the higher-order laws of hypothetico-deductive system. No one will take this seriously, because intuitionists don't mind that people use inductive generalizations for organizing their experience while being ignorant of the formalized theories from which they derive. It is enough for intuitionist purposes that some rule be used for projecting cause and effect onto the sensory given.

Are there, we persist, causes and effects *within* the world? Certainly there are, if we remember that *the world* is only that complex of properties and relations which exists because of its vivacity before the mind. For nothing exists except mind and that manifold which it has differentiated and unified.

Space and time are the last of the three kinds of unity ascribed to the world. They fall into place in a predictable way. There are two alternatives when the differentiations and nomological unity of sensory data are imposed by mind as it thinks them: first, space and time might be independent of mind but empty, because all the differentiations normally referred to them have been relocated within the mind; second, space and time might shrink to the dimensions of our sensory fields, thereby recovering their role as systems of relations for binding sensory data to one another. The first alternative, a mind-independent space and time, serves no theoretical purpose if its only possible contents have been relocated within the mind. Kant has chosen the other view because of having supposed that the manifold is differentiated and unified by the rules which mind uses when thinking it. This manifold also exhibits spatial and temporal relations. If the manifold occurs within mind, as its product, then so is it true that the matrix of spatial and temporal relations is constituted within the mind.

5ciii. SPACE AND TIME

Mind's incorporation of space and time is perhaps the most troubling of all these claims about mind's responsibility for whatever is unified within the world. Intuitionism, with its impatience for dialectic, should have something better than argument to convince us. The metaphor of mind as a theatre is useful now, as we emphasize the immediacy and transparency of spatial and temporal relations. Could space and time be the luminous either within us, hence, the medium in which phenomena of every sort are presented for inspection?

Imagine a brilliant day with no glare but only a sky of deepest blue, swirling trees, and flowers of many shapes, purple, yellow, and red, moving like the trees in a tide of green. Am I sitting in the midst of these things, or is all of it incorporated, somehow, within me? Remembering last night's awful storm, and the distance from my bedroom to this garden, I have no doubt that all these things are seen, not made. Intuitionists disagree; all of it, they say, is within us, for otherwise the transparency and immediacy would be an illusion. Everything occurring within space and time, everything perceived, would be mediated. Nothing could be known as it is in itself. This includes space and time, for everything known of them would derive from inferences drawn from our mediated perceivings of them. All the information that we might extract from these inferences might be a fraction of the information that we acquire by direct inspection, as Whitehead insists that change, hence time, is directly perceived, not inferred from the combination of memory and current perception.

It seems to me that Whitehead is mistaken in thinking that change is inspected not inferred; but let us suppose that he is correct, for intuitionists have still to tell us how it is that mind creates space and time. There is only Kant's proposal that these modes of connection are produced by the transcendental unity of apperception as it binds our sensory data. This would not count as any sort of explanation, if it were not coupled to those sceptical arguments which allege that we cannot know or even speculate about space and time as they might exist independently of our ways of perceiving them. *Esse es percipi* is as true of them as it is of the phenomena related within them. The only space and time that we know are the ones available for inspection because of being the mind's sensorium.

5d. Summary

We now have all three of the considerations which are required if Hegel is to establish that nature exists not as Substance, but only as Substance-for-Subject: there is a differentiated manifold unified under causal and other laws in space time. More than a possible world, this world exists. How? As a qualification of that God who perceives this world and itself.

6. Four additional questions

There are several more things that need to be said if this intuitionist appropriation of Being is to seem plausible. There are four questions: (a) We accept the claim that reality is differentiated and unified by thought as it uses ideas, rules, or theories for thinking the given; but then some reservations follow. Will any theory suffice for creating these differences and relations—i.e., is every theory true? Suppose that this is not so, that is, some theories are false. How shall we identify a true theory, meaning one of those which are utilizable for thinking the differences and relations present within the sensible world? (b) We grant that the existence of other things is dependent upon the mind's own existence. But then it cannot be true that existing states of affairs are the ones set most vividly before our minds, for that turns every nightmare, every delusion into a reality. Intuitionists require a better test for existence. (c) We agree that mind could not know space and time if they were independent of it, hence, unavailable to inspection. Still, we resist the internalization claimed for them until we have a plausible story about their synthesis within the mind. (d) We remark that our own minds are finite and contingent. Mind's role as creator of all Being has required that mind be elevated to

Godhood. How is the *cogito* transformed until it becomes the Absolute? Intuitionist atheists would have to deny this possibility. How are they to justify saying that all of Being is appropriated by our finite minds?

Intuitionist resources for answering these four questions are uneven. There is a more or less convincing response for each one of them, but the questions and answers are not well integrated within a single intuitionist theory. The most accessible formulations are the ones that elaborate on the character of intuiting mind as it evolves from finite human mind to the Absolute. We start, with responses to the fourth question, taking up the other three as they are implied by this ontologically prior claim.

7. Elevating the *cogito* to Godhood

What are the steps to be taken as the *cogito* rises to Godhood? There is no altogether plausible transformation from finite minds to God; but there is a basis for that development within the intuitionist psychology, especially in the distinction between first- and second-order awareness. This is a first glimmering of the claim that God is both immanent and remote, everywhere effective and immediate, but nowhere visible.

First-order awareness inspects whatever given stands before it; we perceive, doubt, conceive, desire, or dream about that thing. These are the acts of a mind, engaged, a mind that is perhaps too preoccupied to think of itself. It is, however, second-order awareness that writes the *Meditations*. This is mind in the posture of reflection, mind withdrawn from whatever is thought or made. Consciousness of both sorts is an acquaintance with the given, but there are some ambiguities. Is second-order awareness merely an observer, or does it have powers for constituting the reality which it observes? Where, for example, are the ideas which differentiate the given, making it thinkable? Is it first-order awareness which deploys these ideas; or is first-order awareness passive to the given, recording and inspecting whatever intimations of form are discovered there but needing second-order consciousness to project its ideas onto the given? Does second-order consciousness merely notice the temporal and spatial order, hence, the unity of things; or does it spin that unity out of itself by creating the network of relations where the given is perceived as one? What is the relation of first- to second-order awareness, such that one has access to the other? Is this only a matter of passive witness, or could it be true that first-order acts are directed by second-order interests?

7a. Descartes

Descartes reserves the greater authority to second-order awareness. The power of judgement lies there, as will restrains us from affirming or denying a judgement until its content is clear and distinct. All the ideas required for discerning differentiations and relations within sensory data are lodged within second-order awareness. For only the second-order power for introducing and arranging these ideas would justify the second order act which restrains judgement until our ideas and their relations are clarified. It is apparently second-order consciousness which establishes a differentiated but orderly sensory world.

7b. Kant

This is probably too Kantian a reading of Descartes' views. For it is Kant, not Descartes, who regards judgement as the act which constitutes experience. Descartes is only halfway to that conclusion as he remarks the difference between sensory data and the ideas with which we construe them. There is, for example, the small disk of our perceiving as against our idea of the sun. Still, Descartes has so empowered second-order awareness as to leave Kant only two assumptions removed from his claim that mind is the synthesizer of experience. The first step requires that space and time be incorporated as the forms of intuition. Second is his redescription of ideas as rules—i.e., schemas—for the spatial-temporal ordering of sensory data. In Kant, as in Descartes, these powers are ascribed to second-order awareness, though with this difference: Our intuited self-awareness is now elevated to the status of transcendental apperception, where mind's activity is inferred from its effects rather than known immediately by self-inspection.

One effect of this emphasis upon second-order mental activities is the devaluation of first-order awareness. In Descartes, our original intendings of the given are a first-order groping in the dark. We perceive, believe, doubt, and deny without the clarity of those ideas on which we depend for everything that is articulate and well-formed.

In Kant the effect is different. On the one side, first-order awareness is overwhelmed by these second-order activities, to the point where first-order acts have lost their integrity. Each one is taken up immediately within the larger setting that is created and sustained by transcendental consciousness. We might suppose, for example, that it is first-order awareness which first entertains unschematized sensory data. But that moment of experience is unrecoverable. Indeed, there might be no first-order of raw sensation. The idea of "unschematized data" might be nothing more than the presupposition that schematized data must have been supplied to mind in an unschematized way. This point implies its complement, that reality so far as it stands before the mind is only the product of second-order consciousness. For transcendental apperception has created a unitary experience. First-order awareness is the naive recording of this given. Yet, first-order awareness is impotent, having no power for making or altering that which it observes.

Here, as in Descartes, all the powers of thought and will lie with second-order mental activity. There is only this reservation as we assess Kant's role within the intuitionist appropriation of Being. He has wanted to secure the persistence and coherence of the intuitionist given. He has done that by crediting second-order activity with powers for creating a sustained, differentiated and orderly experience. But then Kant has also said that we know this second-order activity and its powers only as we infer to it from the experience it creates. Kant's transcendentalism is, therefore, a nonintuitionist guarantee that mind will have an inspectable given, with second-order activity creating the content for unselfreflective first-order awareness.

This view of Kant is an evocation of the immanence and remoteness that are traditionally associated with the notion of God. For notice that the effects of second-order activity are apparent wherever our experience of the world is differentiated but unitary, though we have no direct experience of second-order thought as it creates this result. The efficacy of this higher-order activity is reinforced when Descartes and Kant ascribe the power for willing to second-order thought. All the powers classically ascribed to God are then predicated of this second-order activity: the world is differentiated, unified nomologically and in space and time by a power whose thought expresses its will that the world should exist.

7c. *Three more steps*

We are only three steps short of Hegel's identification of the *cogito* and transcendental ego with the Absolute. First, we need to eliminate the plausible claim that sensory data have a source external to mind. Second, we do not have any reason, just yet, for saying that a God modeled on the *cogito* might exist necessarily. Third, second-order consciousness has been redescribed as the transcendental unity of apperception, where mind needs inference rather than self-inspection to discover itself. This implies, intolerably, that intuiting mind requires a nonintuitionist method to complete its self-knowledge. Here are some intuitionist solutions for these last obstacles.

7ci. Sensory Data Are Made Within the Mind

The extramental source for our percepts might be the one secure bridge to our knowledge of a world that is independent of mind for its existence and character. But Descartes has already half-covered the evidence of that world by saying that thought, rather than perception, is the sole basis for true judgements about matters of fact. Sensory data are sufficiently differentiated and ordered, for the purpose of knowledge, only as we project our ideas onto them. What is more, it is only these ideas, and not the sensory data, which are the content of our judgements. The sensory data themselves are adventitious and unreliable as a basis for judgements about matters of fact.

Kant reformulates this essentially Platonic and Cartesian idea. Sensuous intuitions are fractured and incoherent, he says. They are unintelligible, until they are schematized within space and time. Descartes has allowed that thinking substance is set against an independent, extended substance, with sensory data having their origin within that extended, physical world. Kant destroys this independent footing with the claim that space and time are only the forms of intuition. The claim that mind synthesizes a previously unschematized sensory manifold does invite questions about the mind-independent origin of these data. But their presentation as unschematized is merely a limiting or least condition for experience.

It says nothing to confirm either the reality of an independent world or its agency as generator of sensory data. Reason does postulate the existence of an external source, yet this idea like all the ideas of reason is empty because of having no empirical manifold for its application.

There is also this independent but correlative point: No extramental source could have been the cause of our sensory affections, because causality is only the sequential relation of phenomena within a schematized experience. The notion of an extramental cause operating upon the mind is, again, only the application of a concept beyond its appropriate sensory domain. Extramental causality is, therefore, an idea without a referent.

Kant's argument has a remarkable effect; it should eliminate our questions about an external source for sensory data, because of encouraging us to find their source within the mind itself. How shall we do that when mind does not seem to have the power for generating sensory data? Kant's own views are equivocal. He is committed to saying that phenomena are the representations of things which exist independently of our minds; yet, he is tempted by the view that all of experience might be created out of the mind's own materials.

This is plainest in the A Edition of the First Critique, where Kant emphasizes imagination as a vital activity within mind's synthesis of experience. He credits imagination with a power for organizing the sensory data which derive from perception. But then Kant also distinguishes between reproductive and productive imagination, the one as data are recollected, the other as form is made. Both kinds of imagining are engaged in the making of dreams, as sensory materials remembered from past perceivings are organized in new ways.

Why not liberate productive imagination so that it produces both the content and the form of our dreams, or even the totality of experience? Kant does not press this argument, as Fichte does, because it credits our finite minds with a power that vastly exceeds us. This is no deterrent when God's imagination is the one at issue, for we extrapolate easily to the claim that all of nature and history are contrived by God once it is remarked that our finite minds can sustain the coherence of a dream

This is the argument for saying that intuiting mind can be self-sufficient as the generator of sensory data. Imagination creates them, as it also makes the network of spatial and temporal relations where they are embedded. Perhaps these two acts are one, as the act of synthesizing space and time requires that we should also be imagining some of the things which are spatially and temporally ordered. This is the claim which sets mind free, cutting its tether to a world that exists somehow beyond the reach of direct perception. Mind is unconditioned as it creates experience, hence, all of the world except itself.

7cii. ESTABLISHING MIND'S NECESSITY

This was the first of three problems to be solved if intuitionism was to move beyond finite minds to the Absolute. The second problem is the one of proving mind's necessity. Could it be that the basis for mind's necessity is just its self-sufficiency?

Descartes was happy to emphasize mind's contingency when he wanted to exalt God's greater power. It was plain in this context that the only necessity claimed for us turns about the fact that our thinking presupposes our existence. Descartes could even exploit our contingency by regarding it as evidence for the existence of an unconditioned, perfect, and necessary being, as a finite effect requires an infinite cause. But here, as we magnify the *cogito* until it satisfies the conditions for Godhood, the motive for differentiating God from our human minds is much reduced. Let us go the other way, reconsidering the manner of the *cogito*'s existence, establishing if we can that an Absolute mind might exist necessarily by virtue of features which are already essential to the *cogito*.

Notice that our context is circumscribed. We have not established that God's existence might be necessary because of being unconditioned; necessary, I mean, because of being that act which cannot be suppressed by any power that is consistent with the principle of contradiction. This stronger notion requires that God should exist, because there is nothing possible which could suppress its existence. This we have not proved. Our only claim is that a world created by thought and confirmed by perception requires the mind which has thought and perceived it. We add that this mind's own existence is conditional upon the existence of that contingent thing which it has thought: God deprived of the world would not exist, because He could not think the world, or Himself.

God's necessity is the other side of its self-sufficiency. God is self-sufficient because of being the only source for all the content and form within the world. But then conversely, the world depends altogether upon God for its being. God is its necessary ground, for it would not be if God were not. This is, in the language of Chapter Five and its remarks about cause, an example of existential necessity: Causes are presupposed by effects, because there would be no effect in the absence of the cause it qualifies. Nothing is if there is no mind to think and perceive it. Both are necessary. The world would not exist if it were not created by a God using ideas, rules or a theory to make a differentiated, unified manifold. But also, *esse es percipi.* The world's existence requires that God should perceive what is made. He confirms its existence, and thereby His own.

This argument for thought's necessity, coming after the claim of God's self-sufficiency and before the proof of its self-inspectability, is the second requirement for moving us past the *cogito* to the Absolute. Our objective is close at hand. Descartes and Kant have established the *cogito* as the paradigm for God's activity. They have spoken for existence as it is restricted to matters set forcibly before the mind as it projects differentiation and order onto imagined sensory data, and for that unity which is supplied by projected ideas or integrating rules and by the forms of intuition. God's necessity is assured by the same argument which concludes that the transcendental ego is a necessary condition for a synthesized experience. Hegel has little more to do than assemble and magnify these claims as he completes the intuitionist appropriation of Being.

7ciii. MIND IS EXHAUSTIVELY SELF-INSPECTABLE

There is, however, the third question listed above as we move beyond Descartes' *cogito* to the Absolute: having provided for mind's self-sufficiency and necessity, we have to confirm that a God might be self-inspecting. This question is problematic for Kant has elevated second-order awareness to the status of the transcendental ego where it can only identify itself by inferring from the world made to its own powers as maker. This must be unsatisfactory for intuitionist purposes, because nothing exists, mind included, if it is not perceived. How can we avert the outcome where mind loses touch with itself?

7ciiia. Kant

One might infer from this difficulty that Kant is not part of the intuitionist tradition. Why not say that he elaborates on some of Descartes' ideas while repudiating his intuitionism? This is mistaken. Kant's intuitionism is never shaken, though inference is used to supplement it. The transcendental ego is discovered, for the purposes of the *Critique of Pure Reason,* as we infer to the conditions for experience. Yet, mind is all the while the intuiting spectator of that experience. This point is implicit throughout the First Critique, as Kant argues that sensory data are subjected to categorization so that they may stand before the mind as presentations. This is the content of an experience that is enjoyed in the very act and moment when it is made. Who is there to see it? Only the transcendental ego. Is this second-order thinker restricted to inferring its own character from the experience it has made, or does it have more direct access to itself? Kant is equivocal in the First Critique, but altogether specific in the next one. The powers claimed for self-inspection in the *Critique of Practical Reason* are hardly different from the ones that Descartes acknowledged. The ego directs reason in accord with will, much as volition is to wait for clear and distinct judgements before giving its assent. The ego of the Second Critique is also self-evaluating, as it reflects upon its virtues and desserts. It is self-directing and self-summarizing as these powers for unmediated self-reflection are extended in the *Critique of Judgement,* where ego plans for the future while reflecting upon its own history as a totality.

Kant is more guarded about mind's direct access to itself in the First Critique, because of wanting to avoid the appearance of an argument that is merely impressionistic. His transcendental method is to be impeccably rigorous. He has suppressed claims that might be confirmed by self-inspection in favor of inferential claims about the least conditions for a coherent experience. We are to infer from experience to its conditions, claiming no more for the transcendental ego than is required for explaining those features of experience which inspection has discovered. We report that experience is differentiated, orderly and unified, where it is only the categories, space and time, and the unifying activity of the transcendental ego which are specifiable as we infer from experience to its conditions. Mind's powers for enjoying the experience it creates are assumed. Its powers for self-reflection are, at this point, incidental and largely ignored.

All of this bears on Kant's intuitionism without acknowledging his place at the very foundation of intuitionist thinking. He secures the psycho-centric ontology which Descartes merely extols. Descartes' intuitionism is fragile. The psychological and ontological conditions for it are specified in only a schematic and preliminary way. What is there, for example, to guarantee the relation of first-order intentions to the given which stands before them? Could it happen that first-order consciousness might sometimes face a given that is empty or unintelligible? What are the tasks of self-reflection? Is it merely the observer of first-order events; or does it intrude upon them in additional, more efficacious ways? Kant's transcendental mechanics are an answer to these questions. He cannot assure that there will always be sensuous content for transcendental synthesis. But he secures the intuitionist boat on every other side as it navigates in a void where nothing is intelligible or unitary except mind and the experience it makes.

This is the setting where Kant elaborates upon the intuitionist psychology, and especially upon second-order consciousness and the conditions for receptivity. His solution has these two principal costs: First, knowing mind has intuitive awareness of the experiences made but not of the acts which make them; second, first-order awareness is reduced to the sense of "me" or "mine" accompanying every awareness when all mind's powers are relocated within second-order awareness. This second result is worth remarking, but otherwise negligible. The first one is more important because of being the one obstacle to establishing that the mind creating a thinkable world is altogether accessible to itself. Mind must have this access if it is to exist because of being self-perceived.

7ciiib. Valuing mind discovers itself

How shall we establish that mind might be self-inspecting in the act of making experience? We start by remarking that experience derives its character from that system of rules or concepts which mind has projected onto sensory data in order that the data be differentiated and ordered. For then we remark that these organizing rules have two constituents, pure concepts and their more determinate expressions. First are the concepts, or categories. They are the least regulative conditions that need be satisfied if any possible world is to be thinkable. These are the conditions for possibility, as no world failing to satisfy them is thinkable. If we describe these categories applying across all possible worlds as *determinable,* then we anticipate the need for the second of these two factors. Determinables will need to be further determined if they are to apply to any particular set of sensory data, organizing them in a way that creates one, or a part of one, actual world. Kant describes the rules giving further determination to the categories as *empirical schemas.* It is the complex of categories made determinate by these schemas which generates a particular complex of sensory phenomena—e.g., some dog or cat.

Mind cannot choose whether or not to use the categories; nothing is thinkable, hence, possible, unless we use them. Yet, mind will have to choose among the many empirical schemas available for making the categories so determinate that they may apply to sensory data. How does mind decide which empirical schemas to use? The answer Kant seems to have preferred is that we think sensory data or moral maxims in order that one or a set of values may be exhibited within the world or within mind as it thinks the world. In the case of beauty, we think the data in ways that will produce an aesthetic result. For the sake of good, we order our personal behaviors and social relations by way of the categorical imperative. In the name of truth, we differentiate and order the world in ways that satisfy the demand for consistency and coherence. Suppose that mind is in touch with itself as it reflects upon these values, then uses them to direct its choice of empirical schemas. Only as mind turns from its values and their instruments to make a world does it lose track of itself, needing to infer its own activity and character from the world made. But then mind can recover itself in that other more immediate way by turning from world-making to the values which direct its activity.

Is there some reason that mind should be incapable of turning upon itself when making its experience of the world? Could this be a peculiarly human infirmity; or is the problem deeper, so that God too is barred from self-knowledge in the moment of creating a world in order to see His values fulfilled? There seems to be no obstacle to unmediated—i.e., uninferred—self-knowledge when we finite minds are using a system of concepts to think the given. Intuitionists would say that there are many occasions when we are unproblematically self-conscious about using ideas or rules for interpreting the sensory given. Is there, perhaps, some other consideration which precludes our unmediated self-knowledge when experience is made?

7ciiic. Mind's unavailability to itself when unifying space and time

There is one special problem, a problem that is entailed by the extraordinary powers that Kant ascribes to second-order consciousness; namely, what is mind's relation to itself while it unifies space and time. Is our self-knowledge temporalized, so that our awareness of having unified time comes after the act it knows? If that is so, we shall not be aware of ourselves directly but only by way of self-representation. For the time-unifying act that is known will have passed at the moment when it is registered by mind as it reflects upon itself. Self-knowledge will be mediated by this self-representation, not immediate in the way that intuitionism prefers. We shall have to infer mind's properties as unifier of time from the character of this representation.

We might try to avert this outcome by saying that self-knowledge is not temporalized. That might be so if we are always turned immediately upon ourselves without a finite span of time or a representation to separate us from ourselves. But this hope is confounded by Kant's requirement that everything thought be apprehended in its temporal and sometimes spatial relations. We are made to choose: Allow that self-knowledge is mediated by representations, or agree that the mind's knowledge of itself is exempt from the requirement that every matter of fact, ourselves included, is apprehended as a network of temporal relations.

Remember now that the categories of understanding are only the possible determinations of space and time. Quality is the intensity of a property filling space or time, quantity is the magnitude of the property as it is present there, and relation is a datum's position *vis-à-vis* other data—e.g., before and after, above and below. The categories of understanding—i.e., those determinables prescribing the least properties of any possible world—are founded in mind's unification of space and time. Therefore, we have been too quick to suppose, some paragraphs above, that self-knowledge is unproblematic when mind applies its concepts in behalf of a value while thinking a world. Application of these concepts presupposes the unification of space and time, so that we cannot be altogether self-conscious in applying the categories if we are not self-aware when unifying space and time. This consideration applies all the more to the empirical schemas. For these schemas are only the more determinate specifications of the categories, as the schema for dog is a rule for ordering data that are engaged in space and time because of having quality, quantity, and relation. We cannot be altogether self-aware in using these schemas, for that would require that we have direct access to the categories, hence, to the unification of space and time, as we do not. The obstacle to self-reflection as mind creates the world is, therefore, complete: Mind is barred from knowing itself by direct inspection as it makes experience, and a world, from sensory data. Mind does know itself, but only mediately and inferentially.

This cannot be the final word, because *esse es percipi:* Nothing is if it is not perceived. The very existence of the act creating the web of spatial and temporal relations is at risk if there is no self-confirming inspection of it. A self-inspection occurring in the time which mind has created, hence, mediated by a self-representation, does not satisfy this requirement, because the inference from our self-representation to the act where space and time are made would be fallible. This representation, like every other one, might not have an object; perhaps the act was never done. This is deadly within the context of intuitionist thought, because of entailing that the founding mental activity, the one producing space and time, therefore the categories and experience—dangles in the void without a confirming self-inspection. Kant was willing to settle for less. It was enough for him that we are certain, as Hume was certain, of our sensory experience, so that we may infer from that to its conditions. No matter then if some of those conditions are "transcendental" and uninspectable. Intuitionism, and especially Hegel's Absolute, cannot tolerate an argument which predicates the world's founding act on a speculation. If existing, it must be seen to exist. Where unseen, we have no certainty that it does exist. Without that certainty, we lose the center upon which intuitionism has founded all its claims about knowledge and Being.

7ciiid. Contemporaneity

Intuitionism is left to establish mind's unmediated access to itself in a way that Kant has barred. He argued that everything known to mind is temporalized. This precludes our having knowledge of those acts which create the network of temporalized and spatialized relations. We respond, as intuitionists, by denying his assumption as it applies to the mind's own activities, especially the second-order ones of synthesis, judgement, and volition. We say, instead, that all of these activities, including the ones spanning time and space, are *contemporaneous* with the self-inspections which certify their existence. This is, of course, a special sense of 'contemporaneous.' We normally use this word to mean "occurring at the same time." That cannot be its sense here where the acts creating space and time occur "outside of time," not therefore at the same time as the acts confirming them. These acts are contemporaneous in the different respect that each one is a logical condition for the other. So, mind must be doing something—e.g., creating time—if it is to know itself; but then too, mental activities are like every other thing in the respect that they do not exist if their existence is not confirmed by inspection. The contemporaneity of mind as it creates time and inspects itself is an instance of this mutually conditioning but atemporal relation. Mind is saved from eluding itself. Intuitionism is saved from having to admit that its world-founding act, the one of making a differentiated space and time—hence, experience—cannot be confirmed by our self-perception.

This stipulation is proposed, as I shall suppose that it is accepted, as the way of saving two of the requirements that are vital to intuitionism.

The first one is already plain. The act of creating space and time—hence, space and time themselves and all their contents—will not exist if it is not perceived. We might respond with Kant that this is bizarre when we can attest to the fact that experience does exist, because we have it as a given that is forever inspected. Perhaps we are deluded, for none of the consequences should exist if the founding act does not exist because of being uninspected.

The second point is almost equally vital to intuitionists. They say that mind is autonomous, where responsibility for all that mind does is conditional upon mind's access to—i.e., its perception of—all that is done. No one is responsible for the things he cannot see. Mind will be responsible for everything occurring within it only as nothing there is hidden to it. Only an autonomous mind will be self-enclosing and altogether self-controlling. A mind separated from itself by representations cannot control the state represented, especially if the represented state is past in the moment when it is known. It is on this account that mind's perfect self-control requires that all of mind be visible to itself at every moment, without mediation. This is a condition that must be satisfied if mind is to have the power for redirecting itself in the moment when second-order reflection overrides the determining force of the act it observes. Contemporaneity guarantees mind's access to itself. It is, therefore, a condition for mind's perfect self-control.

7civ. GODHOOD ACHIEVED

A mind altogether visible to and having control of itself is *causa sui.* As source of its own impressions and ideas, and as generator of its experience and history, this mind is complete. This is the cogito elevated to Godhood, with solutions provided for all three of the obstacles to exalting mind: Sensory data have their source in the Absolute's imagination, the Absolute exists necessarily, the Absolute is everywhere and immediately accessible to itself. The result is cosmic: God, nature and self-consciousness are disclosed in their identity. There is God the creator, nature the created, and self-consciousness as the activity of one as it makes the other. The God of *Genesis* is replaced by this intuitionist story of epistemic creation.

7cv. PARMENIDES

This is Hegel's objective, but not his alone. He has embellished the Cartesian-Kantian ego in order to confirm the more abstract and cryptic speculations of Parmenides.

> This alone yet, the account of the route, remains how it is. And on this route signposts further (you), many indeed (indicating) how, being ungenerate and unperishing, (it) is whole, monogeneric as well as untrembling; and incomplete (it) not sometimes was and is not going to be since now (it) is altogether total: One coherent . . . It is not divisible, since all is alike, and it is not here somewhat more, which might prevent it from cohering, or somewhat less, but all is filled up with being. Thus all is coherent, for being concerts with being . . . The same and in the same abiding by itself it reposes. In this manner it abides here steadfast; for mighty Constraint holds it in the restraints of a bond which enfolds it all about. Wherefore there is no Permission

for being to be incomplete. For it is not wanting of anything; nonbeing would be in want entirely. Now these are the same: thinking, and
that on account of which there is the thought-upon. For not apart
from being, in which it is what has been expressed, will you find as
little as if Time is or is going to be alienated from being, since Fate has
shackled it whole and quiescent to be.[9]

What is the Constraint which enfolds Being all about? What is it
that reposes while abiding itself? Only, or most plausibly, self-
consciousness. This is the thinking which is identical with the
thought upon. For as Time runs through all of Being, making it one
and coherent, so is consciousness the medium in which everything is
made one.

7cvi. Plato and some neo-platonists

This reading of Parmenides might seem to be an intuitionist gloss
of a vague text, but for one quite decisive and confirming test. Here is
Plato writing in the *Timaeus* with Parmenides' text as his point of
reference:

> Such was the whole plan of the eternal God about the good that was
> to be; he made it smooth and even, having a surface in every direction
> equidistant from the center, a body entire and perfect, and formed out
> of perfect bodies. And in the center he put the soul, which he diffused
> throughout the body, making it also to be the exterior environment of
> it, and he made the universe a circle moving in a circle, one and
> solitary, yet by reason of its excellence able to converse with itself,
> and needing no other friendship or acquaintance. Having these pur-
> poses in view he created the world a blessed god.[10]

Notice that Plato assigns two roles to the soul. It is diffused throughout the world, as consciousness is the luminous medium within
which all the world's articulations are thought. Soul, as self-
consciousness, is additionally, the unifying envelope within which all
the world is enfolded. Soul is one and solitary, conversing with itself,
and needing no friendship or acquaintance. These are properties
which explain and justify Hegel's description of God as Absolute. For
God is self-reliant and self-sufficient. Every other being exists only as
something created in God's thinking it. Only God exists in Himself.
    Neoplatonism carried this tradition into the modern era, making

it our own. Yet Neoplatonism was metaphysically suspect because of having been appropriated for Christian apologetics. Descartes saves and reanimates the tradition by encouraging the identification of soul with the *cogito*. For the *I think* is familiar, particular, and secular. We have required only Leibniz and Kant to revive and fulfill the Parmenidian legacy: Leibniz as he argues that every characterization of Being gives more or less explicit expression to the perspective of some thinker; Kant as he elaborated on the cogito's tasks, plainly distinguishing first- and second-order thinking, while elevating second-order acts to transcendental status. Hegel integrates these several claims until soul is again located within the midst of Being as its first and sufficient condition. The world is Substance-for-Subject. Soul is in the center, and diffused throughout the body. It fills all of Being, within and without.

7d. *A summary of points that were to be covered*

This is the intuitionist appropriation of Being. It is accomplished as we magnify the powers which Descartes ascribed to the *cogito*. We are to say that mind is self-sufficient as the generator of its sensory content, that it is necessary as ground for the existence and character of the world it makes, and that mind's own existence is confirmed, with certainty, as mind turns perpetually upon itself. We satisfy, by way of these claims, that fourth question asked on page 260: namely how is the *cogito* transformed until it becomes the Absolute? We don't yet have a justification for intuitionist atheists as they assume the incorporation of Being within finite minds.

We also need solutions for the other three problems. First, we have to tell whether every consistent theory is equally good for producing a world. Next, intuitionists have to find something better than force and vivacity as a sufficient condition for existence. This is too vague a test, one that might leave us uncertain about the existence of things seen on a misty day. Finally, Kant's arguments for mind's internalization of space and time are incomplete. How does mind do it? The arguments for mind's self-sufficiency, necessity and self-inspectability have said very little that is useful for settling any one of these questions. Only mind's "synthesis" of space and time is clarified a little. Asking what this means, we are told that atomic sensory data are "grasped," "bound," and "run through."

8. The more rigorous formulation of this result

Perhaps answers would be more forthcoming if intuitionism were to stop relying on notions which are excessively impressionistic or metaphorical. The systematic metaphysics which I have reconstructed in an historical and conceptual way is reconstructed from within as notions once formulated in allusive or vaguely psychologistic ways are restated in language that is less romantic and more precise. For now, when the outlines of the intuitionist program are established and its achievements acknowledged, intuitionists return to the original questions, declaring their solutions in ways that are acceptably rigorous. Can we say, for example, that the given is differentiated and unified by thought without having to invoke introspectable ideas, especially as we realize that introspection is not altogether successful at differentiating these ideas from one another? Is there some other, better articulated device for differentiating and unifying the given—words, sentences, and theories for example? Can we also reformulate the claim that the existence of things "in the world" is provided for within mind without having to say that things exist just by virtue of being set forcefully before us? This is vague when existence is an all or none condition, so that things exist or not, though we cannot be certain at the margins of sensibility that something perceived is forceful enough to count as existent. Perhaps there is some better test.

Intuitionists of our century do reformulate these claims, though not always recognizing their debt to Hegel's project. They do it in the more or less explicit hope that our finite minds may be capable of imposing all of those differentiations and relations which make the world thinkable. Is it implied that finite minds might incorporate all of being within themselves? Nothing so candid is said, where saying it would invite ridicule. For there is no passion among the intuitionists of our time for Hegel's Absolute. There is only the residual embarrassment that Hegel should have been so blatant in proclaiming mind's appropriation of Being.

Interest in the problems left over from Hegel's work is uneven. There is not much devotion to reformulating the claim that space and time are the forms of intuition, or to explaining what mind need do to create them, though this most fundamental claim is rarely denied and often assumed. There is a commitment to telling in very spare language about mind's differentiation and unification of the sensory given. Intuitionist concern for the existence of things seems to be very much less prominent, though the intuitionist motive for locating existence within the mind is disguised under a different name. Rather than say that mind must be the ground for the existence of every other thing, we have intuitionists writing of truth as the inspectable relation among sentences. Discussions of truth are surrogates for the discussion of existence, where existence hovers about the truth of sentences. Here is, first, a characterization of some views about mind's differentiation and unification of the given, then an intuitionist characterization of truth as a surrogate for intuitionist concerns about existence. There will be time at the end for particularizing some of this in a thinker whose eminence is uncontested, though his intuitionism has to this point been ignored.

8a. Using language to differentiate and unify sensory data

Not every twentieth-century intuitionist supposes that words and sentences are the only or best device for differentiating and unifying the given. Husserl regards words as extraneous to the ideas upon which mind reflects. Words are used for expressing, or communicating about, ideas; but it is ideas, not words, which make the world thinkable. Heidegger, whose views about this are not always consistent, argues that words too often mislead and alienate us from the world. That is his message in *The End of Philosophy* where words are said to mask the presence of things. Russell distinguishes knowledge-by-acquaintance from knowledge-by-description, saying that knowledge-by-description is distinctly second best. This is, however, a minority view when the difficulty of distinguishing among ideas compares badly to the ease of distinguishing words, and when the range of available words vastly exceeds the number of plainly distinguishable ideas. Ideas might be idiosyncratic or private, while words seem to be common and public. Words are susceptible to rigorous logical organization in sentences and arguments; ideas too often elude the decidability of logical form. Words are, accordingly, the agreed point of reference for differentiating and unifying matters of fact. Little else is agreed. Is it individual words, sentences, or theories which are to be the vehicles for thinking the sensory given?

One consideration is decisive when the emphasis turns against individual words, in favor of sentences and theories. A dictionary is a list of words signifying possibilities, not actualities, as there might be an entry for "passenger pigeon" though there are no passenger pigeons. Knowledge, so far as we use language to express it, requires sentences and theories, not merely words. Suppose now that the choice is narrowed to sentences and theories; which of them is the better vehicle for knowledge? Individual sentences seem to be self-sufficient, as when we say "The Sun is shining." Every English speaker understands, though nothing else is said. We should not, however, make too much of the difference between the sentences uttered and the others assumed. For no individual sentence stands on its own. There are various contingencies that need be assumed before either the meaning or truth of sentences can be determined. So, this sentence would have a different meaning if uttered by a fish or by someone passing the day in another solar system. Accordingly, we do not know that a sentence is true, or even what it means, without knowing some of the other sentences that would need to be meaningful and true in order that this one should be true under a particular meaning.

8b. Two models for organizing sentences

The relations among sentences are a point of dispute among intuitionists. For consider the sentences known to be true, together with those others they presuppose. How shall we understand the network of sentences asserted, assumed, and implied? Is it like a road map representing large and small towns, each one having a circle of villages around it, with roads connecting each town to most others? Or is the relation of sentences the deductivist one that Descartes recommended in the *Rules?* Either structure will differentiate and unify the given. It is differentiated, when the words and grammatical structure of individual sentences signify different states of affairs; it is unified by the relations among sentences, whether the looser ones of the map or the tighter ones of a deductive system.

We expect humanists to prefer that sentences be organized as a road map, while scientists choose the deductivist format. But natural history is not easily reformulated in a deductivist way, though it used to be considered scientific. Molecular biology may facilitate a deductivist reconstruction of phyla and species; but in the meantime, the road map is still a better representation of medical knowledge. This concedes that progress within a science enhances the utility of the deductivist model; but this assumption might prove illusory if we cannot prove that all macrophenomena are only the aggregated effects of microphenomena. A science criss-crossed by bridge-laws—i.e., rules that coordinate the domains of microphysics, biology, psychology, and economics—will be closer to the road map than to Descartes' *Rules*. There is also the fact that practical life seems permanently alien to the formalized theories of science. Problem-solving may have a structure which applies universally, whether we are fixing the car or managing the car company. Yet, deductivist reconstructions of what we do may be incidental to the circumstances where local details and routines are learned and applied. We may want to minimize the common features though we acknowledge the affinities, as we enjoy the special qualities of one city while agreeing that cities are very much alike.

The road map is also better than a deductive system as a representation of spatial relations, if one values the iconic similarity of the map and the terrain represented. Notice, however, that we use mathematically formulated, deductively organized theories rather than spatially organized navigational charts for sending rockets to the moon. We may draw the trajectory in that spatialized way, but only after using a deductively organized theory to calculate it. This practical fact helps to explain the motivation when intuitionists, and others, choose the deductivist model for organizing the sentences of a theory. This is the preferred model for differentiating phenomena, and for exhibiting all three of the unities for which intuitionists must provide: cause and effect, space and time, and the nomological unities—e.g., $F = MA$.

A formalized theory may provide for each of the three unities if we assume these two things: first, that individual cause and effect relationships have been subsumed under causal laws; second, that positions and relations in space and time are represented by that succession of four-place variables which locates phenomena on the coordinate system mapped by a theory. Every unification of sensory data is then nomological, meaning that relations among phenomena are signified by those test sentences which are deduced from the higher-order sentences of the formalized theory.

8c. *The preference for deductively organized theories*

Deductively organized scientific theories are the preferred vehicles for thought, not primarily because of a fascination for nature, but rather because of intuitionist respect for those conceptualizations which differentiate and unify some vast domain of sensory data. Remember the task for a prescriptivist intuitionist: He is to generate or find the ideas which make the sensory data thinkable. He could hardly be unimpressed with a theory which does that while enabling us to predict and explain phenomena of great diversity, including some which are otherwise unanticipated—e.g., comets and eclipses. Philosophers who abandoned nature to physics, deriding nature and science by saying that all our beliefs about it are speculative and contingent, can admire these theories without qualification. Why? Because these are devices for recovering all that is intelligible within nature, relocating it within our minds.

There are very few intuitionists who remain, like Ryle,[11] outside the circle of converts, forever wanting to reinterpret scientific conceptualizations in the language of ordinary discourse. Other intuitionists embrace these scientific theories like the grail. For them science is thinkable form. Some of these philosophers have considerable scientific learning. Most others are efficient "philosophers of science," meaning that they are skilled in the analysis of deductive systems and the "logical" problems that accrue as these systems are used for thinking the sensory given.

There are conceptual problems as scientists use hypotheses for explaining matters of fact, so that philosophers rightly devote themselves to these questions. Still, this interest is different from the intuitionist use of scientific theories for projecting form onto the given. Both sides may worry, for example, about the criteria for regarding a theory as well-confirmed. But realists distinguish the evidence for a theory from the states of affairs to which the theory applies. They may emphasize crucial experiments, where failure to obtain a predicted result is a sufficient basis for rejecting a theory when experimental error or errors in calculation are discounted. Intuitionists are not impressed by crucial experiments, because they do not agree that a theory is ever confounded by some alien reality, one that it misrepresents. They believe instead that there is a degree of latitude for interpreting individual sentences, and a degree of tolerance in the relations among a theory's sentences. Evidence is irreparably disconfirming only if we cannot alter one or more of a theory's sentences within these tolerances, where the last-ditch apology for a theory is the fact that we can ignore the falsifying evidence because of being able to think an intelligible world by using the theory. There may be several theories that might be used in this way. The best theory is the one having the greatest range of applications, that is, the one which differentiates while integrating the greatest diversity of sensory data.

8d. Goodman on truth

This intuitionist point of view is the one proposed by Nelson Goodman. He has wanted to subvert the idea that theories are measured against an independent reality. He prefers to say that we may have innumerable theories, each one claimed as "true" for reasons which are internal to the theory or to relations among theories. This is a plausible notion of truth only if one has destroyed the possibility that theories might be true because of being satisfied by some aspect of a world that is independent of the fact that we think about it. Goodman supposes that this realist program is defunct.

> The devastating charge against the picture theory of language was that a description cannot represent or mirror forth the world as it is. But we have since observed that a picture doesn't do this either. I began by dropping the picture theory of language and ended by adopting the language theory of pictures. I rejected the picture theory of language on the ground that the structure of a description does not conform to the structure of the world. But I then concluded that there is no such thing as the structure of the world for anything to conform or fail to conform to.[12]

This last sentence explains altogether the intuitionist passion for scientific theories: Nature has no form in itself, so that there are as many "true" views of it as there are coherent theories for thinking the sensory data.

8e. Truth as a surrogate for existence

This is the place for confirming that the intuitionist account of truth is a surrogate for the demand that existence be incorporated within our minds. Consider this argument. There is at least one true sentence signifying every thing existing, namely the sentence which affirms that thing's existence. We would know all that exists if we were to know all the true sentences signifying those things. Knowing these sentences, we would prefigure, *within the mind,* all that exists. How shall we do that? By deriving these sentences from a theory. But which theory? Only a comprehensive theory, one applying to every circumstance throughout every domain of nature. Why this emphasis on comprehensiveness? So that nothing existing should elude our theory's competence for generating a sentence to signify it. There is, of course, no theory of this depth and scope. Intuitionists wanting to generate true sentences must resort to whatever theories are available to them. Asking them what things exist, we get this answer: only such things as are signified by the sentences derived from our accepted theories.

Do these things exist independently of our theories, or is it true instead that the only reality is the fact that sentences "about" them are deduced from a theory? Intuitionists reply that this is a confused question, for there is only a semantical distinction to mark the difference which I am phrasing in an ontological way. We are to distinguish between the *material* and *formal* modes of speech, not between realism and idealism. In the material mode, we speak unqualifiedly of things as they are. In the formal mode, we say that a sentence is true. There is a claim to be uttered in the material mode for every claim that is made in the formal mode, as snow is white wherever "Snow is white" is true; but this is the only parity that intuitionists acknowledge. Where theory is the vehicle for thinking the world, the formal mode is prior, because the existence of things thought is just the fact that we can deduce the sentences describing them from an accepted theory.

Intuitionists would not object if there were two or more of these theories. For there is nothing inconsistent in having several comprehensive theories, even theories that are not intertranslatable. Intuitionism abhors surprises. It does not want to be embarrassed by some existent that is nowhere anticipated by theory. But it does not mind that there be different theories, each of them adequate for thinking all of the sensory given. Its principal concern is the one of having some conceptual device for knowing the world. Two or more such theories are merely the extravagance of an already good thing. We have only to acknowledge that our thinking is warped by the theory we use. The thing which is created when thought by using one theory will not be the "same" as a thing which is objectified by using a different one.

These are the results as intuitionists formulate a linguistic expression for the systematic metaphysics received from Hegel. A unified science is to differentiate and unify the sensory given. The true sentences derived from this theory are to prefigure every existent. We have eliminated the ideas and rules that are so hard to discern within our minds, and the still more problematic claim that existence is only the forcible presentation of things inspected. The world's differentiation, unity, and existence are reestablished in terms that are sober but still inspectable. Being is appropriated by our finite minds.

8f. Quine

This reformulation of the intuitionist metaphysics is incomplete only because of needing personification. Is there a contemporary philosopher who provides for all three of the considerations which are demanded if mind is to claim the power for creating a world by thinking it? Is there someone who locates the entire basis for the world's differentiation, unity, and existence within language? Professor W.V.O. Quine has a fair claim to being that man.

One may have the impression when reading Quine that language is the all pervading ether in which we live.

> What comes of the association of sentences with sentences is a vast verbal structure which, primarily as a whole is multifariously linked to non-verbal stimulations. These links attach to separate sentences (for each person), but the same sentences are so bound up in turn with one another and with further sentences that the non-verbal attachments themselves may stretch or give way under strain. In an obvious way this structure of interconnected sentences is a single connected fabric including all sciences, and indeed everything we ever say about the world.[13]

One might infer that all Being is differentiated, unified, and even made to exist by way of language; but Quine does sometimes deny that this is so.

> [W]e must not jump to the conclusion that what there is depends on words. Translatability of a question into semantical terms is no indication that the question is linguistic. To see Naples is to bear a name which when prefixed to the words "see Naples," yields a true sentence; still there is nothing linguistic about seeing Naples.[14]

Notice, however, that Quine has also said that "Semantic ascent, as I speak of it, applies anywhere."[15] He adds, by way of explanation: "I accept (Carnap's) distinction between the material and the formal mode."[16] Quine's debt to Carnap is fundamental.

Carnap maintains that ontological questions, and likewise questions of logic or mathematical principle, are questions not of fact but of choosing a convenient conceptual scheme or framework for science; and with this I agree only if the same be conceded for every scientific hypothesis.[17]

Carnap, himself, is altogether explicit about the reality of Naples and every other thing.

The concept of reality occurring in these internal questions is an empirical, scientific, non-metaphysical concept. To recognize something as a real thing or event means to succeed in incorporating it into the framework of things at a particular space-time position so that it fits together with the other things recognized as real, according to the rules of the framework.[18]

Those who raise the question of the reality of the thing world itself have perhaps in mind not a theoretical question as their formulation seems to suggest, but rather a practical question, a matter of a practical decision concerning the structure of our language. We have to make the choice whether or not to accept and use the forms of expression for the framework in question.[19]

Quine locates Naples among the other facts; it exists to the extent that there is a bound variable specifying it within sentences which are coordinated to other sentences within that "single connected fabric"—i.e., language. We may speak of Naples in the material mode only as we have a rule for introducing this word and its complex definite description in the formal mode.

It is all the more plausible now that Quine should provide within language for the differentiation, unification, and existence of things in the world. He does emphasize that our choice of predicates determines the universe of discourse within which to think the world. Every differentiation that might be credited to it originates in one or another semantical framework. Quine also supposes that every sort of unification ascribed to the world is founded in the coordinated law sentences of the science or practice used for thinking about it. Language even provides for the unity of space and time. It does that by including a more or less explicit metric, so that we may give values to the spatial and temporal parameters of the events to which our law sentences apply. Existence, Quine has said, is only the value of a bound variable, though he adds that quantified sentences occur within a network of other sentences so that it is not quantification alone but also the relation of a quantified sentence to the other sentences of a theory which secures our right to make the existence claims. Language is, in all of this, the instrument for making the world thinkable. Mind is the measure as it chooses one or another semantical framework.

Quine's holism and his idealism are not much in doubt. He is remarkable for satisfying the demand that Being be appropriated by our finite minds, without having to invoke God's mind to do it. For Quine, with Carnap and Goodman, argues that every finite mind having its choice of frameworks can provide for all the differentiation, unity, and existence of any world rendered thinkable by a language. Does it follow that Quine the idealist is an intuitionist? How could that be true when Quine's behaviorism is explicit?

Consider his remarks about "stimulus meaning"[20] and "surface irritations."[21] These are behaviourist notions. They imply that we humans are located within a physical world where our eyes and ears are affected by the things about us; that circumstances or need provoke our linguistic responses; that the meanings of the words to which we respond are a function of how we respond when seeing or hearing them. This is the story that Quine seems to be telling, though he has no right to defend it as the final truth about language. There are two reasons for saying this.

On the one side are Quine's remarks about semantical frameworks and the relativity which distinguishes them. Their variability entails that we may interpret both our sensory data and our linguistic behavior in a variety of ways, each one determined by the semantical framework that is assumed by the interpretation. A behavioristic reading of these two is, therefore, just one of the several that are possible.

The other reason is that Quine so often reflects upon the available frameworks from the standpoint of a subject trying to estimate the most plausible interpretation of the phenomena visible to it: are these the effects of physical causes or might they be sensory data having no ulterior causes? He asks this question regularly, giving different, usually pragmatic, reasons for choosing one framework or another.

Quine's behaviorism is, therefore, either of two things: It is the interpretation that we render after choosing one among the several possible frameworks for thinking about ourselves; or it is merely a kind of rhetoric, one that implies no commitment whatever to the ontology of physical agents located within a public world. "Surface irritations" are just the sensory data set before our inspecting minds.

That we have these data is perhaps the one thing about them which we cannot doubt. Everything else that we might say of them is an interpretation, one that is founded in our interests and purposes.

> From among the various conceptual schemes best suited to these various pursuits, one—the phenomenalistic—claims epistemological priority. Viewed from within the phenomenalistic conceptual scheme, the ontologies of physical objects and mathematical objects are myths. The quality of myth, however, is relative: relative, in this case, to the epistemological point of view. This point of view is one among various, corresponding to one among our various interests and purposes.[22]

Could it be that Quine's "behaviorism" is a myth? To what end? Perhaps intuiting mind wants to objectify its circumstances so that it may turn away from itself, locating itself—like Wittgenstein in the *Philosophical Investigations* and Heidegger in *Being and Time*— within the business of the everyday world.

There are, finally, two additional, still speculative reasons for thinking that Quine may be an intuitionist.

The first is language and our use of it. Language is to supply both the universe of discourse within which we think the world and the lines of inference that terminate in those true sentences which mark the world's existents. These are linguistic frameworks that someone must formulate, then use for thinking the world. We can hardly keep ourselves from inferring to the existence and character of that mind which creates and uses them. Isn't Quine appealing in a tacit way to these two things: first, to second-order consciousness as it formulates the language used for creating a thinkable world; then to first-order awareness as it affects the attitude of a naive realist—i.e., enjoying a world it has not made?

The other consideration is a fact that would be remarkable if it were fortuitous. Quine provides within language for all three of the facts for which intuitionism is responsible if it is to establish that all the thinkable world is relocated within our minds, namely differentiation, unity and existence. Why would Quine want to fulfill the intuitionist program in this very detailed way if he were not impelled by intuitionist motives?

The evidence for Quine's intuitionism, I agree, is only circumstantial. Is there some place where Quine reveals himself more directly? Quine is frequently guarded and allusive; but there is one passage which describes our circumstances in a plain and simple way.

> The philosopher's task differs from the others', then, in detail; but in no such drastic way as those suppose who imagine for the philosopher a vantage point outside the conceptual scheme that he takes in charge. There is no such cosmic exile. He cannot study and revise the fundamental conceptual scheme of science and common sense without having some conceptual scheme, whether the same or another no less in need of philosophical scrutiny, in which to work. He can scrutinize and improve the system from within, appealing to coherence and simplicity; but this is the theoretician's method generally. He has recourse to semantic ascent, but so has the scientist. And if the theoretical scientist in his remote way is bound to save the eventual connections with non-verbal stimulation, the philosopher in his remoter way is bound to save them too. True, no experiment may be expected to settle an ontological issue; but this is only because such issues are connected with surface irritations in such multifarious ways, through such a maze of intervening theory.[23]

For "he" read "mind," for then it seems that this is the characterization of the thinking subject as it projects order onto sensory data so that it may have access to a thinkable world. Second-order consciousness is to create the semantical framework—hence, the world—that first-order consciousness will enjoy.

9. Idealism is the consequence of intuitionist method

This reading of mine does not confirm or even suggest that Quine is self-consciously an intuitionist metaphysician. He would likely object to the noun as much as the adjective. But then some other things remain to be said, for we as philosophers have lost sight of this most fundamental truth about our history and procedures: Idealism thrives only because mind is sceptical about the character and existence of every thing which it cannot inspect. When a thinkable world is not set before us with all its deeper structures apparent on its face, intuitionism would rather create a thinkable world than speculate, fallibly, about a world whose existence and character are independent of the ways we think about it. It follows that intuitionist method has idealism as its consequence. Quine, the idealist, is oblivious to his intuitionist roots. Like Plato, he almost succeeds in depersonalizing mind as it knows the world. He cannot altogether succeed, because there is some agent who steps back from every semantical framework in order to choose the one most likely to serve its interests. That spectral agent is the self-encircling mind presupposed by intuitionist method. Like the black hole at the center of our galaxy, everything turns about this mind though little or nothing of it is perceived.

10. Why intuiting mind disappears

Why does mind disappear, even from itself? There are several reasons. First is the Platonic tradition and its hope that *nous* might have no identity additional to the things it knows. Second is Kant's role in dividing second- from first-order consciousness, while ascribing all of mind's world-making powers to second-order thinking. Add now that a mind thinking upon itself will do that within time, though mind in the act of making time exists somehow outside of time. If knowing mind operates within time, then it never will have direct access to itself in that "moment" when it spins the time within which it thinks. This highest-order thinking never will be inspected; it might as well be ignored. Carnap and Quine fall exactly within this dilemma, for how shall mind know itself: by way of the conceptual framework it has made or in some direct and unmediated way? Mind cannot know itself directly, for it cannot know anything, they assume, without using one or another of the linguistic frameworks which mediate our thinking about everything. The result is that mind is simultaneously elevated and reduced; it is the all-empowering creator of semantical frameworks, but then its existence is suspect because it is invisible to itself. Only as it reflects upon its purposes and the framework appropriate to realizing them does mind recover itself.

Quine, Heidegger, Wittgenstein, and Derrida all seem determined that mind should disappear, even as we enjoy the world to which it gives us access. These first two reasons do explain something of their motivation. The third excuse for mind's disappearance is more a privation than a reason. There is a certain amnesia that affects us. We would rather use the intuitionist method than reflect upon it. Doing that is easier when our disinterest in the history of philosophy combines with the assumption that our method is neutral, with no psychological or ontological presuppositions of its own.

This is the shallow water where idealism breeds. Reality, we say, is only the sensory given or the experience created when ideas, rules, or theories project differentiation and order onto the sensory data. Mind disappears because self-understanding is fractured or suppressed. We do not want to know that our idealism has intuitionist roots. We say, in all candor, that intuitionist method is exposed and discredited. We renounce it, even as we use it. For this method is a vortex. It draws us into itself so long as we insist that nothing shall be claimed for knowledge if it is not presented and confirmed before our inspecting minds.

Everyone committed to this claim turns perpetually within the circle of intuitionist method, its psychology and ontology, never escaping the psycho-centric postulate that I am, I exist. Idealism is the sure result, so that anyone who renounces intuitionism while espousing his idealism is very likely an intuitionist despite himself. There might be some other method sufficient to generate idealist theories, though it remains to tell what that method is and how it varies from the intuitionist one. Can this be a method where mind disappears because of being irrelevant to the making of a thinkable world? I doubt it.

11. Intuiting mind as the paradigm for reality

There are, of course, some intuitionists, like Whitehead, for whom mind never disappears. These are the idealists who go the other way: Rather than say that reality is only the given as thought or perceived, they identify it with mind, saying that reality is constituted of myriad finite minds or the Absolute. These other idealists are also motivated by the sceptical question, how do we know a world that is separate from us? Their answer is that all of reality is like us. Having inspected ourselves, we generalize to other things, saying that every monad or actual occasion is a more or less articulate, more or less self-conscious drop of experience. Never disappearing, our finite minds become the centerpiece or paradigm for all of Being.

12. An alternative to intuitionist idealism

These two are the faces of idealism and the consequences of intuitionist method: All of Being is relocated within our minds as we create a thinkable given; or we populate the world with minds that are generically like our own. Either way, nature is repudiated. It is, says intuitionism, the alien thing-in-itself, or the object of meaningless speculation. But what if nature is everywhere about and within us? How shall we establish our access to it? We do that by choosing a method which regards perceptual data as the effects of their causes, while it identifies the generative and sustaining conditions within the things perceived. Repudiating intuitionism, we say that all our knowledge of the world is hypothetical. We formulate hypotheses which signify possible states of affairs. True hypotheses are the ones signifying possibilities instantiated. We test and revise our hypotheses, wanting to determine whether the evidence for them is sufficient to justify our saying that the possibilities they signify are actual.

Philosophy has supposed that this hypothetical method is sufficient for the purposes of science and practice, but that philosophy itself requires something better. Intuitionism was to be that superior instrument. It was to assure that every philosophical claim satisfies the more demanding requirement that our judgements are confirmed to the point of certainty. Now, with intuitionism renounced, philosophy is to settle for knowledge claims which are only probabilistic. There may be some conclusions which are demonstrated—i.e., their negations are contradictory—but they are rare. Every other claim will be as contingent as the assumptions on which it is based. All our hypotheses will be speculative, because each of them signifies some possible matter of fact that is, in every case, distinct from the evidence which provokes or justifies our making the hypothesis.

The speculative and probabilistic character of our thinking must have considerable effects throughout philosophy. Intuitionism in logic, value theory, and all of mind's self-reflections gives way to hypotheses and constructions. Constructions are familiar enough among intuitionists, as Carnap uses them for projecting form onto sensory data. Now, we distinguish between the things we make and the hypotheses used for thinking the things which are merely represented. So, a moral theory may combine hypothesis with construction, as we hypothesize about human nature and society while proposing the laws and organization which should constrain our behavior. We may also hypothesize about the character of eternal moral laws, though we shall not be able to justify our claims about them by saying that these laws are known to rational or empirical intuition.

If every philosophical study is affected by changing our method, it is metaphysics especially that is transformed. Rather than being first in the order of knowledge metaphysics will come late or last. When practice and science have exposed some part of the world's features, metaphysics will extend the generality of their hypotheses in the direction of nature's categorial form and conditions. Reflections that may have started in private self-regard will evolve until we have located ourselves within that nature and society where we secure and satisfy one another and ourselves.

This hypothetical method, like the intuitionist one, will have psychological and ontological presuppositions. But these are tolerable complications when mind is liberated. No longer having to make the world or model its form, we have only to know the world while finding our way within it.

Notes

Introduction

1. David Weissman, *Eternal Possibilities: A Neutral Ground for Meaning and Existence* (Carbondale: Southern Illinois University Press, 1977).

2. Also see, Weissman, "The Spiral of Reflection," in *News Essays in Metaphysics,* edited by R. Neville (Albany: State University of New York Press, 1986), 275–310.

3. Weissman, *Hypothesis and the Spiral of Reflection* (Albany: State University of New York Press, forthcoming).

4. Martin Heidegger, *Being and Time,* translated by J. Macquarrie and E. Robinson, (New York: Harper and Row, 1962), p. 187.

5. Heidegger, *The End of Philosophy,* translated by J. Stambaugh (London: Souvenir Press, 1975), p. 10.

6. Ibid., p. 21.

7. Ibid., p. 32.

8. Ibid., p. 38.

9. Bas van Fraassen, *The Scientific Image* (New York: Clarendon Press, Oxford University Press, 1980), p. 3.

10. Jacques Derrida, *Speech and Phenomena* (Evanston: Northwestern University Press, 1973), pp. 129–160.

11. Also see, Stanley Rosen, *The Limits of Analysis* (New Haven: Yale University Press, 1980).

Chapter One

1. Rene Descartes, *Rules for the Direction of the Native Talents,* in *Rene Descartes: The Essential Writings,* translated by John J. Blom (New York: Harper, 1977), 30.

2. Ibid., 22.

3. Ibid., 24.

4. Ibid., 36.

5. Ibid., 36.

6. Ibid., 37.

7. Ludwig Wittgenstein, *Tractus Logico-Philosophicus,* translated by D.F. Pears and B.F. McGuinness (London: Routledge and Kegan Paul, 1961), paragraphs 4.014 and 1.13.

8. Weissman, *Eternal Possibilities* 247–56.

9. Descartes, *Meditations,* in *Rene Descartes: The Essential Writings,* p. 206.

10. Ibid., 209.

11. Ibid., 208.

12. Ibid., 204.

13. Descartes, *Rules for the Direction of the Native Talents,* p. 24.

14. Descartes, *Meditations,* pp. 199–200.

15. Descartes, *Rules for the Direction of the Native Talents,* p. 31.

16. Descartes, *Mediations,* p. 199.

Chapter Two

1. Wittgenstein, *Tractus Logico-Philosophicus,* paragraph 5.6.

2. Thomas Kuhn, *The Structure of Scientific Revolutions* (Chicago: University of Chicago Press, 1965), 23–34.

3. William James, "Does 'Consciousness' Exist?" in *The Writings of William James,* edited by J.J. McDermott (New York: Modern Library, 1968), 169–183.

4. J.L. Austin, *Philosophical Papers* (London: Oxford University Press, 1970), 130.

5. Ibid., 130.

6. Hans-George Gadamer, *Truth and Method* (New York: Crossroad, 1985), 401.

7. Ibid., 399.

8. Ibid., 497–498.

9. Ibid., 297.

10. Ibid., 297.

11. Ibid., 405–406.

12. Ibid., 29.

13. Ibid., 430.

14. Ibid., 440.

15. Ibid., 439–440.

16. Ibid., 442.

17. Ibid., 445.

18. Gadamer, *Reason in the Age of Science,* translated by F.G. Lawrence (Cambridge: MIT Press, 1983), 12.

19. Rudolf Carnap, *The Logical Structure of the World,* translated by R.A. George (Berkeley: University of California Press, 1967), 8.

20. Ibid., 6.

21. Ibid., viii.

22. Ibid., 10.

23. Ibid., 109.

24. Ibid., 107–108.

25. Ibid., 282.

26. Ibid., 89.

27. Ibid., 288.

28. David Hume, *A Treatise of Human Nature* (Oxford: Clarendon Press, 1967), 1.

29. Ibid., 70.

30. Ibid., 79.

31. Ibid., 79.

32. Edmund Husserl, *Cartesian Meditations,* translated by D. Cairns (The Hague: Martinus Hijhoff, 1970), 69.

33. Ibid., 70–71.

34. Jean-Paul Sartre, *Being and Nothingness,* translated by H.E. Barns (New York: Washington Square Press, 1969), 3.

35. Ibid., 7.

36. Ibid., 11.

37. Ibid., 14.

38. Ibid., 17.

39. Ibid., 240.

40. Martin Heidegger, *Being and Time*, 257.

41. Ibid., 257.

42. Ibid., 255.

43. Ibid., 263.

44. Ibid., 256.

45. Ibid., 252.

46. Nelson Goodman, *Problem and Projects* (Indianapolis: Bobbs-Merrill, 1972), 30–31.

Chapter Three

1. Hume, *A Treatise of Human Nature* 71.

2. Wilfrid Sellars, *Science, Perception and Reality* (New York: Humanities Press, 1963), 140.

3. C.S. Peirce, "Questions Concerning Certain Faculties," *Collected Papers,* edited by C. Hartshorne and P. Weiss (Cambridge: Harvard University Press, 1965), 2:135–155.

4. Daniel Dennett, *Content and Consciousness* (London: Routledge and Kegan, Paul, 1969), 96: ". . . there are no pains; 'pain' does not refer."

5. Ludwig Wittgenstein, *Philosophical Investigations,* translated by G.E.M. Anscombe (New York: Macmillan, 1966). par. 1–23.

6. Wittgenstein, *Tractatus Logico-Philosophicus,* par. 5.631–5.633.

7. Heidegger, *Being and Time,* 400.

8. Peirce, *Collected Papers,* 6:237.

9. Descartes, *Meditations*, 198.

10. Weissman, *Eternal Possibilities,* 84–95.

11. Ibid., 57–108.

12. Franz Brentano, *Psychology from an Empirical Standpoint,* translated by A.C. Rancurello, D.B. Terell, and L.L. McAlister (New York: Humanities Press, 1973), 324.

Chapter Four

1. Rudolf Carnap, "Empiricism, Semantics, and Ontology," in *Semantics and the Philosophy of Language,* edited by L. Linksy (Urbana: University of Illinois Press, 1952), 211, 219–220.

Williard V.O. Quine, "Notes on Existence and Necessity," in *Semantics and the Philosophy of Language,* 80: ". . . the question of ontological presuppositions reduces completely to the question of the domain of objects covered by the quantifier."

2. Carnap, "Empiricism, Semantics and Ontology," 217–218.

3. Carnap, *The Logical Structure of the World,* 104.

4. Ibid., 261.

5. Ibid., 260.

6. Ibid., 205.

Chapter Five

1. David Weissman, *Dispositional Properties* (Carbondale: Southern Illinois University Press, 1965), 43.

2. Wittgenstein, *Tractatus Logico-Philosophicus,* par. 1.13.

3. Richard B. Braithwaite, *Scientific Explanation* (Cambridge: Cambridge University Press, 1964), 293–294.

4. Carl Hempel, *Philosophy of Natural Science* (Englewood Cliffs, N.J.: Prentice-Hall, 1966), 53.

5. Ibid., 48.

6. Braithwaite, *Scientific Explanation,* 343.

7. Ibid., 354.

8. Hempel, *Philosophy of Natural Science,* 53.

9. Braithwaite, *Scientific Explanation,* 339.

10. Ernest Nagel, *The Structure of Science* (New York: Harcourt, Brace and World, 1961), 323.

11. Ibid., 324.

12. Alfred North Whitehead, *Process and Reality* (New York: Harper and Row, 1960), 113.

13. Ibid., 135.

14. Ibid., 78.

15. Descartes, *Meditations,* 198.

16. Whitehead, *Process and Reality,* 83.

17. Ibid., 246.

18. Ibid., 241.

19. Ibid., 243.

20. Ibid., 241.

21. Ibid., 124.

22. Ibid., 524.

23. Ibid., 30.

24. Ibid., 127–167.

25. Ibid., 136.

Chapter Six

1. G.W.F. Hegel, *The Phenomenology of Mind,* translated by J.B. Baillie (New York: Harper and Row, 1967), 80.

2. Ibid., 808.

3. Ibid., 802.

4. Descartes, *Meditations,* 202–203.

5. Ibid., 199.

6. Hume, *A Treatise of Human Nature,* 66–67.

7. Ibid., 32.

8. Ibid., 67.

9. Parmenides, *On the Being One,* translated by Peter Manchester, *The Monist* (January 1979), vol. 62, no. 1, 84–85.

10. Plato, *Timeaus,* in *The Collected Dialogues,* translated by B. Jowett (New York: Pantheon, 1964), 34b: 1165.

11. Gilbert Ryle, *Dilemmas* (Cambridge: Cambridge University Press, 1966), 68–81.

12. Nelson Goodman, *Problems and Projects,* 31.

13. Willard V.O. Quine, *Word and Object* (Cambridge: The M.I.T. Press, 1967), 12.

14. Quine, "On What There Is," in *Semantics and the Philosophy of Language,* 203.

15. Quine, *Word and Object,* 271–272.

16. Ibid., 272n.

17. Quine, *The Ways of Paradox* (New York: Random House, 1966), 134.

18. Carnap, "Empiricism, Semantics, and Ontology," 210.

19. Ibid., 211.

20. Quine, *Word and Object,* 32.

21. Ibid., 22.

22. Quine, "On What There Is," 206.

23. Quine, *Word and Object,* 275–276.

Index

rejected, 243, 289–291

James, William, 7, 66–67, 69, 79, 82, 84, 87, 149, 158, 172, 174, 192, 235
judgement
as analytic and synthetic, 36
and Descartes, 22
intuitionist, 136–138
justifications
for intuitionist method, 55, 97–106, 107

Kant, Immanuel, 7, 14, 35, 38, 39, 61, 62, 72, 77, 78, 86, 89, 90, 102, 103, 107, 112, 113, 114, 115, 117, 120, 133, 135, 137, 140, 142, 147, 148, 149, 152, 165, 172, 176–177, 179, 182, 186, 188, 190, 192, 193, 227, 232, 233, 235, 247, 248, 249, 258, 261–262, 263, 264, 266, 267–268, 269, 270, 271, 272, 273, 275, 288
knowledge
as acquaintance, 31
and belief, 154
and certainty, 97, 151, 152, 154, 155, 290
and constructivism, 180
and Descartes, 41–42, 122, 124
and existence, 167
and hypotheses, 1, 195
as hypothetical, 290
and inspecting mind, 107, 115, 289
and intuition, 92
as invulnerable, 102
and language, 278
mediated by signs, 1
its objects, 54, 98, 171
and phenomenological description, 106
philosophical, 54
as probabilistic, 170, 290
and psychologism, 23–29
as self-knowledge, 152
of transcendental synthesis, 272
and verification, 253
as warranted assertibility, 195
and Whitehead, 232
Kuhn, Thomas, 62

language
and Austin, 67–69
and behaviorism, 285–286
and Carnap, 75–82
and sensory data, 277, 283, 284
and Gadamer, 71–75
and Goodman, 281
and Quine, 283–287
and space and time, 284
and Wittgenstein, 61, 71
see also ordinary language
laws
causal, 205–206, 209, 221–223
of logic, 165–166
and material and formal modes, 256
of nature, 5, 8, 9, 208–209, 211, 223–224
and rules, 209
law sentences, 284
least energy principle, 217–219
Leibniz, Gottfried W., 7, 41, 149, 185, 193, 197, 235, 238, 275
Lewis, Clarence I., 150
Locke, John, 89, 164, 231, 232

Marx, Karl, 5
material cause, 215, 216, 217, 219
materialism, 5
material mode, 51, 256, 257, 282, 283, 284
matter, 5
meaning
and psychologism, 23
metaphysics
and history of philosophy, 11
and intuitionism, 246
of nature, 4, 5, 204, 220
subjectivist, 181
systematic, 197–198, 245
topical, 197–199, 245
transformed, 291
method
and theory, 44–52
see also hypothetical method
intuitionist method
mind
its activity, 152
its agency, 194
its autonomy, 253, 273
as being, 246–291

and truth as surrogate for existence,
281–282
as used by intuitionists, 226–229
theory
and the given, 135
and method, 44–52
thermodynamics, 230
thinking
and a determinate world, 2
and making, 1
Thomas Aquinas, 10
thought
as a sign process, 118
transcendentalism, 101–105
transformation
and causality, 206–209
tribalism, 155
truth
and Aristotle, 92
and conceptual systems, 158
contingent, 25–27
and correspondence, 26–27
and Descartes, 19
and disclosure, 92–93
and existence, 277, 281–282
and Goodman, 281
and Heidegger, 92–93
and inspecting mind, 42, 167
necessary, 24–27
and Plato, 33–34
and psychologism, 23–29
and theories, 224–225, 259

Weiss, Paul, 10
Whitehead, Alfred N., 4, 5, 7, 11, 16,
76, 168, 185, 197, 200, 207–208,
231–243, 258, 289
will, 36–37
Wittgenstein, Ludwig, 21, 56, 61, 62,
71, 113, 116–117, 139, 158, 193,
210, 286, 288
wholism
in Quine, 285
world
and actuality, 2
and causality, 8
as determinate, 1, 2
as inspected, 3, 157, 257
and interests, 9
as known, 2, 3, 291
of minds, 290
and perception, 1
and possibilities, 2
a sceptical question about, 289
as Substance-for-Subject, 247,
259, 275
and thought, 1, 2, 8
world-making, 106

unity
as an aim, 146–147
of cause and effect, 257–258
and forms of intuition, 190
and the given; 140–148
irreducible, 145–146
and mind, 147–148
nomological, 255–256
and plans. 148
spatial and temporal, 258–259
of things known to intuition, 255–259

values
and the given, 180
and ideas, 146–147
van Fraassen, Bas, 14–15